POSTCARD HISTORY SERIES

Marion County

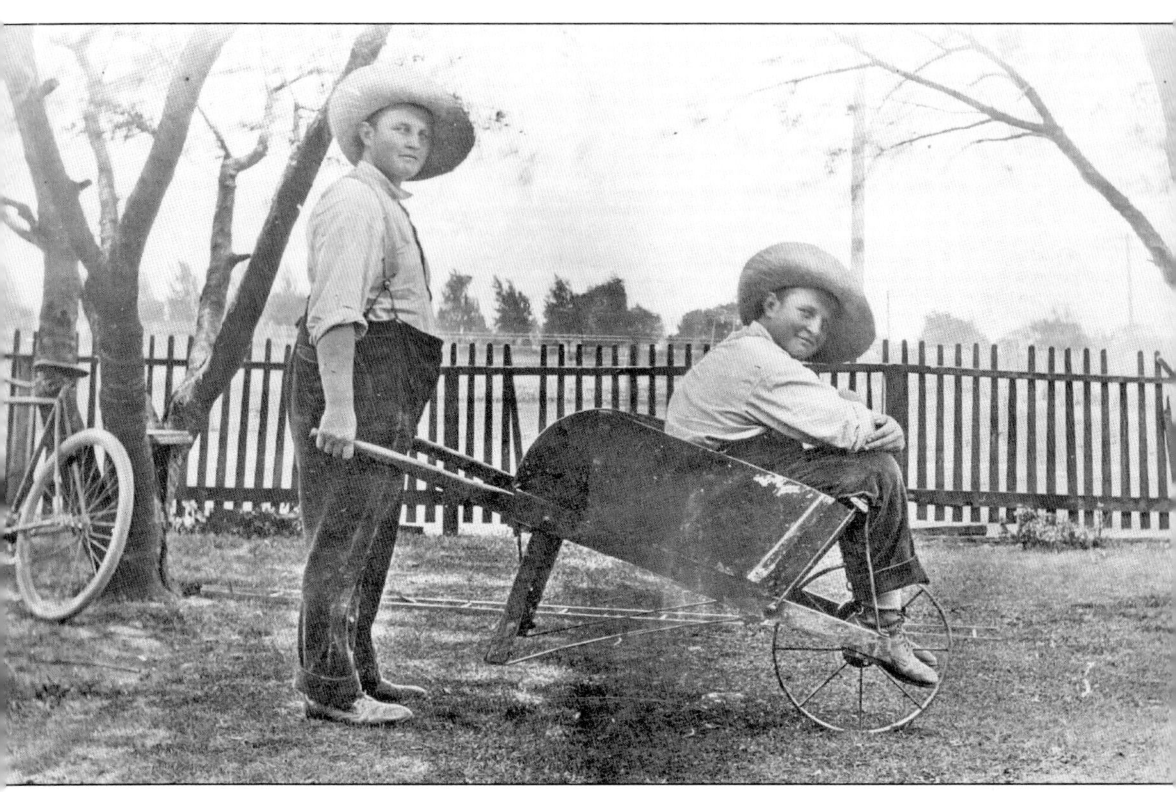

Twins or Trick? What at first glance appears to be a photograph of identical twins is actually a creative use of double-exposure photography. The technique, which merges two subjects into a single photograph, has been around since the late 1800s. The identity of the young man is unknown, although he may have been from the LaRue area based on the address and postmark on the card. (Courtesy of Richard Carey.)

On the Front Cover: Off to Market. Prospect farmer Ferd Gabriel (center) brought a wagonload of sheep to a brief halt to allow this photograph to be taken near the Central Hotel in Prospect. The fly nets hanging from the horses' harness consisted of small strips of leather designed to move as the horses walked, thus keeping away annoying flies and other insects. (Courtesy of Jane Burkett.)

On the Back Cover: Hardware and Implement Sales. The farm equipment and hardware needs of Morral area farmers and residents were likely taken care of via these two stores located in the Morral Bank building. The rich, dark soil produced bountiful crops but required sturdy equipment pulled by strong horses to work it into suitable condition. (Courtesy of Ellis and Margaret Hudson.)

POSTCARD HISTORY SERIES

Marion County

Randy Winland

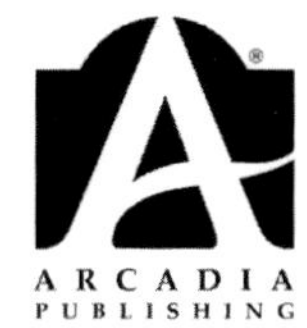

ISBN 978-1-4671-2621-2

Published by Arcadia Publishing
Charleston, South Carolina

Printed in the United States of America

Library of Congress Control Number: 2016959855

For all general information contact Arcadia Publishing at:
Telephone 843-853-2070
Fax 843-853-0044
E-mail sales@arcadiapublishing.com
For customer service and orders:
Toll-Free 1-888-313-2665

Visit us on the Internet at www.arcadiapublishing.com

Dedicated to the collectors of memories
of Marion County—be they past, present, or future

Contents

ACKNOWLEDGMENTS

The efforts of a group can often successfully accomplish what may have been overwhelming for an individual. Such was the case with the compiling, researching, and writing of this book. Many people graciously shared their resources, including postcards, historical documents, knowledge, and time. The end result is something that will hopefully be used and enjoyed by its readers.

The postcard images were compiled from the collections of several individuals. Nearly half of the images came from Richard Carey, who has amassed an amazing collection of Marion County ephemera and memorabilia and willingly shares it for projects such as this. The desire to allow others to view many of his perhaps one-of-a-kind postcards was a driving force behind the publishing of this book.

Others who shared their collections are Mike and Linda Perry; Bob Turner; Ellis and Margaret Hudson; and Kim Hall, owner of the Ralph and Erdine Eaton postcard collection. Jim Anderson, Wayne Apt, Jane Burkett, Kensel Clutter, Richard Johnson, Rebecca Johnson Oldham, John and Virginia Murphy, Terry Kreis, Rebecca Jacobs Rynders, and the Marion County Historical Society also provided images.

The research for this project proved to be a daunting task, as reliable sources of information were often conflicting or simply not available. Extensive efforts were made to ensure the accuracy of information, but as with most historical research, discrepancies may exist. Dennis Fabian, Stuart Koblentz Haley, and Bob Turner provided invaluable assistance, and their efforts were greatly appreciated. Research assistance was also provided by Jim Anderson, Jane Burkett, Michael Crane, Douglas and Marjory Denzer, Charlie Evers, and Jim Forry Jr. Others who provided assistance include Gary Hite, Richard Johnson, Mark Melroy, John and Virginia Murphy, Rebecca Johnson Oldham, Wayne Porter, Willis Thomas, and Jack Whiteamire. Dale Stage and other employees of the Marion County Engineer's Office provided answers to numerous inquiries. My sincere gratitude is extended to all.

Finally, and most importantly, I truly thank Sandy Winland, my wife of 41 years and my best friend. Her acceptance and support of the many days I spent scanning, researching, compiling, and writing were greatly appreciated. Her suggestions for possible improvements in the content and grammar of the captions certainly made for a more concise and informative end product.

Introduction

The seven villages of Marion County and their surrounding locales are home to almost half of the total population of the county. A previous Arcadia Publishing book in the Postcard History Series featured the city of Marion but did not include these smaller communities and rural areas. They are the focus of this book, *Marion County*.

The geographical area that is now Marion County was sparsely inhabited, primarily by Native Americans, into the early 1800s, mostly due to the Greenville Treaty Line. The treaty line had been established in 1795 as part of an agreement signed with several Native American tribes that set off much of the northwestern part of Ohio for their use. The line passed through what is now Marion County about a mile north of the current villages of Prospect and Waldo.

By 1806, explorers and squatters had begun to venture north near the treaty line. The Wyatt and Brundige families both settled just south of Waldo in Marlboro Township, Delaware County. As tensions mounted with Great Britain, the federal government negotiated with the Native Americans for permission for a "war road" to be built from Delaware County to Lower Sandusky (Fremont). Surveyors marking the road traveled through the wilderness and established stopping points such as Jacob's Well, located in what would one day become the city of Marion.

The War of 1812 brought the threat of hostilities from Native Americans, who had largely allied themselves with the British based on the promise of the return of their land if the Americans were defeated. Troops by the thousands began traveling the war road to Lower Sandusky and on to Lake Erie, which engendered the need for a safe haven for the settlers living in the area as well as a supply depot for the troops. Fort Morrow was built at Wyatt's Tavern, just south of what is now Waldo, to serve these purposes. Following the end of the war in 1815, travelers continued to pass through the area, with some settling on land they did not own. In 1817, the northwest part of Ohio was purchased from the Native Americans and became known as the New Purchase. This ended the Greenville Treaty Line's barrier to expansion for white settlers.

The land north of the treaty line began to be surveyed in preparation for land sales. Marion County was officially created in 1820 by the state legislature, with land sales beginning soon after. It remained attached to Delaware County for legislative and judicial purposes until 1823. Over the next several years, the county's boundary changed as adjacent counties were created or modified. The final change came in 1848, when Morrow County was created in part with five townships taken from Marion County. As compensation for this, the area south of the original Greenville Treaty Line was transferred from Delaware County to Marion County.

Marion County has seven incorporated villages: Caledonia, Green Camp, LaRue, Morral, New Bloomington, Prospect, and Waldo. There are several unincorporated communities, at least one of which has a larger population than some of the incorporated villages. Among these communities are Big Island, Brush Ridge, Claridon, Kirkpatrick, Martel, and Meeker.

The criteria for village incorporation has changed significantly since the original formation of Ohio's state government in 1803 but generally includes a minimum number of residents, at least two square miles of territory, and other specific requirements. The primary difference between incorporated and unincorporated communities is the system of governance. In general, an incorporated village will have some version of a village council and mayor, while unincorporated communities are normally under the jurisdiction of the township trustees. Throughout this book, the author made efforts to use "village" only for those areas that are incorporated and "community" or "settlement" for the unincorporated areas, although exceptions may have occurred.

A review of historic maps of Marion County also reveals many communities that are either no longer in existence or perhaps were never more than a "paper town." Some examples include Blow's Grove, Buzzard's Glory, Clyde, Goose Pond, Harvey, Newmans, Owens, Parr Town, Slick's Station, Stringtown, and Tully City, just to name a few.

Two significant challenges presented themselves in the course of writing this book. The first involved locating postcards that included as many of the Marion County villages and communities as possible. Since this book is part of Arcadia Publishing's Postcard History Series, only postcard images were used. Finding usable postcards for the smaller communities presented a significant difficulty. Some of the larger villages may have had photographers who either lived in the area or chose a specific village to photograph for use on postcards. The quality of the available images also needed to be taken into account, as pictures that were blurred or printed on a certain type of stock did not meet the publication standards. Many wonderful images are available as photographs but could not be used for this book. One specific example entailed the Oorang Indians National Football League team based in LaRue. Pictures were available of team captain Jim Thorpe and his Native American teammates, but no clear images could be found on postcards. This lack of availability led to the exclusion of images featuring several places, people, or events that would have been interesting to include but did not meet the standards required for publishing in this book.

The second challenge was the difficulty of compiling accurate information about many of the subjects of the postcards. Resources such as the 1883, 1907, and 1979 Marion County histories, as well as smaller histories of many of the communities, were invaluable yet often contained discrepancies, especially regarding dates. Newspaper compilation databases provided interesting information but were somewhat questionable in their accuracy in numerous instances. Interviews with those who now or once did live or work in the various areas helped flesh out much of the information gathered elsewhere, although they were also prone to some inaccuracies, as memories change over the years. Many hours were spent checking and verifying information to create a final product that is as historically accurate as possible. In the end, errors may have occurred but not for lack of an effort at accuracy.

This book is the fourth from Arcadia Publishing that focuses on the city and county of Marion, Ohio. Together, they form a visual history of the people, places, and events of the area. Many memories have been preserved and shared that may otherwise have been lost. If the readers of this book have developed an increased interest in learning more about our rich heritage, then the final statement can be "mission accomplished."

One

Caledonia and Claridon Area

The area that would become Caledonia was surveyed and platted in 1834 at the request of landowners John Parcel and William T. Farrington. Lots were sold, and a settlement soon developed. As was true with many early communities, the name of the postmaster was used to identify the settlement. VanBuskirk was formed from its association with Lawrence E. Vanbuskirk, an early postmaster in the area. Many of the early settlers traced their roots to Scotland. Legend has it that a Scotsman, perhaps pining for his native land, soon suggested the name Caledonia, a Celtic word used as a romantic term for Scotland. The name was made official in 1835. The community grew steadily, and it reached the required number of residents to officially be classified as a village in 1873. Rail service helped the village grow, as its location (essentially equidistant from Bucyrus, Galion, Mount Gilead, and Marion) made it a good choice as a shipping center.

Col. James Kilbourne platted the settlement of Adelaide in the township of Claridon, located on the banks of the Whetstone River, in 1821. It was one of the earliest communities in what would soon become Marion County. Kilbourne felt that its location (near the center of the proposed county, which, at that time, included townships to the east of his settlement) was ideal for a county seat and developed the plats accordingly. The settlement covered more than 100 acres and had a large square in the center of the platted area. The square was to be used as the site of county buildings as well as a park. Other land was designated for buildings that would have a "literary purpose," such as a library. Avenues measuring 99 feet wide and streets measuring 66 feet wide were laid out in expectation of the heavy usage found in a county seat. Eventually, the small village of Marion was chosen as the county seat, bringing all the political and economic advantages associated with it. Kilbourne's settlement in due course adopted the name of the township and became known as Claridon. It remains an unincorporated community, as it has never achieved the minimum number of 1,600 residents required for incorporation.

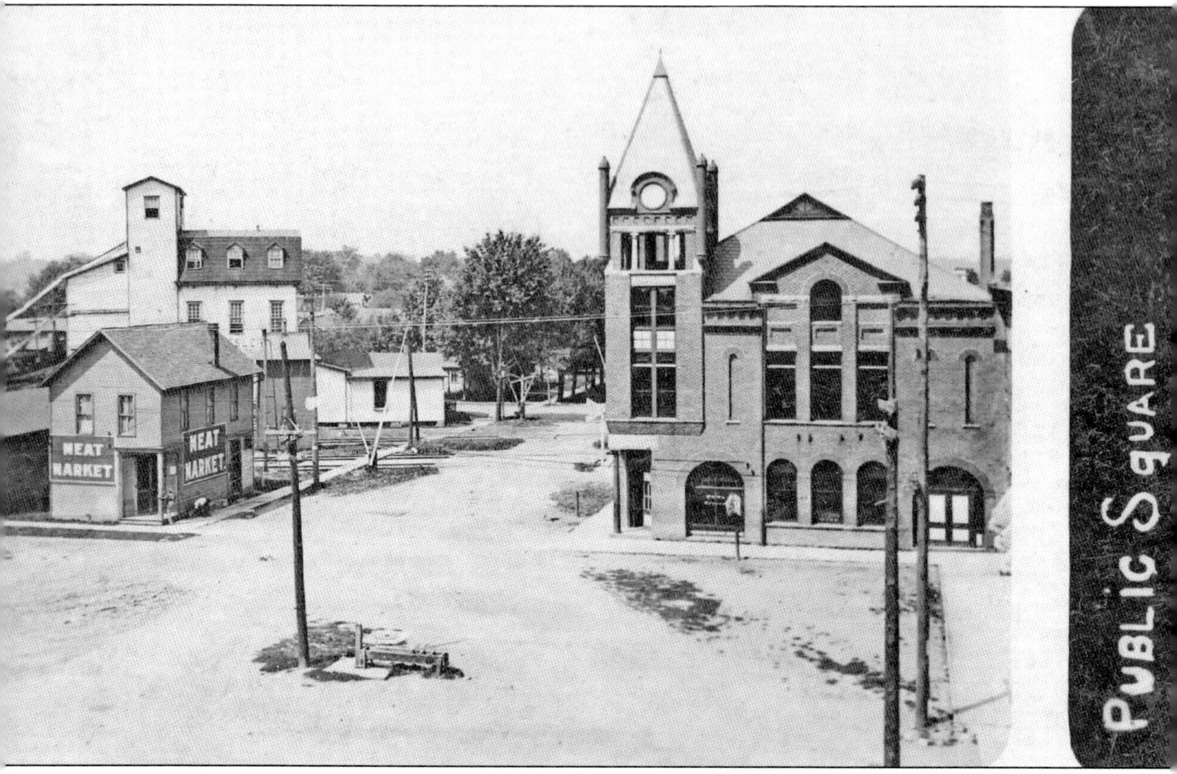

On the Square. Caledonia's public square served as an anchor for businesses and government buildings. Many of the original buildings were destroyed in an 1883 fire, after which the square was rebuilt in essentially the same configuration. The town hall was built in 1891 on the northeast corner of the square on a site once occupied by the Methodist church. It featured Romanesque elements, including arches, stained-glass windows, and a unique tower with a bell used to summon volunteer firemen. Council chambers, the mayor's office, the jail, the post office, and an assembly hall were all located in the building. The second-floor assembly hall hosted events such as traveling medicine shows, high school plays, and agricultural corn shows. A watering trough for horses was located in the center of the square, while merchant buildings such as the Underwood Block and a meat market lined its borders. Today's visitors will find the town hall still being used, while a veteran's memorial stands where the meat market once was. (Courtesy of Richard Carey.)

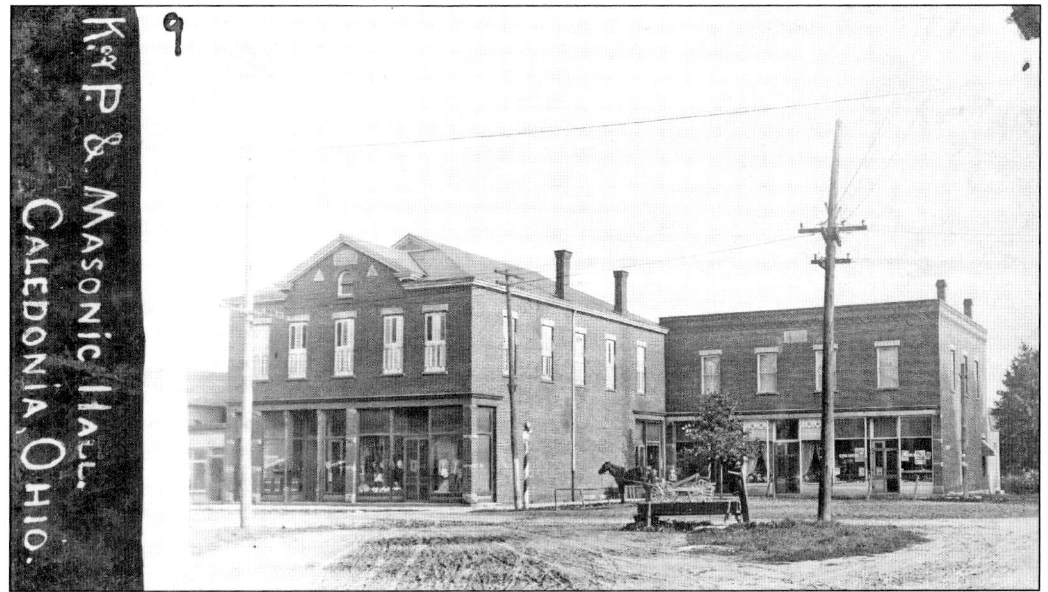

Knights and Masons. The Knights of Pythias Lodge No. 116 (the building on the left) was granted its charter in 1879, while the Oliver Lodge No. 447 of the Free and Associated Masons (at right) was chartered in 1870. The buildings the two fraternal organizations would occupy were built in 1879 on East Marion Street. The organizations occupied the upper floors, while retail establishments occupied the ground-level space. (Courtesy of Richard Carey.)

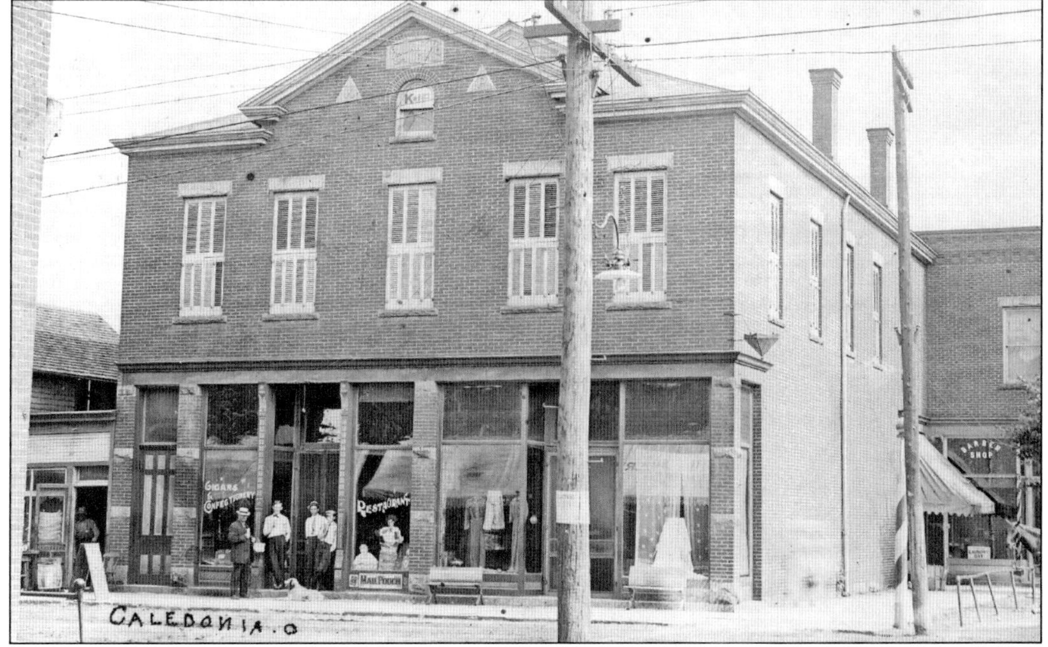

Roll Out the Barrel. The man standing in the shadows of the doorway at far left (next to the restaurant building) is John Kite Landes, a cooper who was well known for his mulberry-wood barrels. Landes was a Virginia native who did not believe in slavery and moved to Caledonia with his family to avoid being conscripted into the Confederate army. (Courtesy of Ralph and Erdine Eaton collection.)

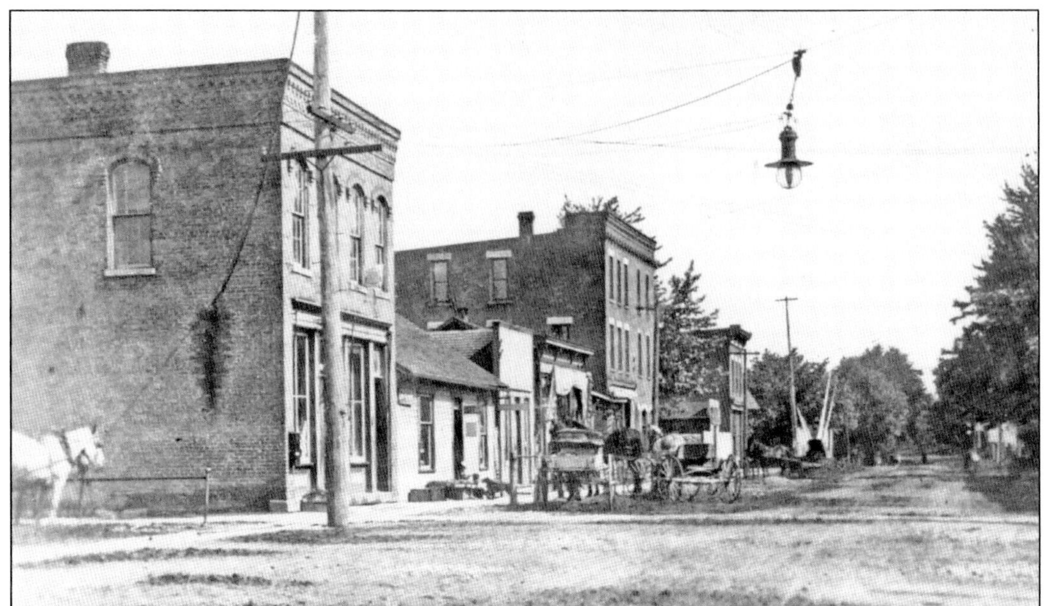

Shops and a Hotel. This view looking north on Water Street shows several merchant establishments in the days when the horse and buggy served as the primary means of transportation. The large building toward the back with white stone window lintels was the Hanley House Hotel. Since the railroad depot was nearby, the hotel was a popular stop for travelers in the early 1900s. (Author's collection.)

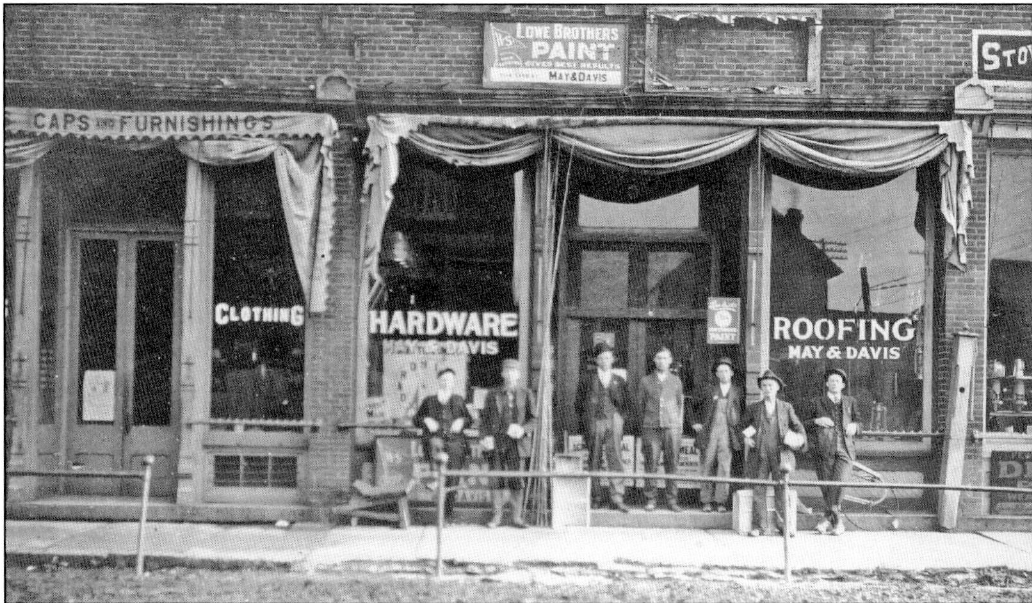

May & Davis. Joseph and Nora May opened a roofing, spouting, and tin shop in 1909. They later bought out the stock of the Scott E. Irey Hardware Store on South Marion Street and moved their business there. George Davis, a longtime employee of the Mays, became a partner for a few years before leaving the partnership in 1915. Sales were brisk, and additional space was added after the purchase of an adjacent building. May Hardware Company remained a fixture in Caledonia until it closed in the early 1990s. (Courtesy of Richard Carey.)

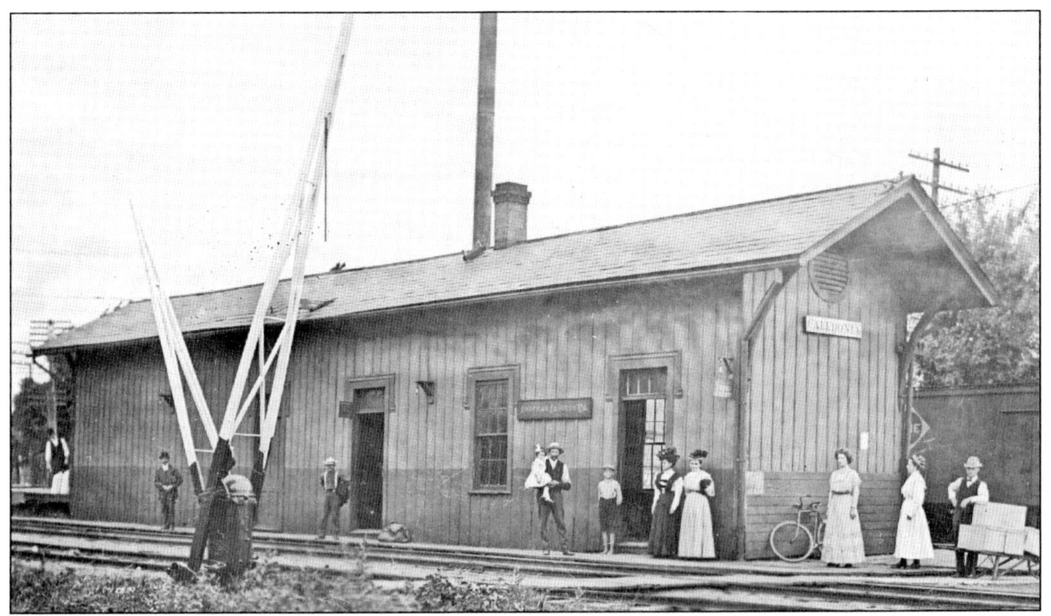

Patiently Waiting. The Caledonia Depot, located near the business district between North Main and Water Streets, served both the Erie and Big Four Railroads. Village residents often "took a local" to Marion or other destinations for the day to shop or enjoy entertainment. (Courtesy of Richard Carey.)

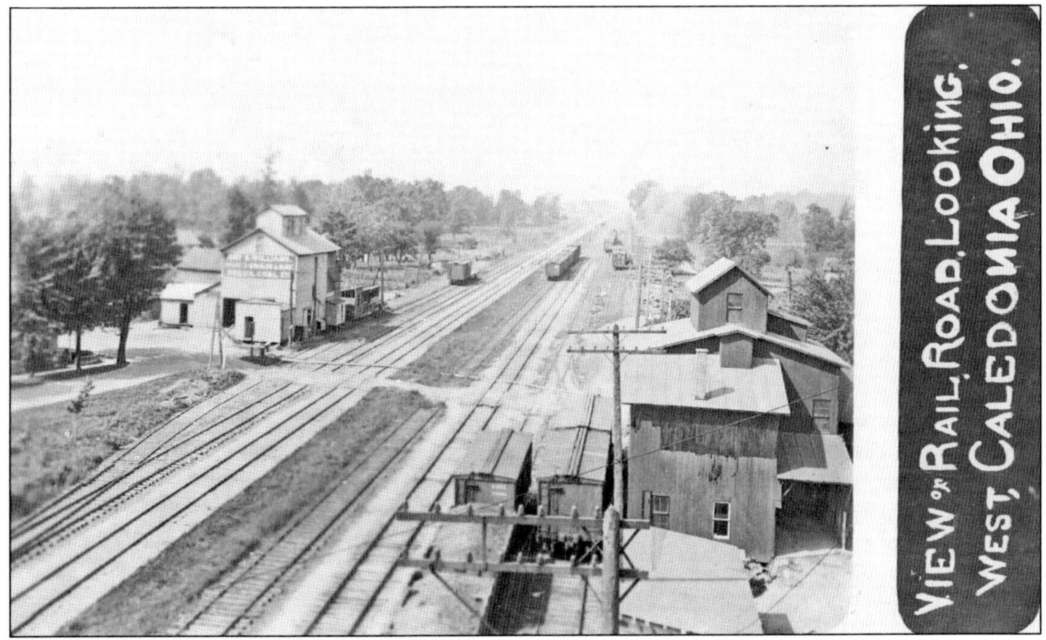

Railyard. Caledonia's small railyard provided sufficient room on its sidings for loading and unloading at two grain elevators and for sorting or storing railcars. Workers at the elevators may have used the "Improved Hand-truck for Sacking Grain, and Moving the Same" patented by Caledonia resident William Brocklesby Jr. in 1869. (Courtesy of Richard Carey.)

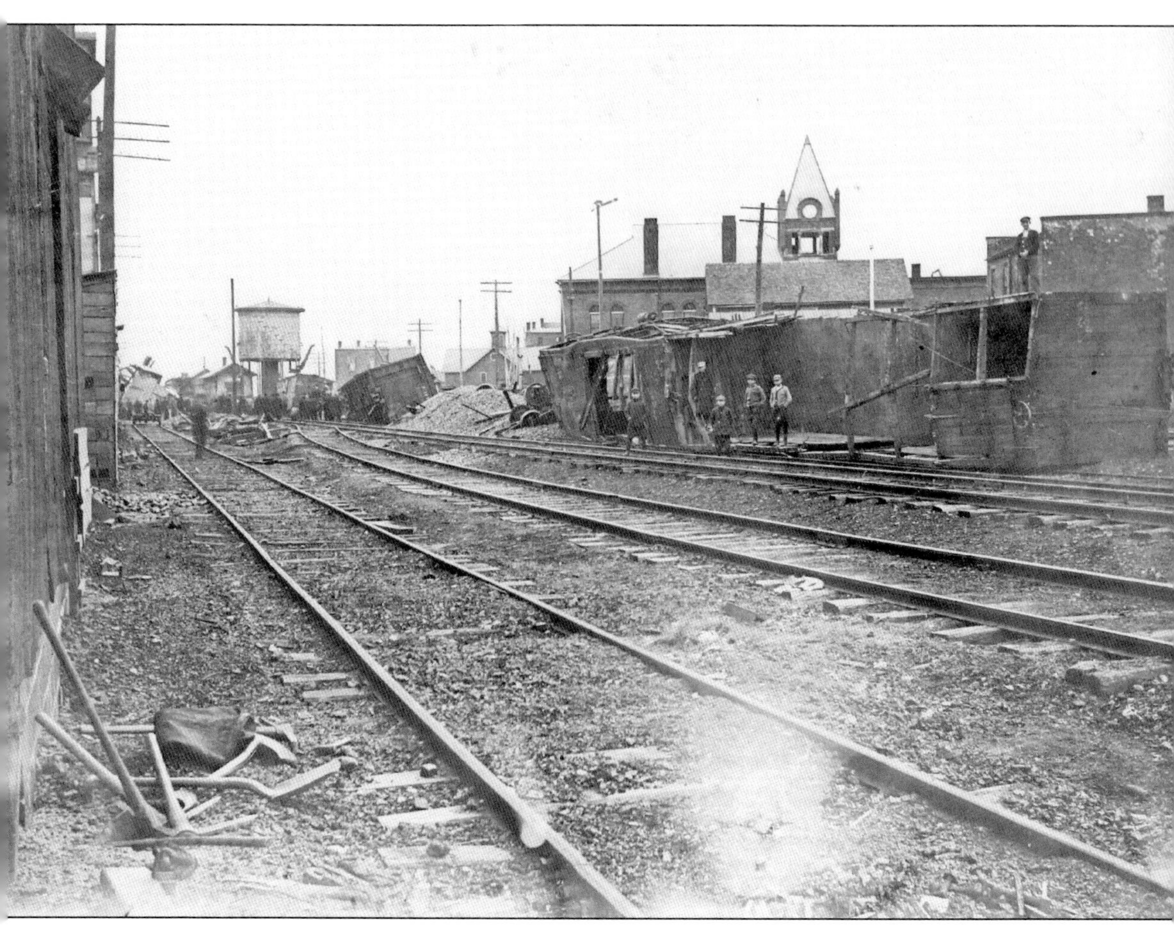

TRAIN WRECKS. In 1913, tragedy was narrowly avoided when a westbound Erie Railroad freight train hit a broken rail, causing seven cars of hard coal to derail at the Main Street crossing. Some of the cars piled up at the crossing (as shown in this image), while others rolled against the tower, causing it to shift. No one inside the tower was injured. This was not the case in 1910, when a Big Four passenger train apparently ran a red block at Martel and crashed into the rear of a stopped freight train a short distance east of Caledonia. The engineer was killed, and the 150 passengers on the ill-fated flyer were shaken up, but none reported serious injuries. An investigation into the crash determined that the engineer had reversed his engine prior to the collision to little effect. Two hundred sacks of mail were saved by the quick action of the mail clerks, who smothered a fire that broke out in the mail car. They were forced to grab axes to chop their way out of the crushed car. (Courtesy of Richard Carey.)

OIL RUSH. Oil was discovered on the farm of Frank Ulsh about two miles southwest of Caledonia in 1916. Several wells were drilled on the property over the next few years, with records showing that more than 75,000 barrels of oil were removed. This resulted in a rush by speculators and developers to lease and buy the surrounding land, but many of them found little success. (Courtesy of Mike and Linda Perry.)

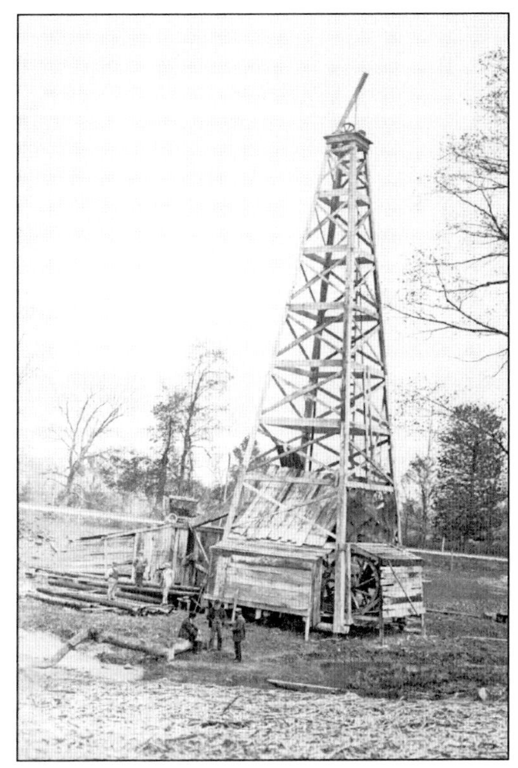

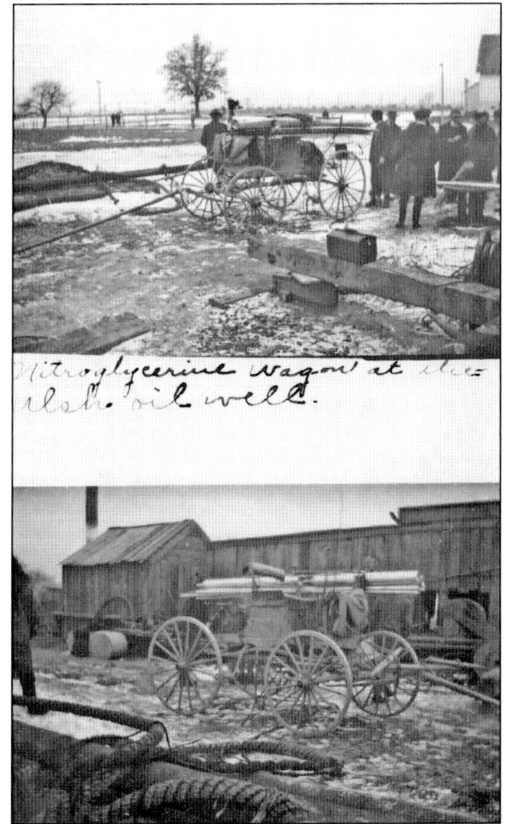

DRIVE CAREFULLY. Oilfield work was sometimes dangerous. This was especially true when a well needed to be "shot" by dropping a "torpedo" filled with explosives down the shaft before triggering it. The resulting explosion fractured the rock, allowing the oil and natural gas to escape more freely. For the Ulsh "shooting," 40 quarts of nitroglycerin were transported 60 miles in a wooden-wheeled wagon. (Courtesy of Richard Carey.)

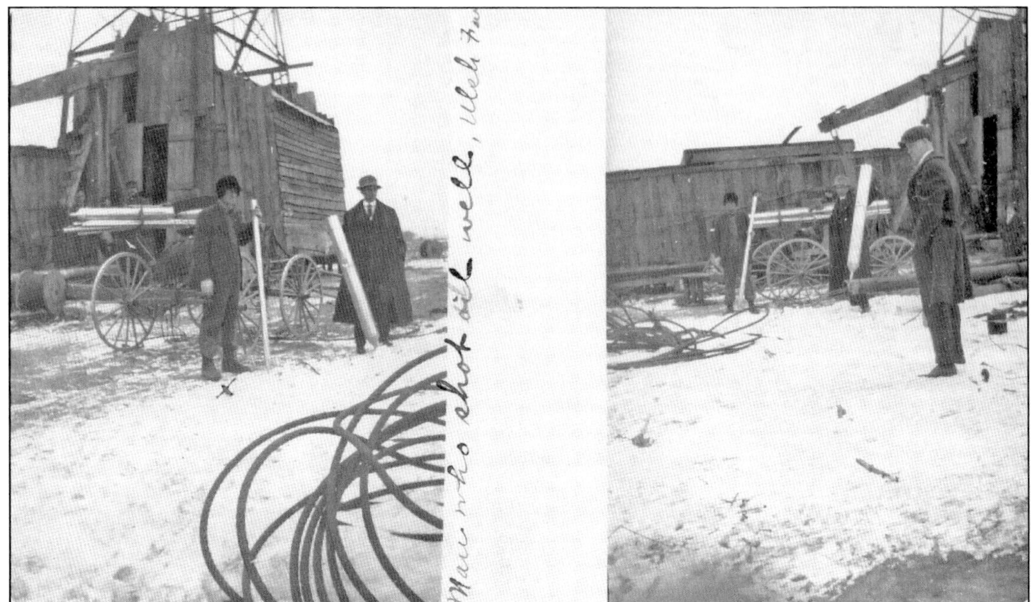

Big Boom. The man who shot the Ulsh well is identified with an "X" mark on the left side of this postcard. The Marietta Torpedo Company provided the torpedo, which is being held by the man in the overcoat. Although the scheduled time of the well shooting was not supposed to be public knowledge, an estimated 500 people were on the scene to watch the explosion and possible oil gusher. (Courtesy of Richard Carey.)

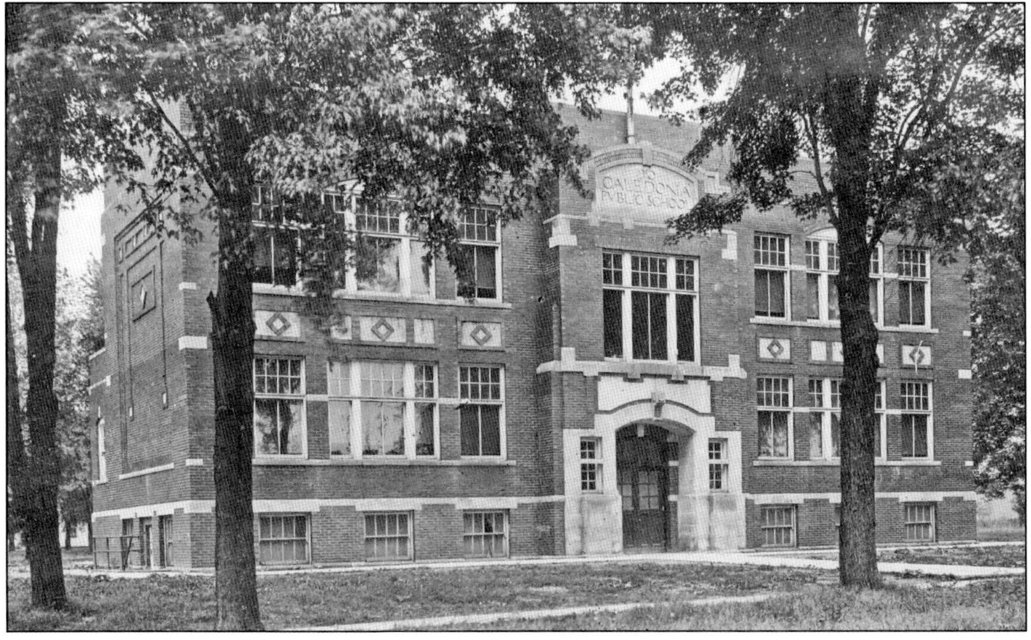

First Class. Residents of Caledonia took great pride in their Caledonia Public School. Completed in 1910 at a cost of $20,000, the school was at first considered to be a "second grade" school due to the lack of certain facilities. As a result of centralization in 1915 and increased attendance, the school added an auditorium, resulting in it being reclassified as a "first grade" facility. (Courtesy of Ralph and Erdine Eaton collection.)

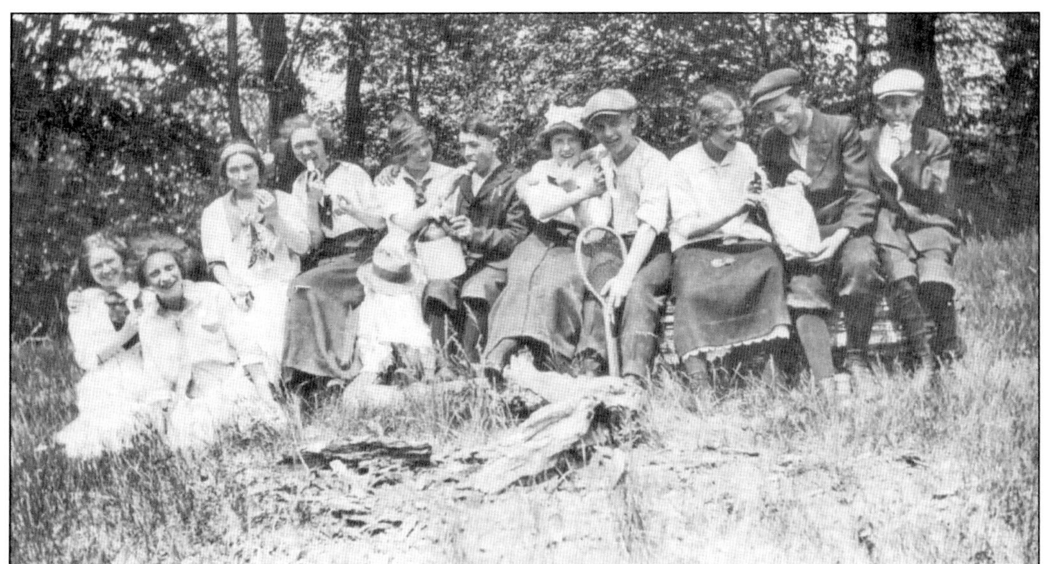

Class Picnic. Students from Caledonia enjoyed a class picnic with bananas as a special treat. One young man is holding a jug with unknown contents (although it's likely not lemonade). Another has his tennis racket at the ready, perhaps to play a quick game on the court once located behind the Caledonia Memorial United Methodist Church. (Author's collection.)

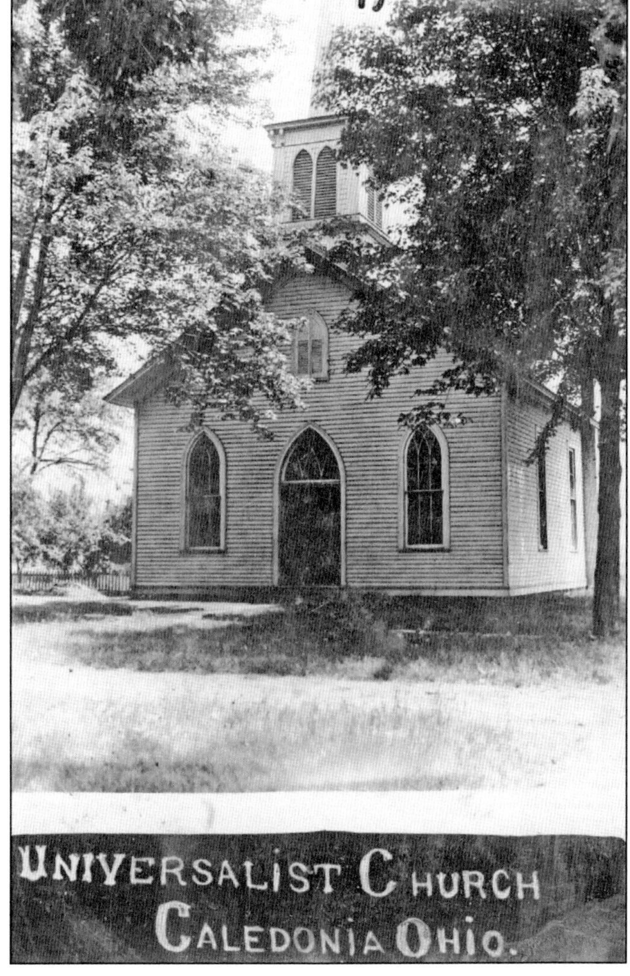

Universalist Church. Located on North Water Street at Liberty Street, the Universalist church was built in 1871 at a cost of $3,284. Universalists believed in the ultimate salvation of all mankind with the premise that truth and righteousness are controlling powers. The building was sold to the Nazarene congregation in 1950. It is now a private residence. (Courtesy of Bob Turner.)

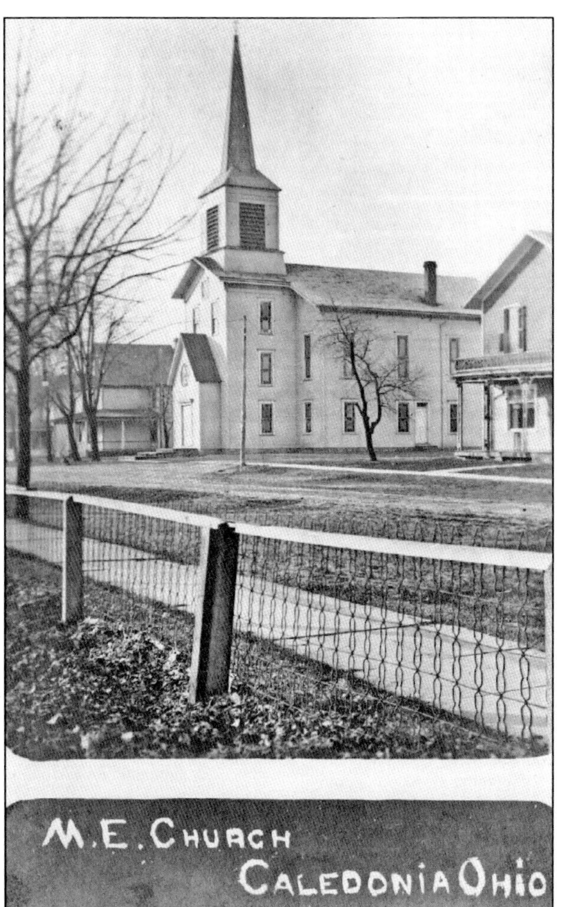

METHODIST EPISCOPAL CHURCH. The first Methodist Episcopal church was located on the northeast corner of what is now the village square. In 1863, the rapidly growing congregation built this 40-by-50-foot, two-story building on the southwest corner of Main and South Streets at a cost of $2,500. It stood until 1908, when it was razed to make way for a massive new church. (Courtesy of Richard Carey.)

SETTING OF THE CORNERSTONE. Anna Harkness, widow of Stephen V. Harkness (one of Standard Oil Company's original investors), offered a gift to the village of Caledonia in honor of her mother, Anna Marie Underwood, a lifelong resident. When the village rejected her offer for a memorial library, Harkness approached the Methodist Episcopal congregation with an offer to build a new church. They readily accepted, and the cornerstone was set on October 24, 1908. (Author's collection.)

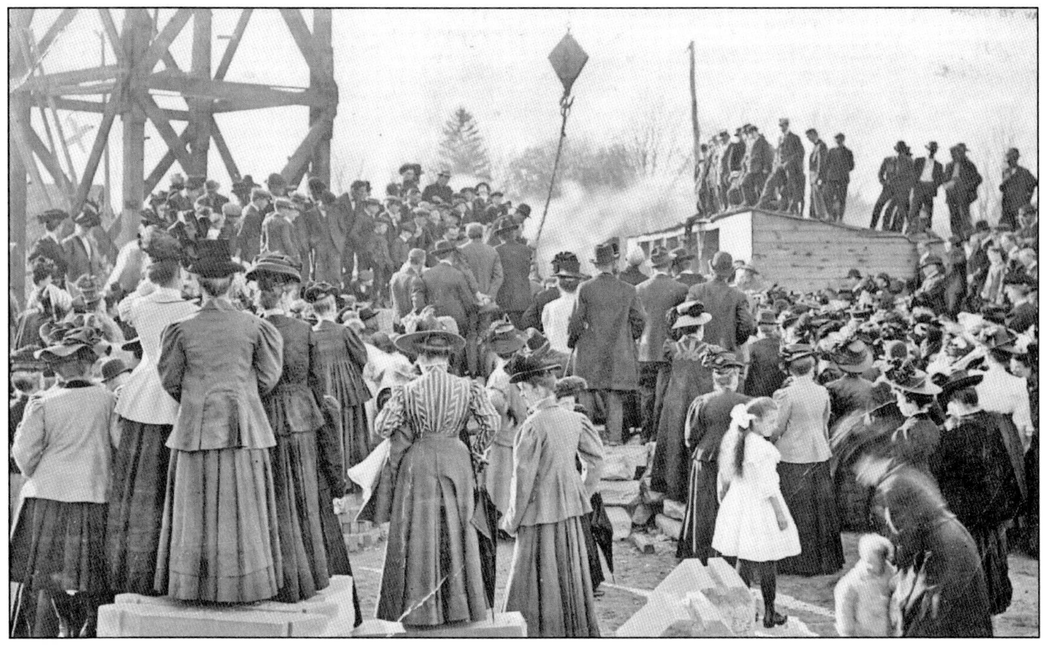

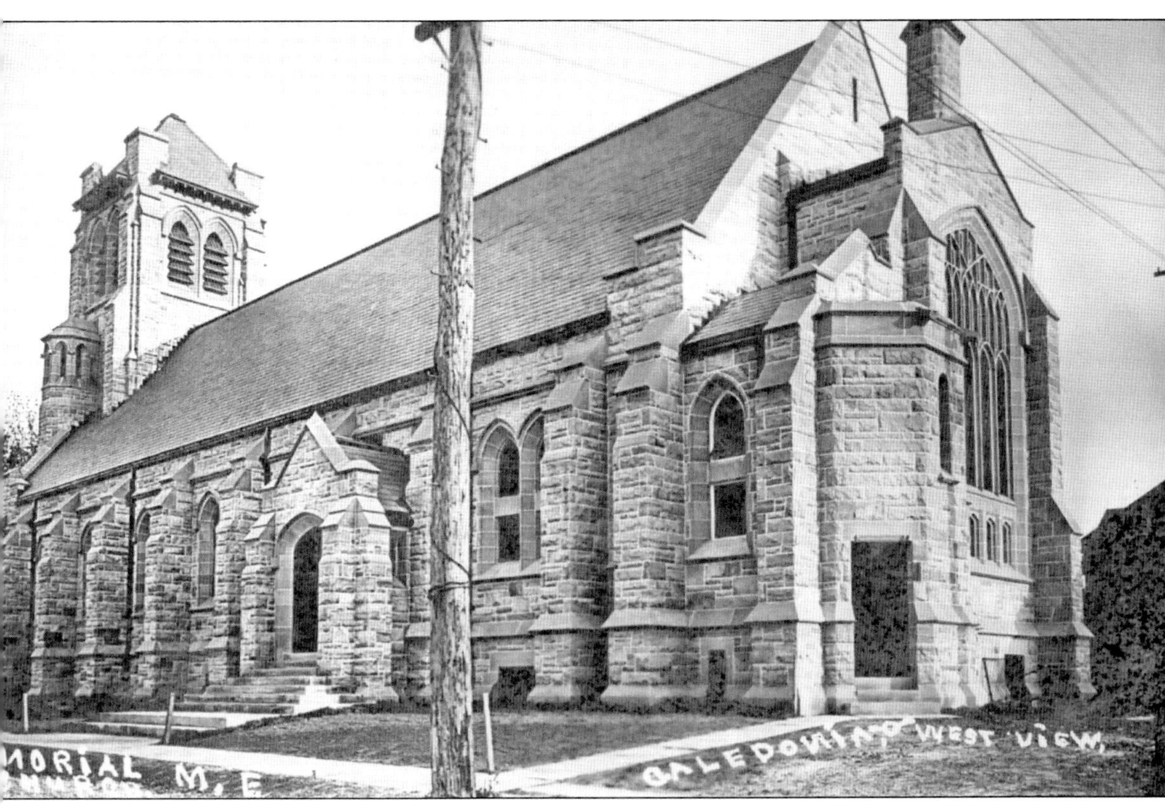

Completed Project. The Caledonia Memorial Methodist Episcopal Church took its design from 15th-century Norman cathedrals in Scotland. Abram Garfield, son of Pres. James A. Garfield, was chosen as the architect. Skilled stone masons from Cleveland cut the stone by hand. The bell tower rose more than 75 feet into the air, while the massive cut-stone walls provided a sense of strength and permanence. A vaulted wooden ceiling highlighted the interior, which also featured iron chandeliers. A set of 18-foot tall interior doors could be closed to create separate spaces for Sunday school classes or other purposes. Narrow spiral staircases cut from white sandstone wound upward from the altar to the choir loft and organ chamber and also down to a basement. The basement featured a massive sandstone fireplace with a carved sculpture of a mother and child. The building was completed in 1909. (Author's collection.)

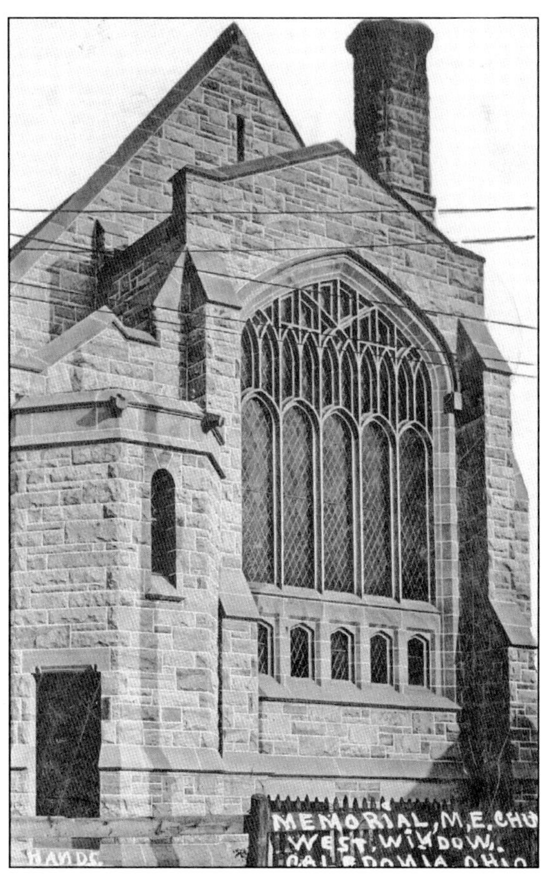

Let the Light Shine In. The large west window of the Caledonia Memorial Methodist Episcopal Church was designed to allow natural light to fill the sanctuary. Despite the generosity of the gift from Anna Harkness, some village residents felt the church leaders should not have taken the money. Much of the original Harkness fortune was earned by her late husband Stephen's distillery business, which led to this structure's derisive nickname of "the whiskey church." (Courtesy of Richard Carey.)

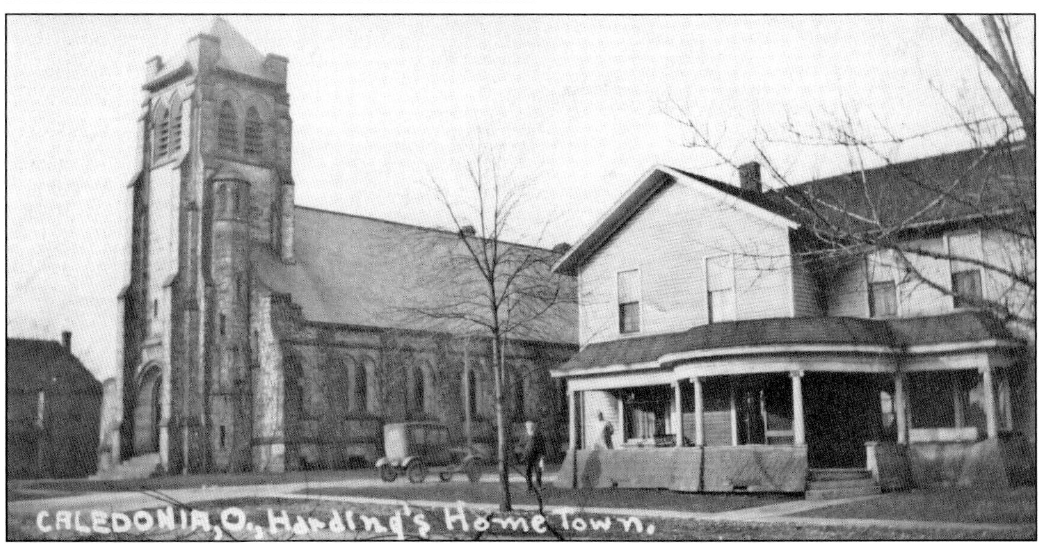

Future President's Home. Warren G. Harding was 10 years old when his family moved into this home in 1875. Harding entered Ohio Central College in nearby Iberia at age 14 and graduated with a bachelor of science degree in 1882. While at the college, he served as editor of the school newspaper, which helped prepare him for his early career as the owner and editor of the *Marion Star* newspaper. (Courtesy of Richard Carey.)

North Canaan Church. Located just east of Caledonia in Morrow County, the North Canaan Methodist Episcopal Church traces its roots to 1833. In 1846, a log church building was erected on land donated by Jacob Strawser. The church flourished, and in 1861, the log structure was replaced by this building, which is still in use today with an active congregation. (Courtesy of Ralph and Erdine Eaton collection.)

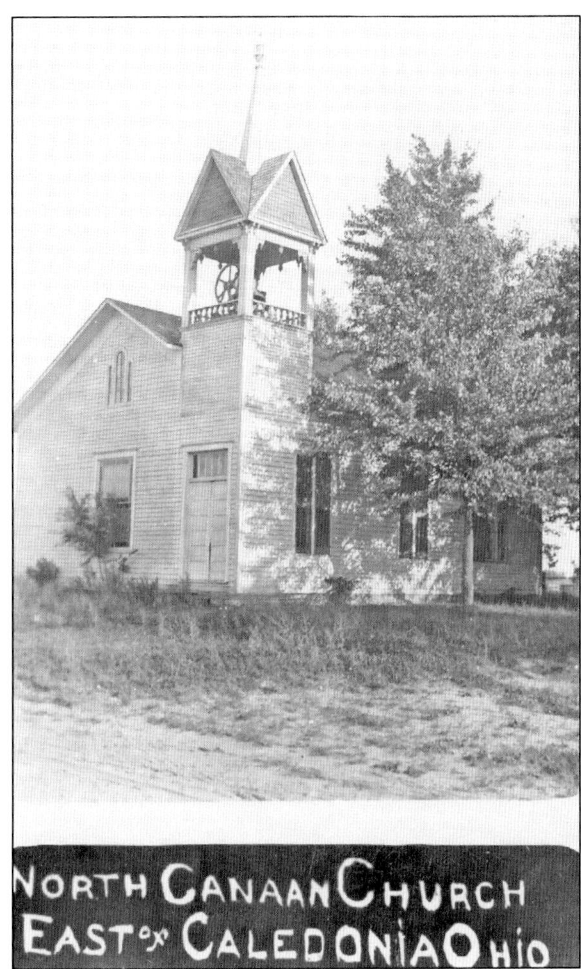

Memorial Mausoleum. Despite the similarity of its name, the Caledonia Memorial Mausoleum had no direct connection to the Caledonia Memorial Methodist Episcopal Church. The structure was built in the early 1900s by a mausoleum association. The lack of a perpetual care fund led to difficulties in maintenance, and the building deteriorated. In 1984, the bodies were removed, cremated, and buried in the Caledonia Cemetery, and the structure was then demolished. (Author's collection.)

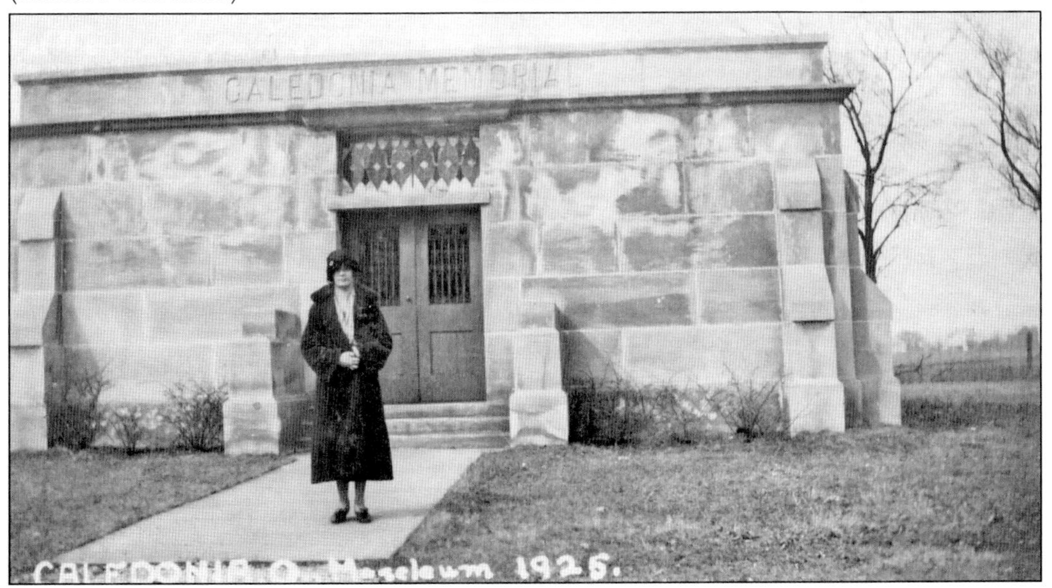

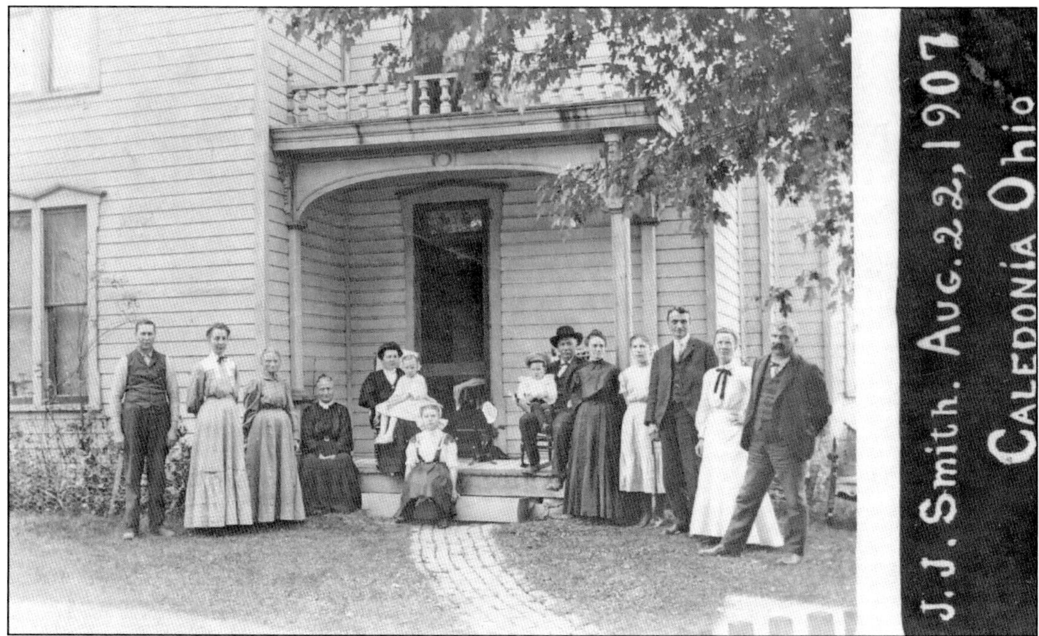

Family Gathering. The family of John J. Smith gathered at the Smith home for this photograph in 1907. Smith and his wife, Rebecca, moved to the area prior to 1880. They had at least five children, with two dying at a young age. Smith served in the Civil War with the 64th Ohio Volunteer Infantry, after which he became a farmer. (Courtesy of Mike and Linda Perry.)

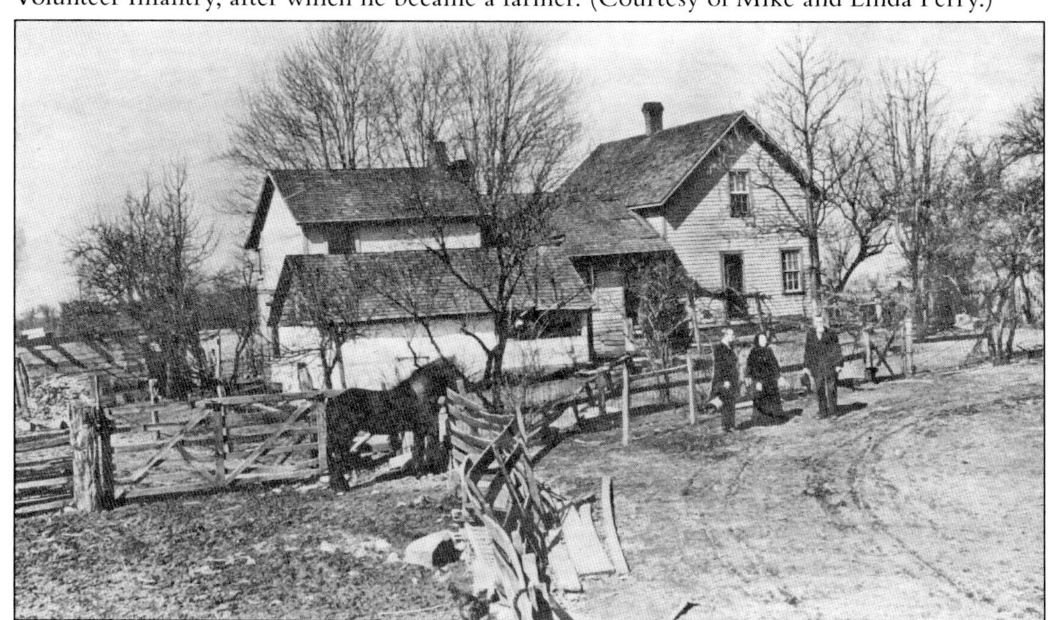

Going to a Reunion? Perhaps these people, who appear to be waiting for a ride at the Hipsher farm northwest of Caledonia in 1910, are on their way to a family reunion. The Hipsher families in Marion County traced their roots to three brothers from Wurtenburg, Germany, who immigrated to America in 1750. Family reunions were important events, as evidenced by the more than 100 people who attended the 1907 Hipsher reunion at the school grounds in Caledonia. (Courtesy of Marion County Historical Society.)

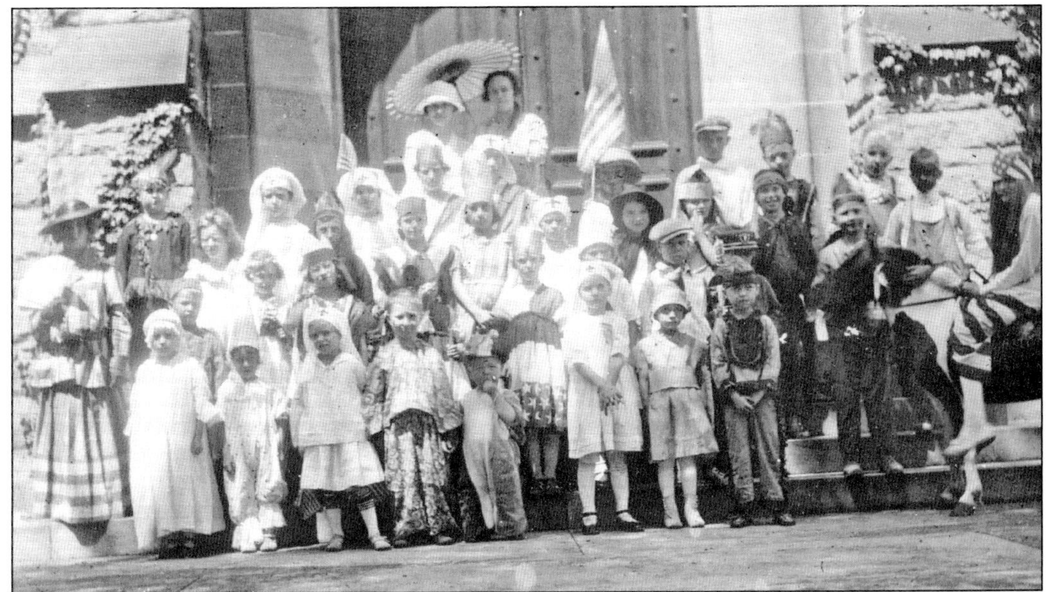

Ready for a Parade. Children in costumes gather in front of the Caledonia Memorial Methodist Episcopal Church prior to participating in a Chautauqua parade. The Chautauqua circuit was active in Marion County from 1910 until around 1929. The primary location was in Marion, which had a pavilion with room for 2,300 attendees. Villages such as Caledonia and Green Camp occasionally hosted their own events with speakers and entertainment. (Courtesy of Richard Carey.)

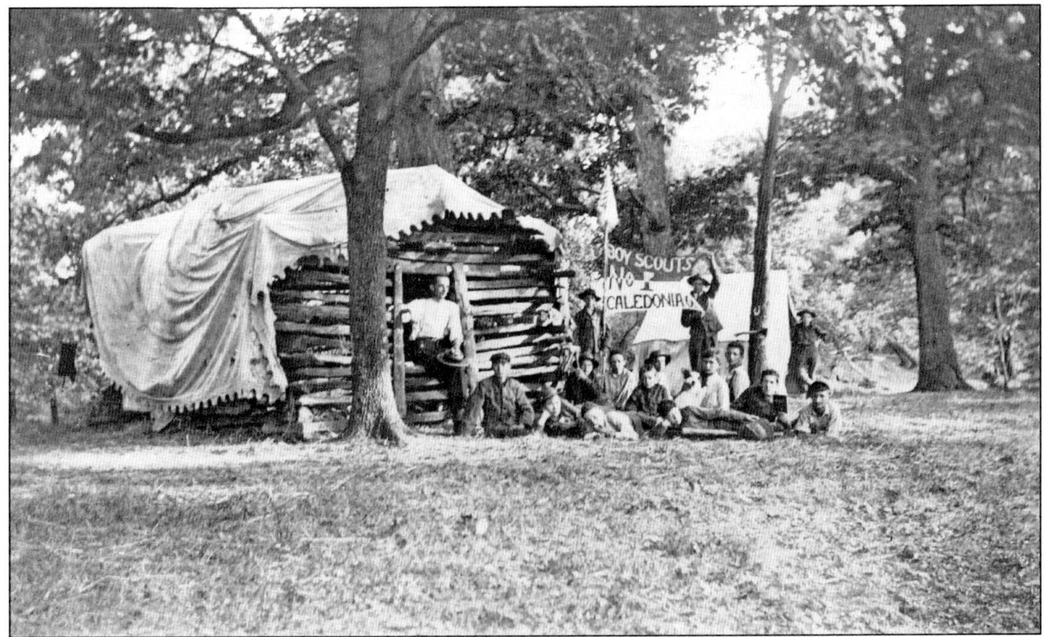

Camping Trip. Boy Scout Troop No. 1 is shown settled at its campground in 1913. The location may have been at a Boy Scout camp on the east side of the Whetstone River near an area that is now designated as the Caledonia Nature Preserve. The preserve is the site of a historical bowstring bridge that was moved from Green Camp in 1976. (Courtesy of Richard Carey.)

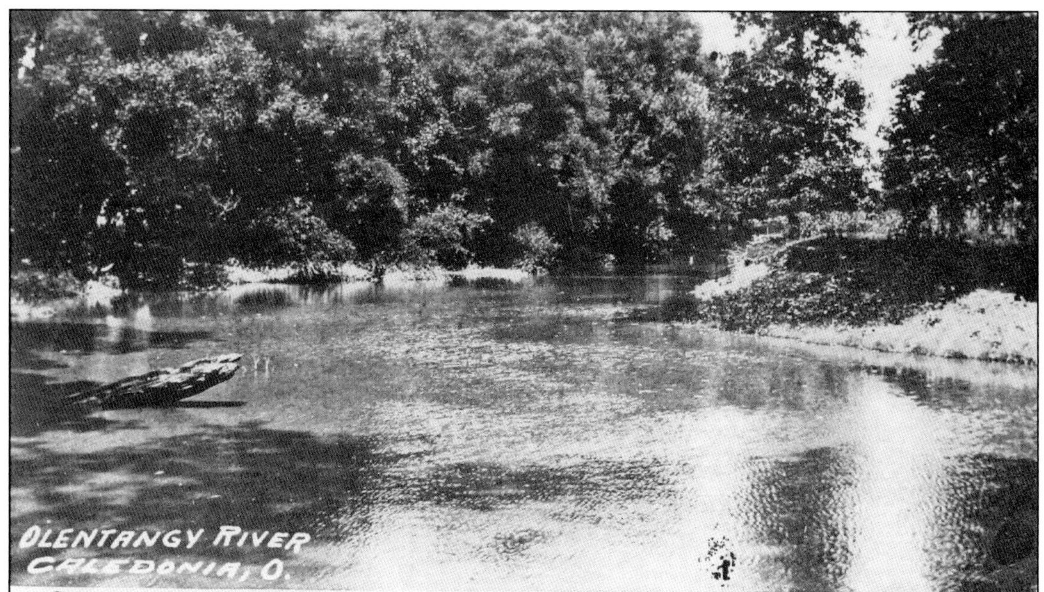

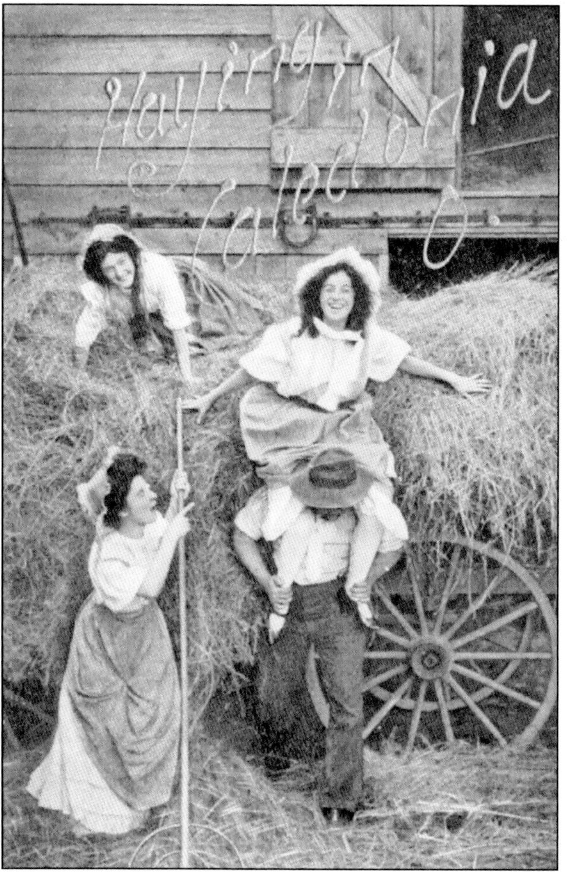

TAKE A DIP. Future US president Warren G. Harding spent many summer days in his favorite swimming hole while living in Caledonia. Its exact location is unknown, but it was probably north of the Caledonia railroad bridge in one of the deeper pools in the otherwise shallow river. (Courtesy of Richard Carey.)

MAKING HAY. Postcard manufacturers often utilized a stock photograph with personalized labeling. This card, with its double entendre picture and caption, would have been considered a bit risqué for its early-1900s publication. (Courtesy of Richard Carey.)

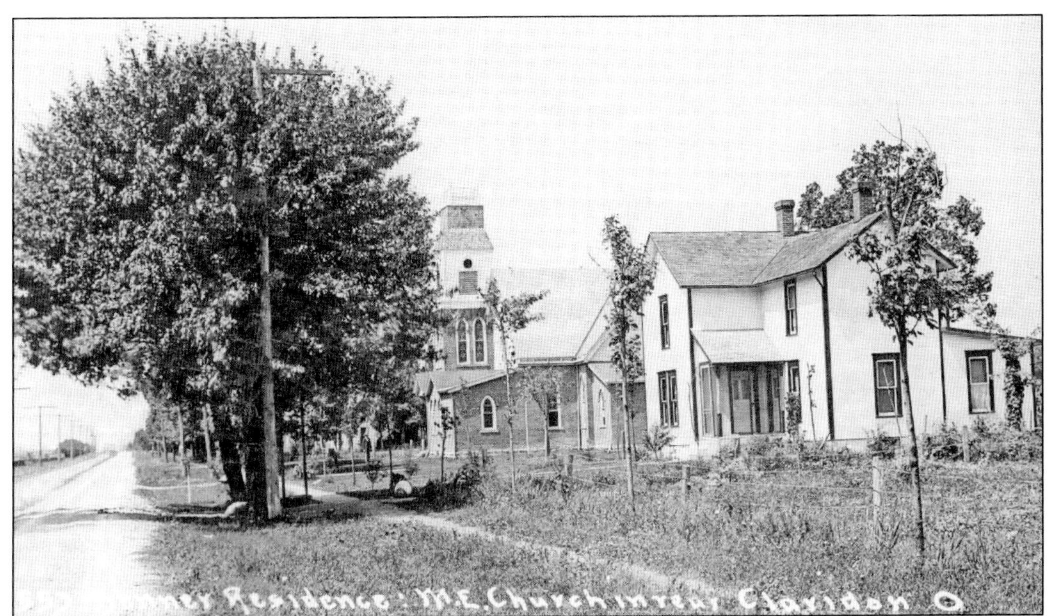

Claridon Methodist Church. The Claridon Methodist congregation traces its roots to 1820, when worshipers, many of whom had emigrated from England, gathered in the home of Jacob Aye Jr. This church, which was dedicated in 1885, was the third built by the congregation. Remodeling completed in 1967 consisted of Sunday school classrooms, a pastor's study, and restrooms. (Courtesy of Terry Kreis.)

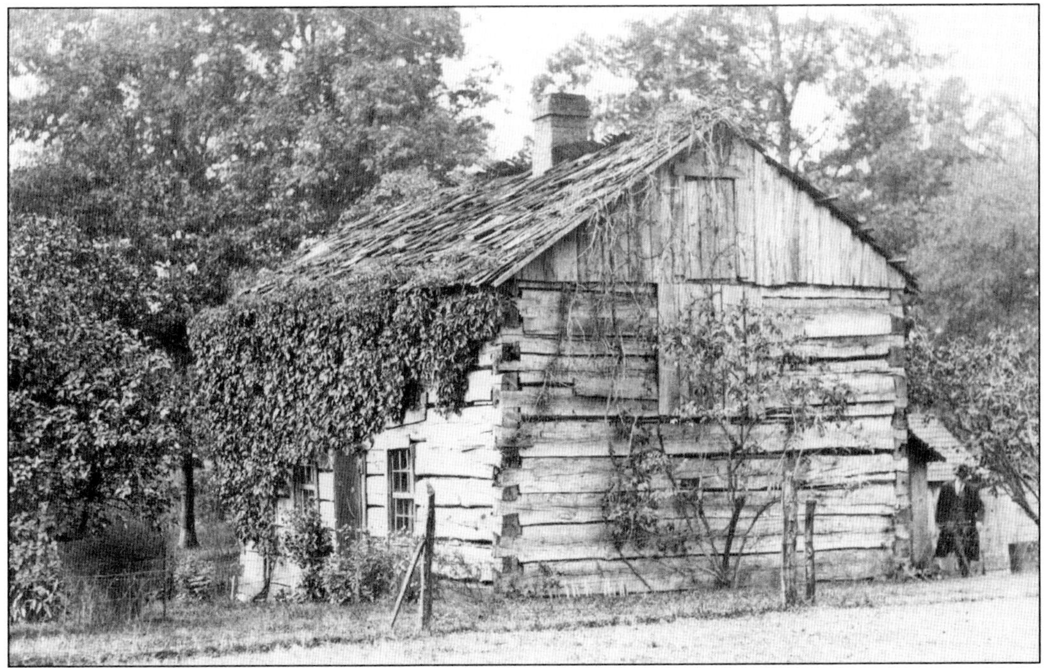

Smithson Log House. Joseph Smithson owned this log house south of Claridon near the Whetstone River. Smithson was known as an abolitionist and offered his property as a burial site for an escaped slave who died of illness while on her trip to freedom. She was buried in a grove of trees west of the house at a site marked by a triangle of stones. (Author's collection.)

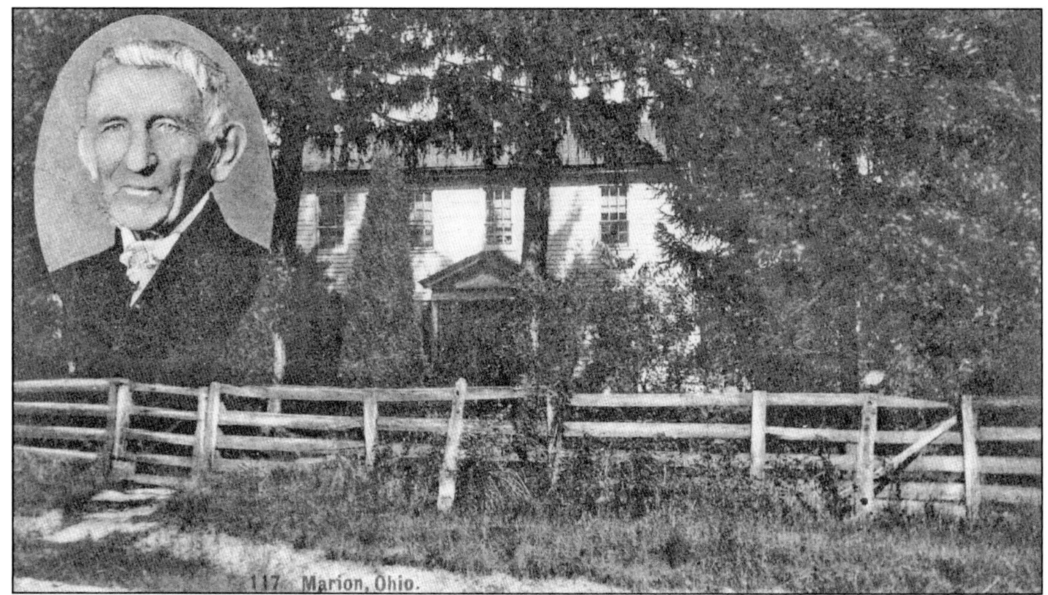

MORRIS RESIDENCE. Joseph Morris operated one of the better-known stations on the Underground Railroad at his farm and plant nursery in northeast Richland Township. The home featured hidden chambers in the cellar as well as tunnels leading to outbuildings. Morris, who was a Quaker, traveled around the country delivering material aid and distributing religious publications to orphanages, prisons, and communities of former slaves. (Author's collection.)

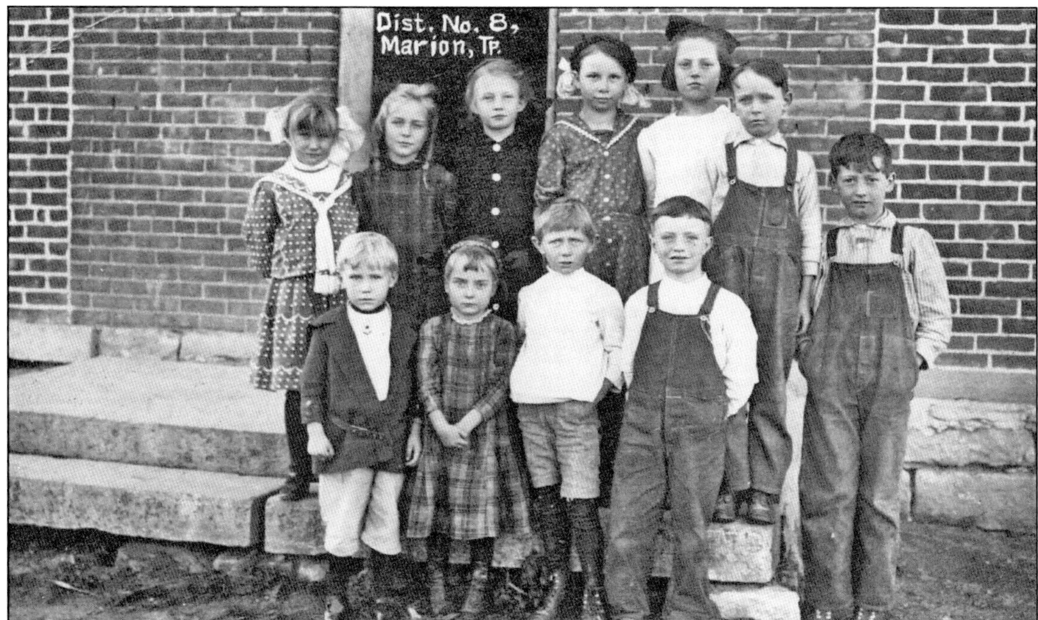

ADDITION REQUIRED. This group of students gathered for a picture at the Marion Township District 8 School, the exact location of which is unknown. Districts continually changed their numbering systems as the population in their areas grew or declined. Records of these changes are often not reliable or even available. The school was apparently in an area that was increasing in population, resulting in an addition to the building, as evidenced by the mismatched brick. (Author's collection.)

Two

Green Camp and New Bloomington Area

The beginnings of the village of Green Camp can be traced to the War of 1812. Soldiers under the command of Capt. Daniel Green camped near Horseshoe Bend on the Big Scioto River north of the present-day village. The site became known as "Green's Camp," with the name eventually being adopted for the township. Among the first settlers in the area was Alexander Porter, who arrived in 1819. He settled on land north of the Greenville Treaty Line that was not surveyed and thus could not be purchased until 1820, when the state legislature of Ohio began to allow land sales. When sales opened, Porter purchased 80 acres in the area that would become the village.

In 1838, David Beach plotted a settlement on 40 acres he had purchased on the banks of the Scioto River. He named it Berwick in a likely reference to the village of Berwick, Pennsylvania, where his father had lived. The community continued to grow, and in 1875, it met the standards for incorporation at the time, which required at least 300 residents and 50 qualified voters. Approval for incorporation was given by the county commissioners, who also agreed to the residents' request to have the village named Green Camp to help alleviate confusion with another village called Berwick (located in Seneca County).

Brothers Wingate and W.W. Carey, along with C.A. Darlington and Armstrong Smallwood, plotted a settlement in 1856 in southeastern Montgomery Township. It was located about half-mile west of a Bellefontaine & Indiana Railroad section camp known as Carey's Camp. The first name given to the settlement was Bloomington, but over the next 89 years, it was renamed numerous times along with the post office and railroad station. Agosta, Belfast, and New Bloomington were all used by the different entities at some point in various combinations. The availability of rail service in 1856, along with the construction of a depot in 1879, spurred development of the new settlement. By the late 1890s, a thriving community included a stave factory, a tile factory, several grocery stores, a hardware store, a blacksmith shop, a grain elevator, and a rail depot, among other businesses. In 1883, Agosta became the official name for the village, railroad, and post office. Locals also sometimes used the nickname "Cy Plunk" in reference to the village. Agosta remained the village name until 1945, when residents changed the name once again, to New Bloomington, after rail service was discontinued during the previous year.

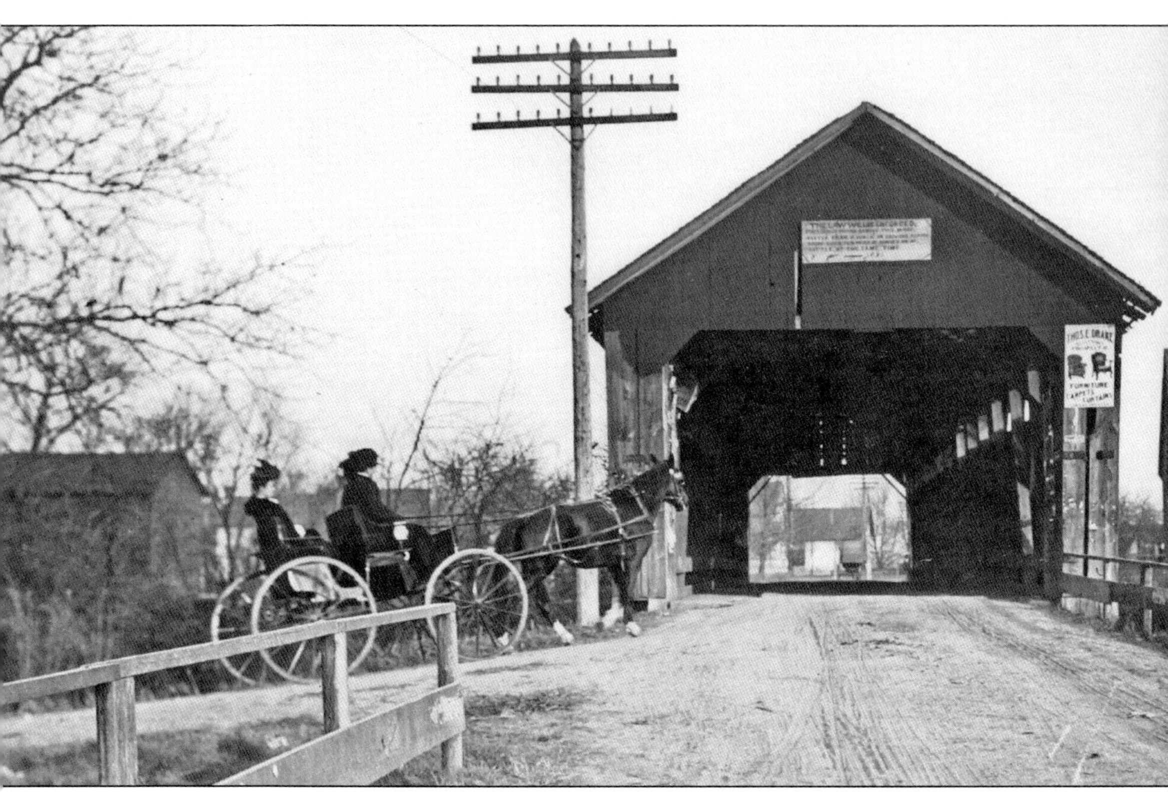

BERWICK CROSSOVER. This covered bridge served as the gateway to the village from the time of its construction in 1869 until it was replaced following a devastating flood in 1913. Village residents apparently wanted to be sure the bridge remained safe and established a set of prominently displayed restrictions, such as how many cattle could be taken across at one time. An image of a pistol was added to the sign to encourage compliance. The bridge stood on what was once a turnpike (also known as a toll road) that connected Bellefontaine and Marion. Turnpikes were so named because a long pole or pike that was mounted on a post could be turned across a roadway to prevent usage without payment of a fee. Turnpikes were common in the late 19th century, when entrepreneurs saw a way to profit from the combination of a growing population and few developed roadways. Government regulation soon became necessary, with most turnpikes eventually being purchased by local or state governments to allow for citizens to travel freely. (Courtesy of Mike and Linda Perry.)

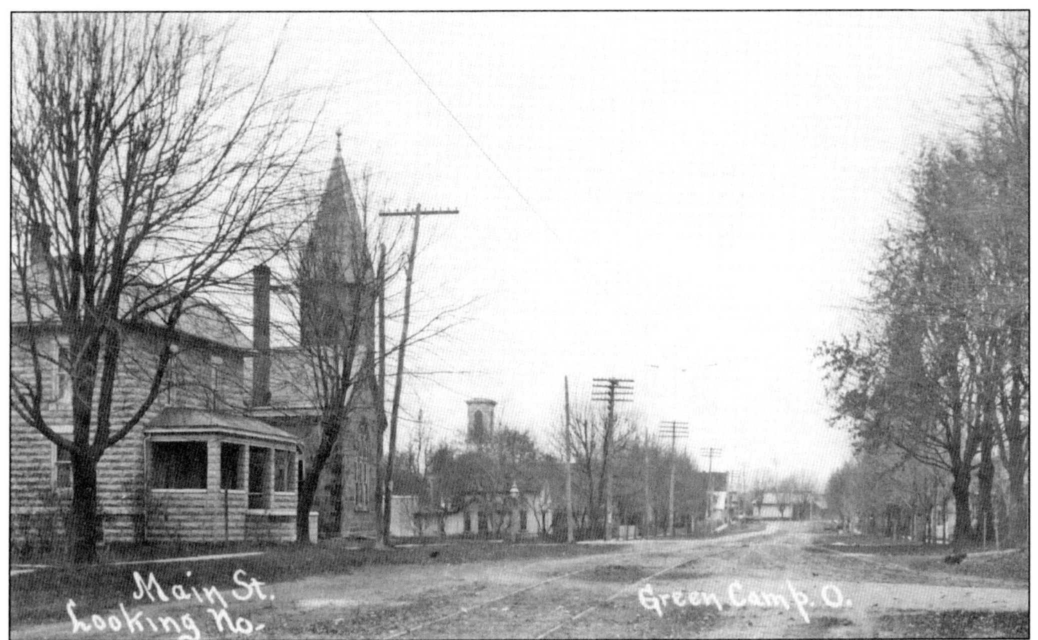

Looking North on Main Street. In this photograph, the tracks for the interurban rail service are clearly visible in the dirt surface of Main Street. The house at far left was the Baptist congregation's parsonage and was adjacent to its church. The steeple of the Methodist church is visible in the background. (Courtesy of Richard Carey.)

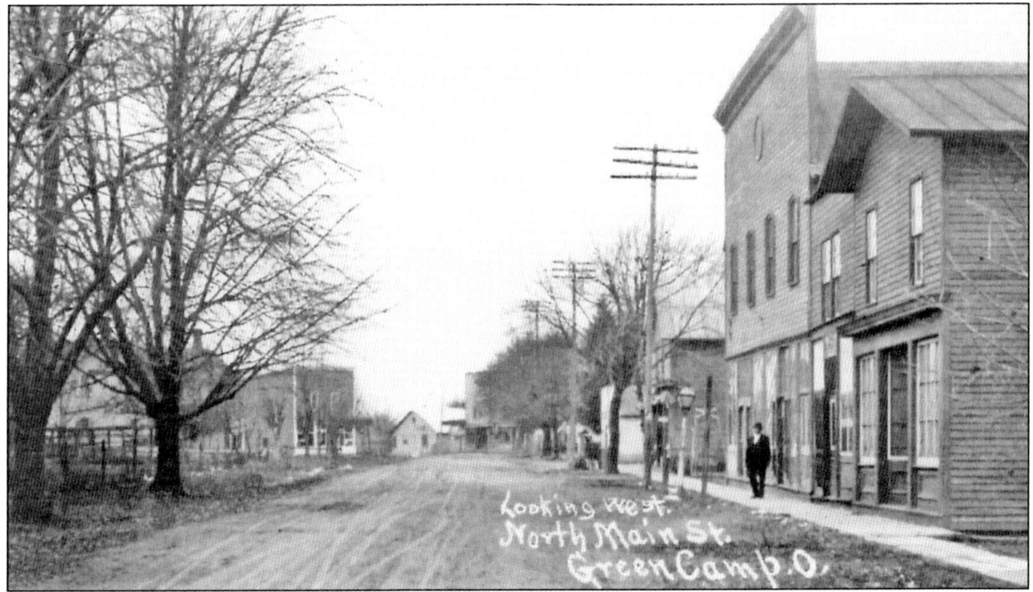

Uptown. The sandstone sidewalks installed around 1900 made shopping at the "uptown" merchants on North Main Street a cleaner and more enjoyable experience. One merchant hoped to lure potential clients with his use of a false front designed to make his establishment more impressive. That building was home to the post office for many years and later housed a hardware store. The village park is on the left. (Author's collection.)

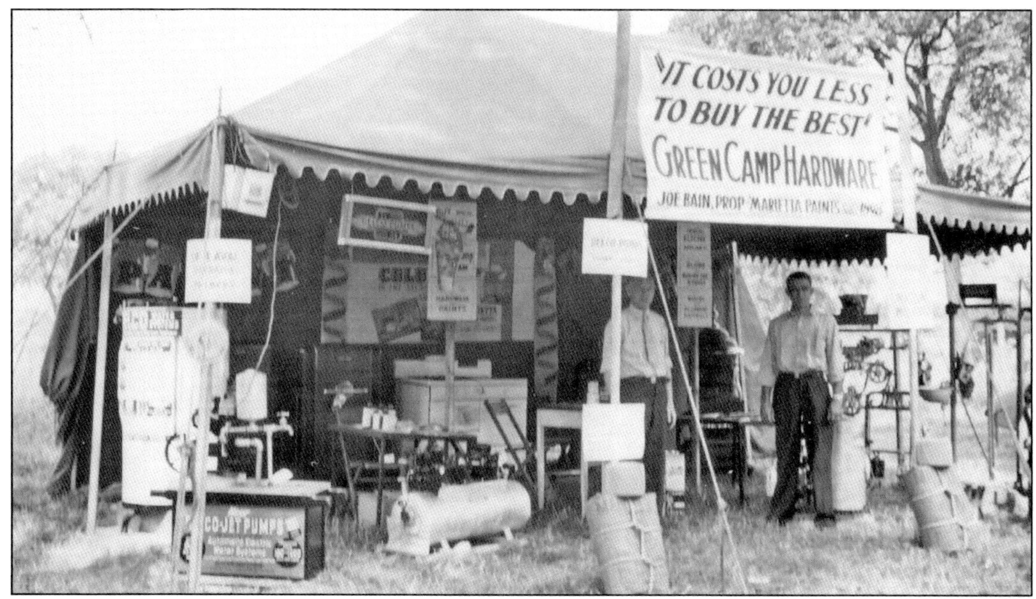

TENT SALE. Green Camp was home to a variety of businesses over the years. One that lasted many years was Green Camp Hardware, under the proprietorship of Joe Bain, with the sales motto, "It costs you less to buy the best." Other Green Camp businesses included the Hopkins House Hotel, Thomas Berry Grocery, Kimmil and Stratton Hardware, Berwick Flouring Mills, Schultz's Store, and Henry Lanius's Shoemaking. (Courtesy of Bob Turner.)

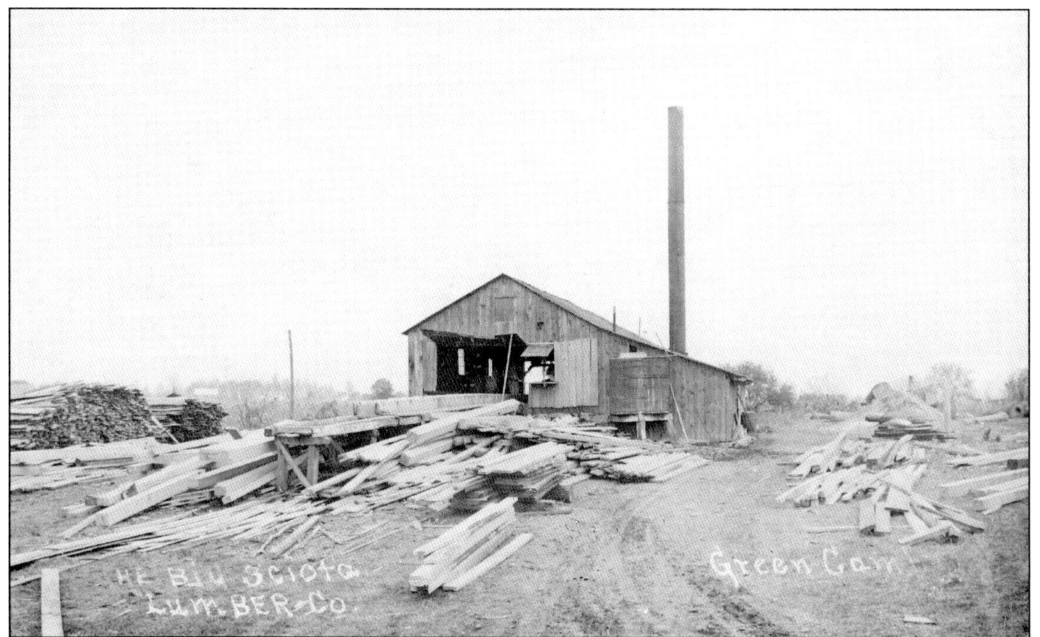

SAWING WOOD. Several sawmills, including the Big Scioto Lumber Company, operated in the area. The first one is believed to have been started around 1838 by Halderman and Fisk on the banks of the Big Scioto River inside what are now the village limits. It was powered by water drawn from the river and channeled through a race to turn a wheel for power. Flour and grain mills were also in operation for many years. (Courtesy of Ralph and Erdine Eaton collection.)

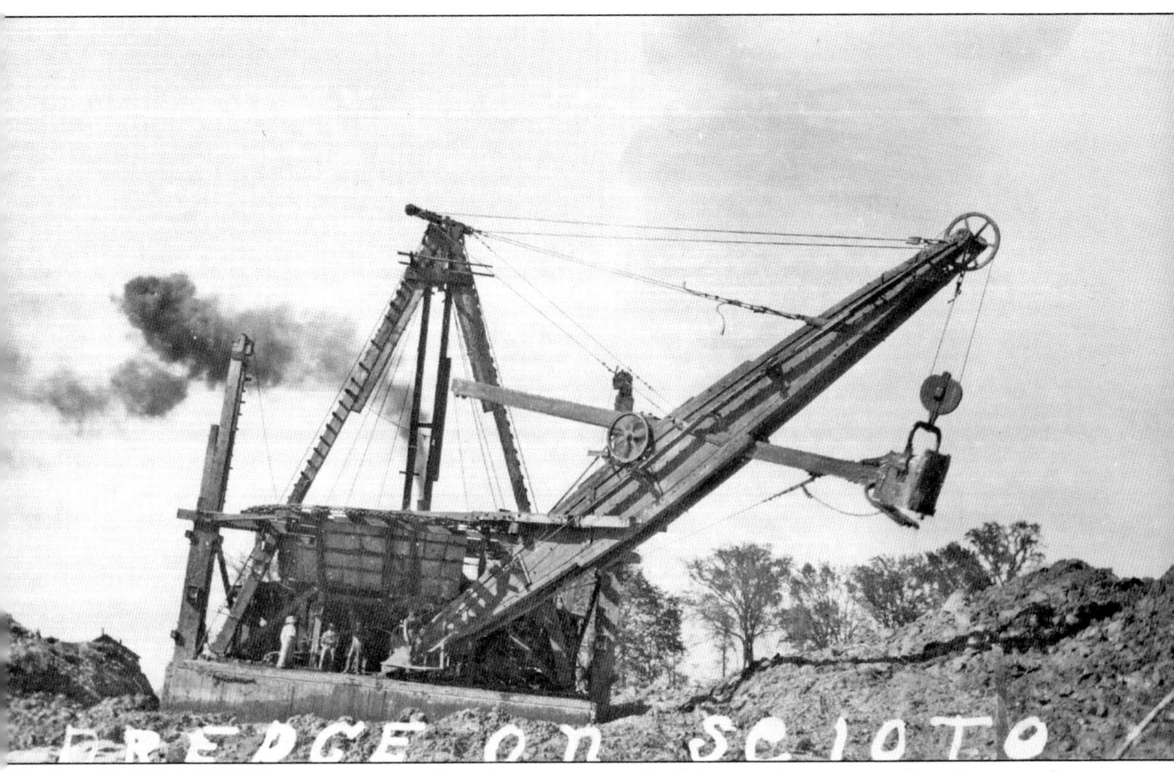

Dredging. In an effort to reduce flooding, a major dredging project was undertaken on the Little Scioto River in 1912–1913. The river was widened and deepened to keep water within its banks. Men working on the project lived in white tents west of the river in what became known as "White City." One of the more innovative living arrangements used on other dredging projects was utilized by the Fairbanks Steam Shovel Company of Marion. A large floating bunkhouse, which could be towed through a recently cleaned or dug waterway as the dredges moved forward, provided both eating and sleeping convenience for workers without the necessity of pitching tents. Fairbanks, the Osgood Company, and the Marion Steam Shovel Company were all located just a few miles to the east in Marion. Upon completion of the project, this dredge was disassembled, and the cab was used to help build a house that still stands at 507 Walnut Street in Green Camp. (Courtesy of Richard Carey.)

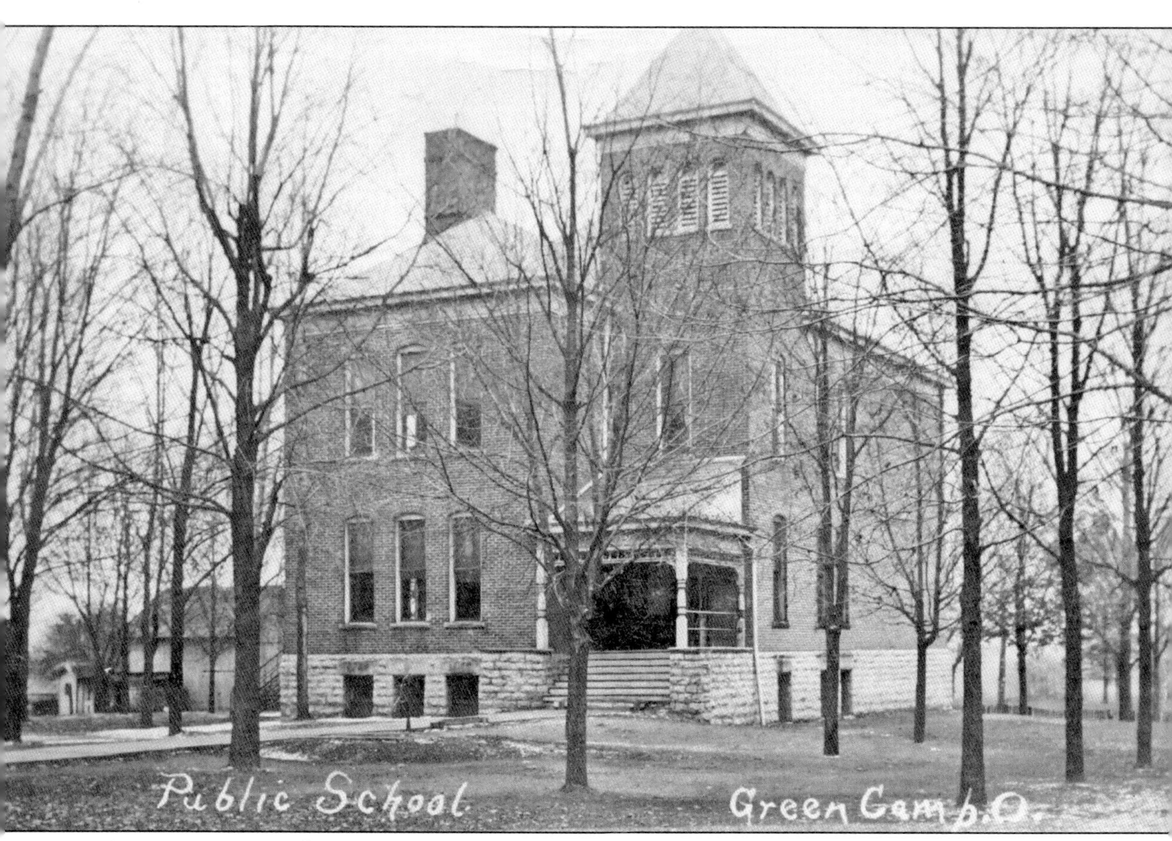

School Days. The Green Camp Special School District was created in 1862. It included the village as well as adjoining territory to the north and west. An octagonal school was soon built on High Street at a cost of $4,000. Prof. J.C. Poland served as the first instructor. In 1891, the school was torn down and replaced with the building shown here. A merger with the township school districts occurred in 1919, necessitating an addition to the building. An elaborate cut-stone entryway was a prominent feature of the addition. Some villagers felt its reputed cost of $10,000 was an extravagance, while others believed it was a fitting way to celebrate the revamped building. More changes and additions were made over the next 50 years, including an underground gymnasium. The school served a variety of grade levels over the years, with the last several classes using it as a high school. The last class graduated in 1962, and the school then sat vacant until it was razed in 1969. The building caught fire while it was being torn down, resulting in a bit of irony when the stone entryway remained standing after the fire was extinguished. (Courtesy of Mike and Linda Perry.)

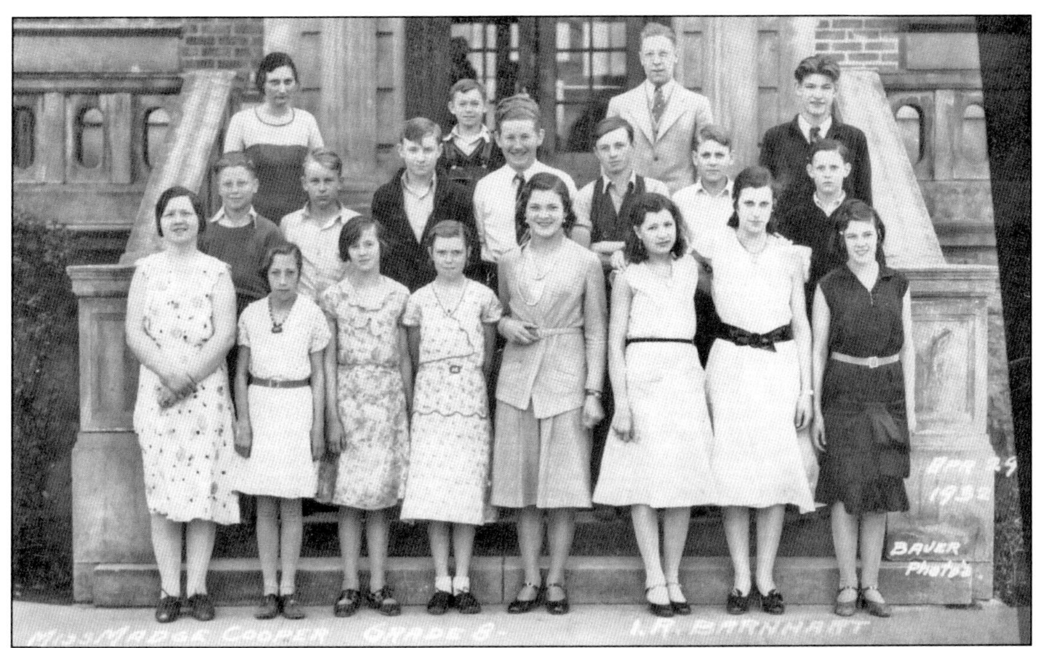

CELEBRITY IN WAITING. At the time this picture was taken in 1932, a young Madge Cooper (standing in the upper left corner) likely had little clue that her days as a teacher would soon be over, and her new career would begin. She left teaching to join local radio station WMRN, where, as Madge Cooper Guthery, she would become one of Marion's most beloved on-air personalities with a career spanning more than 52 years. (Courtesy of Marion County Historical Society.)

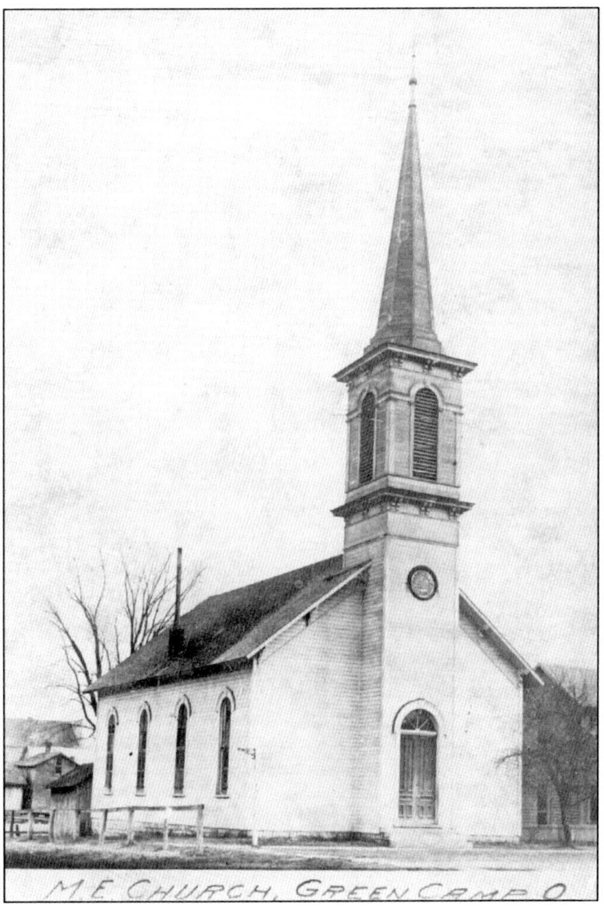

METHODIST EPISCOPAL CHURCH. The Methodist congregation of Green Camp has worshipped in the village for more than 170 years. Its original church was erected about 1850 but was later moved for use as a private residence. It was replaced in 1879 by the current structure (shown here prior to extensive expansions and renovations). The changes to come included the addition of stained-glass windows, a full basement, and an expanded front entrance. (Courtesy of Richard Carey.)

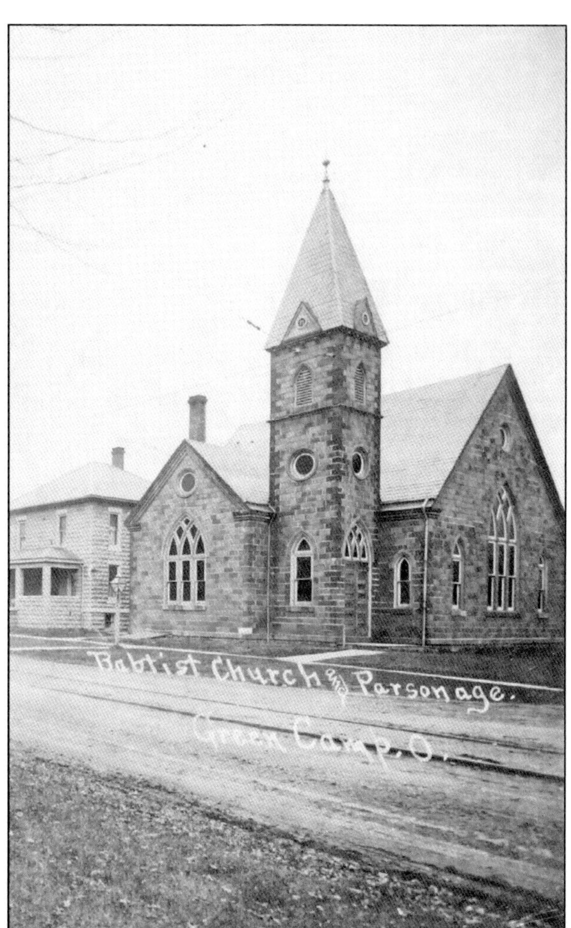

Baptist Church. The Baptists of the Green Camp area built their first church around 1852 about two miles east of the village. Some 20 years later, it was moved to the site of this tile building, which replaced it in 1895. A parsonage was added in 1907. In 1920, this building was razed when it was deemed a fire hazard. It was later replaced by a brick structure that still stands, although it is no longer used as a church. (Courtesy of Richard Carey.)

Mt. Olive Methodist Episcopal Church. The Mt. Olive Methodist Episcopal Church grew from a small group of worshipers who were served by circuit-riding ministers. A church and cemetery were eventually located on land donated by Charlotte Kersey on the condition that the name be Mount Olive. The current building was erected in 1893 but is no longer used as a church. (Author's collection.)

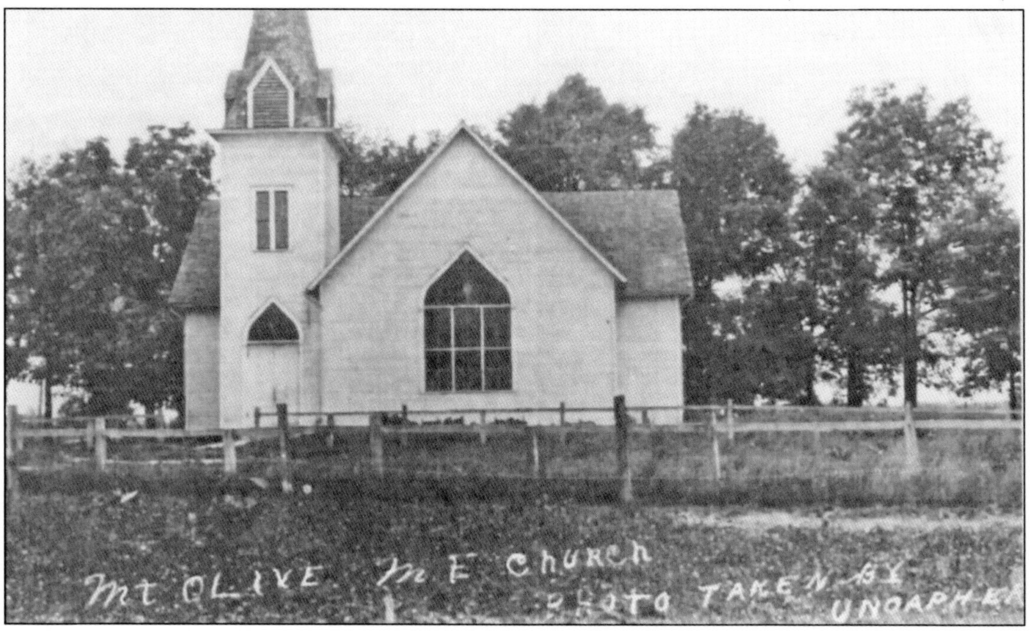

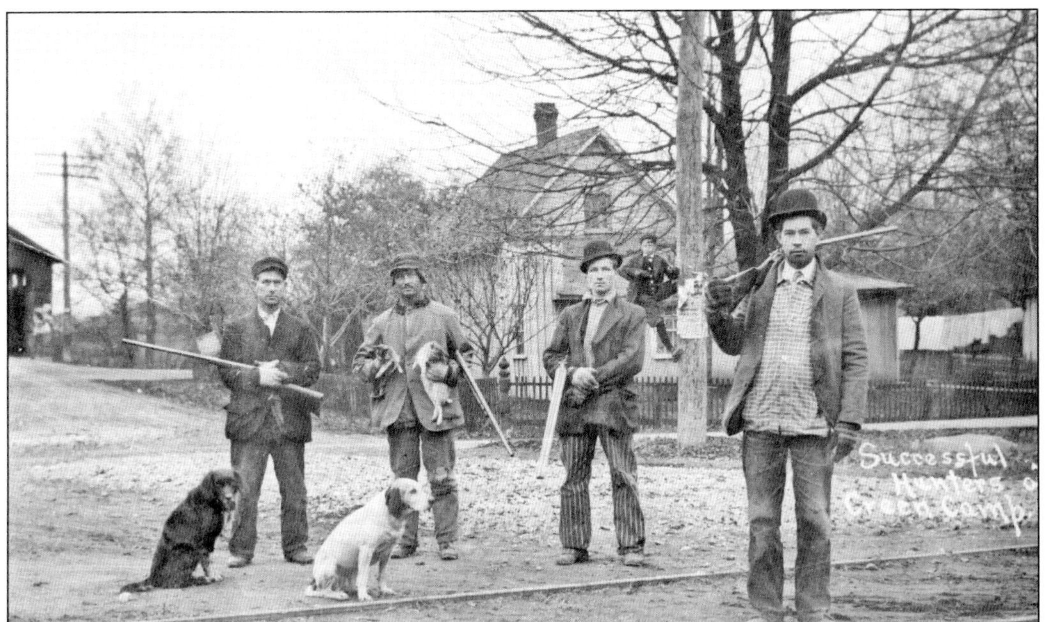

A Good Day. These hunters posed for a group picture on the outskirts of the village near the covered bridge along with their dogs and evidence of success. The youngster on the telephone pole in the background is Paul Dudley, son of renowned landscape artist Frank Dudley. Paul's mother died when he was a child, after which he lived with relatives in Green Camp. (Courtesy of Richard Carey.)

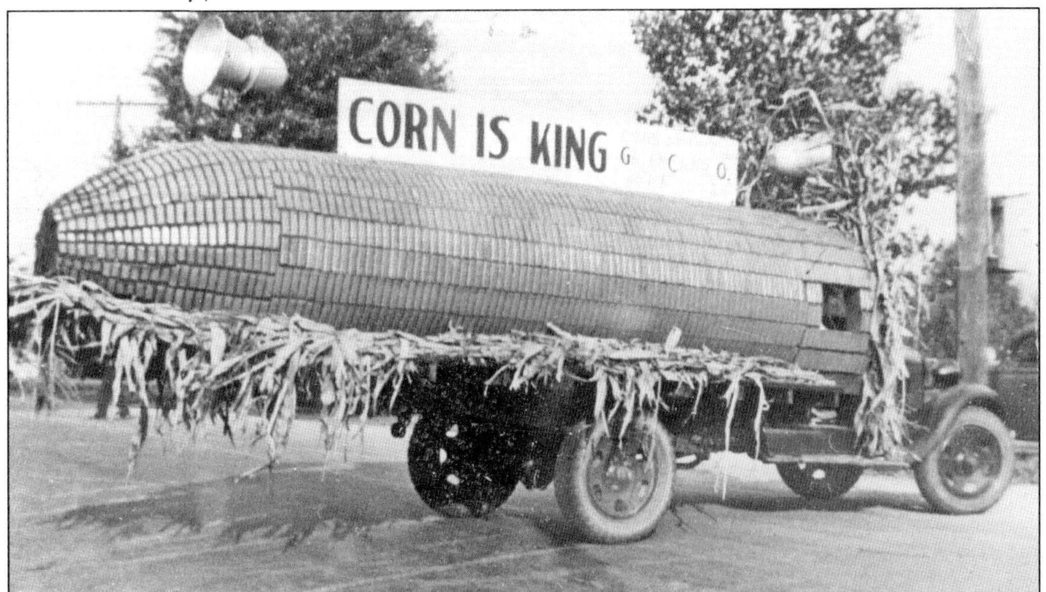

Corn Is King. Green Camp honored its centennial in 1938 with a three-day celebration that drew an estimated 100,000 visitors to the village of approximately 375 residents. At the time, the Associated Press said it was the biggest celebration per capita staged by any town in the nation. Hoping to build on that success, Green Camp held a Corn Festival the following year, with advertising provided by this 25-foot-long ear of corn, which traveled to other festivals to promote the event. (Courtesy of Marion County Historical Society.)

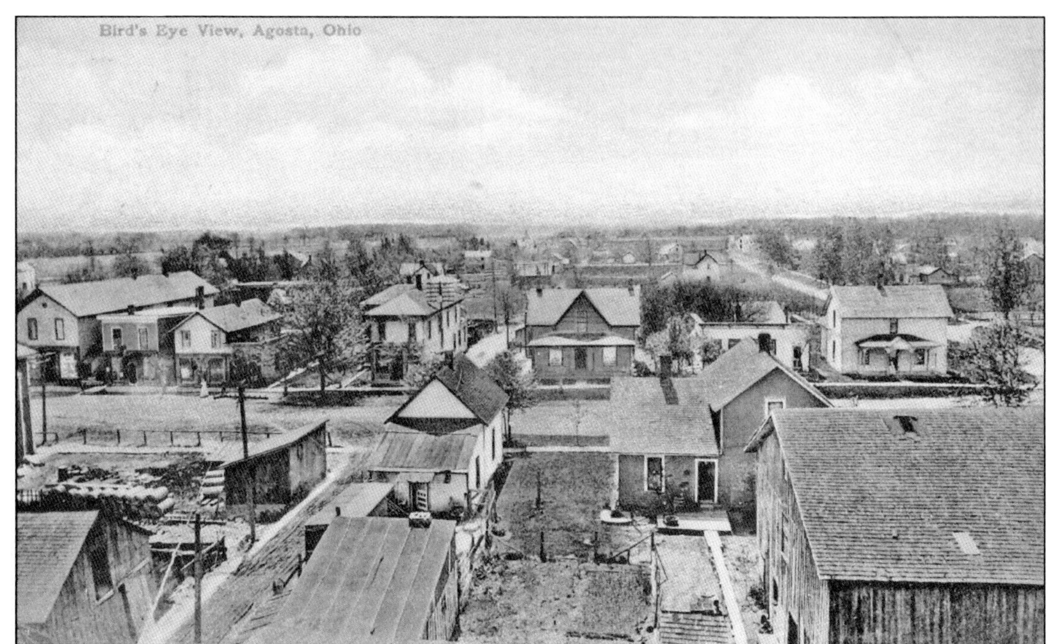

BIRD'S-EYE VIEW. The bustling village of Agosta was home to a wide variety of businesses in the 1880s, including grocery stores, a hardware store, a drugstore, a doctor's office, a post office, and an ice cream parlor. Industries, including a stave factory, tile factory, stockyard, and grain elevator, relied on the Big Four Railroad to transport products. (Courtesy of Richard Carey.)

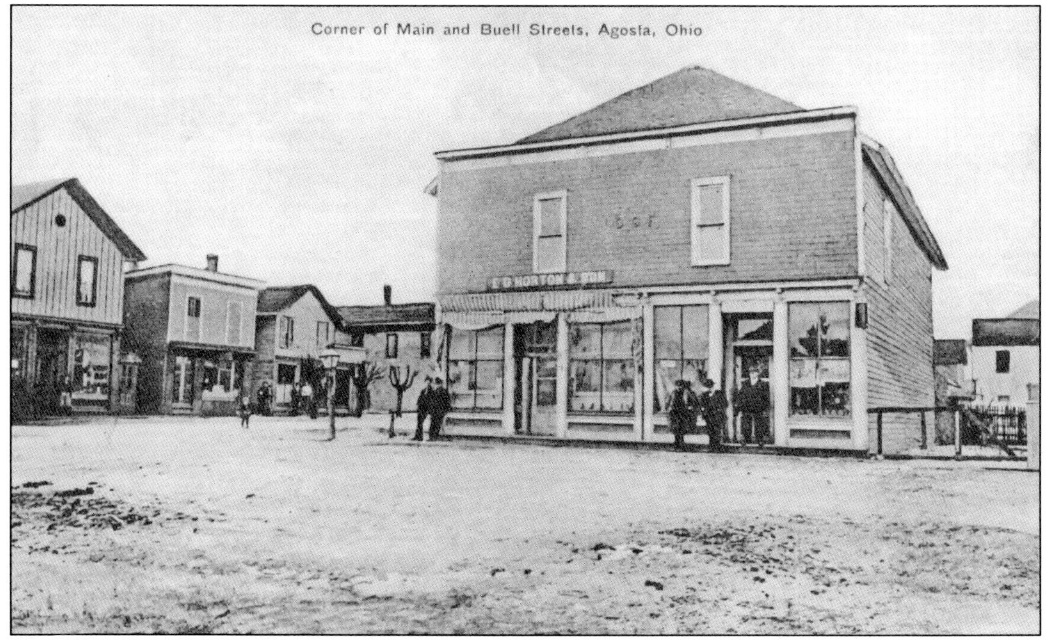

STANDING ON THE CORNER. The E.D. Horton and Son store at Buell and Main Streets was a popular gathering place for village residents. The second floor served as home to Agosta Lodge No. 451 of the International Order of Odd Fellows. Clark and Ollie Longshore later operated their Serv-U-Wel Market grocery store and filling station in this location. The building is no longer standing. (Courtesy of Richard Carey.)

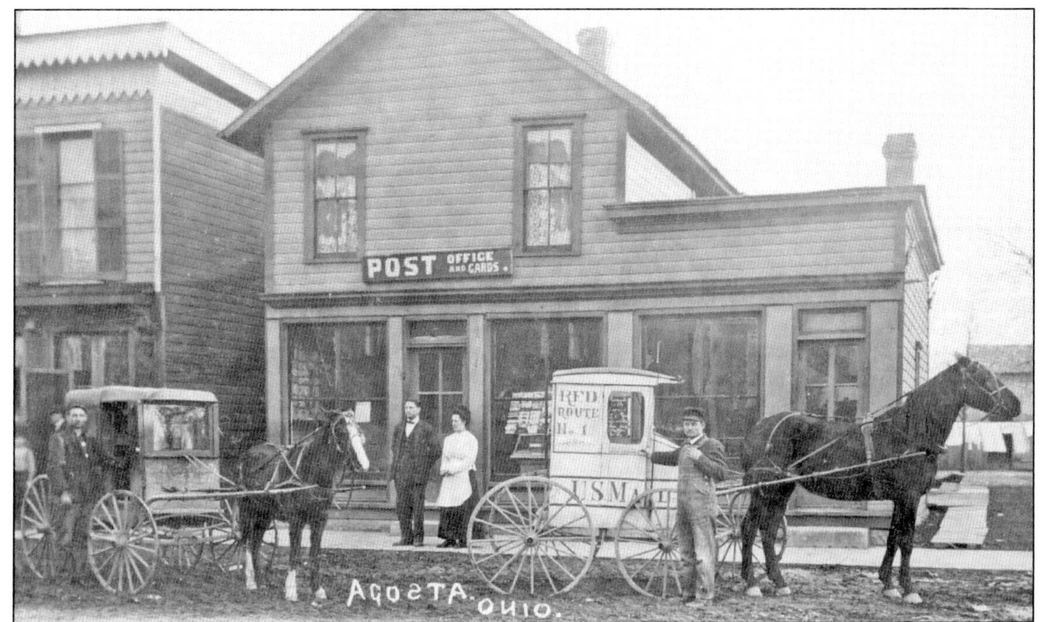

Mail Carrier. A mail deliverer at the Agosta Post Office prepares to begin his Rural Free Delivery (RFD) route. The RFD service delivered mail directly to rural farm families who, prior to the service being mandated in 1893, would have needed to come to the post office to pick up their mail or pay a private carrier to have it delivered. Many local shopkeepers opposed the service, as they feared it would result in a loss of business. (Courtesy of Bob Turner.)

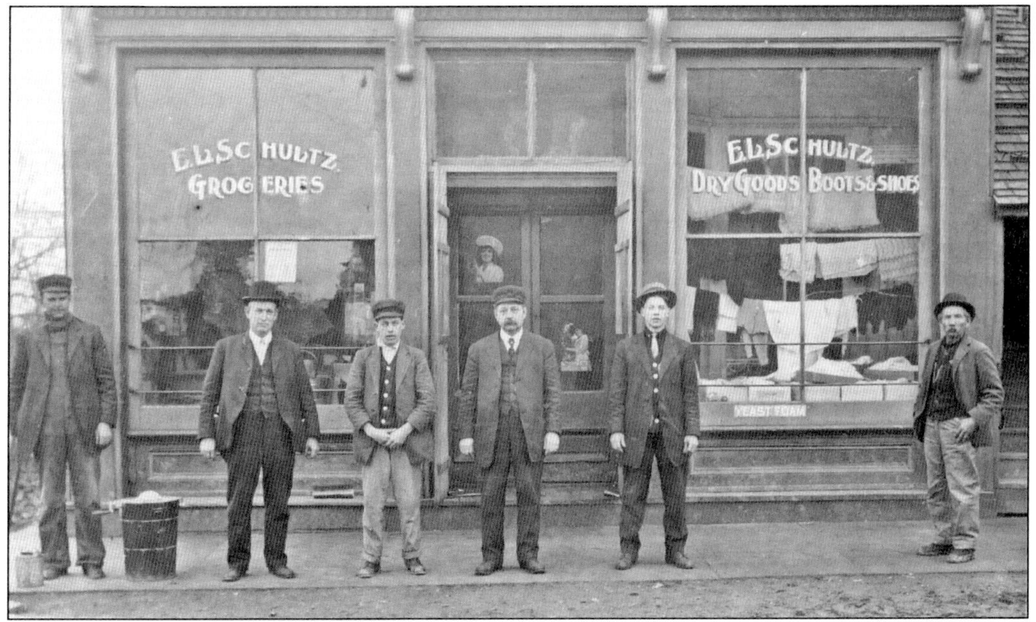

Schultz's Store. James Elliott opened a grocery store in 1871 on the corner of Main and Buell Streets. The building was soon sold to the first of a string of owners, with E.L. Schultz eventually taking ownership. The first telephone line in the village ran from this store to Meeker, where Schlultz's brother also had a store. E.L. Schultz owned an IGA store in Green Camp in the 1930s. (Courtesy of Richard Johnson.)

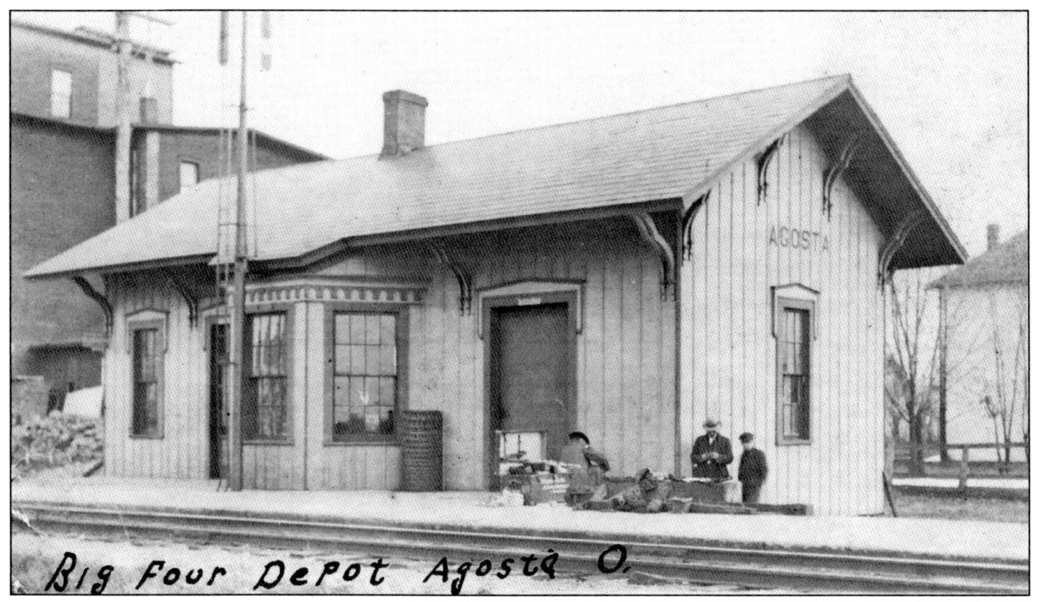

BUSY PLACE. Built in 1879 at a cost of $1,000, the Agosta Depot soon became a busy place. Records show that in the first half of 1883, more than 790,000 pounds of freight was received here, with over 1.7 million pounds shipped from the depot. In addition to providing rail service, the depot also housed a telegraph office. Passenger service ended around 1942, and the depot closed soon thereafter. (Courtesy of Richard Carey.)

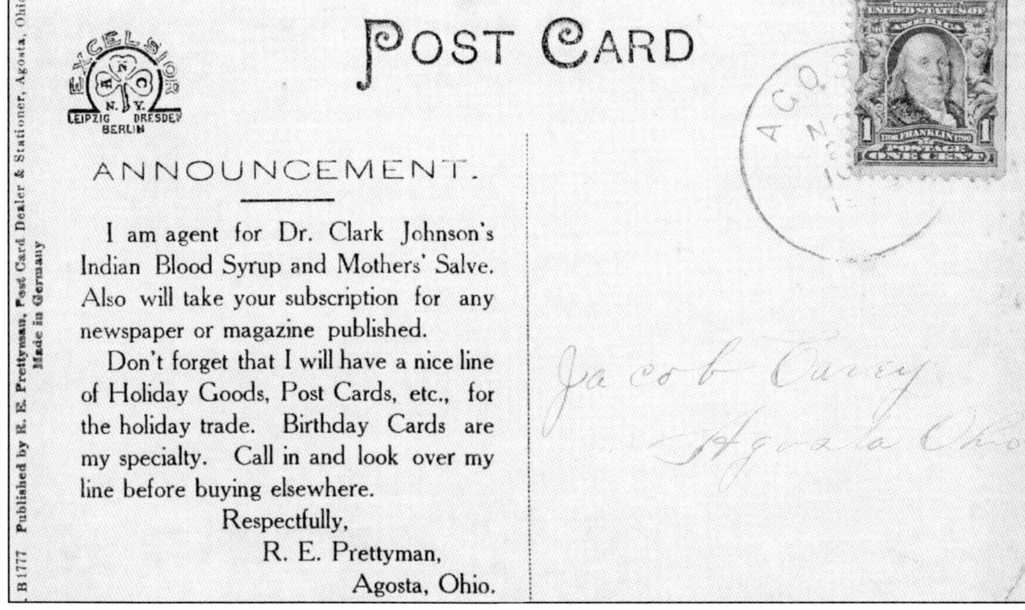

B 1777 Published by R. E. Prettyman, Post Card Dealer & Stationer, Agosta, Ohio
Made in Germany

EXCELSIOR
N.Y.
LEIPZIG DRESDEN
BERLIN

POST CARD

ANNOUNCEMENT.

I am agent for Dr. Clark Johnson's Indian Blood Syrup and Mothers' Salve. Also will take your subscription for any newspaper or magazine published.

Don't forget that I will have a nice line of Holiday Goods, Post Cards, etc., for the holiday trade. Birthday Cards are my specialty. Call in and look over my line before buying elsewhere.

Respectfully,
R. E. Prettyman,
Agosta, Ohio.

Jacob Carey
Agosta Ohio

SALES PITCH. The R.E. Prettyman store in Agosta used postcard advertising to increase its sale of Johnson's Indian Blood Syrup. The syrup was advertised as a nostrum to cure "all diseases of the liver, stomach, kidneys, bowels, skin, and blood." Among the illnesses cured were "dyspepsia, rheumatism, constipation, heart disease, female weakness and general disability." This was one of thousands of patent medicines that flooded the country after the Civil War. (Courtesy of Richard Carey.)

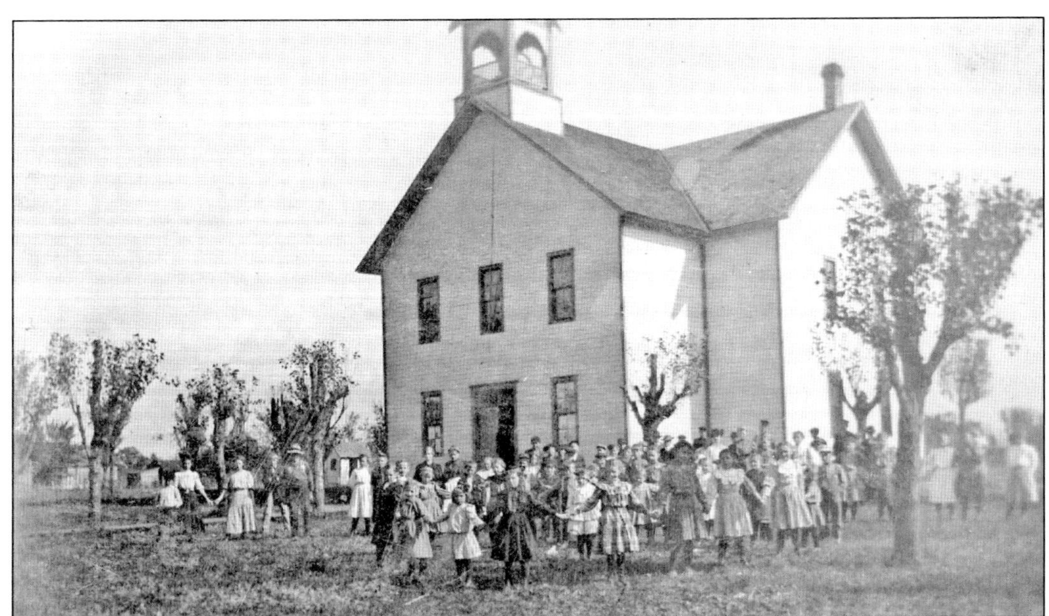

All Hold Hands. The young ladies gathered outside the second Agosta School building joined hands as the young men stood behind them in the background. The first school in Agosta was built on land donated by Wingett Carey. It was later replaced with this building, which cost $2,500 to build and $1,000 to furnish. Agosta also housed the Agosta Normal School Academy for teacher education in the 1880s and beyond. (Courtesy of Richard Carey.)

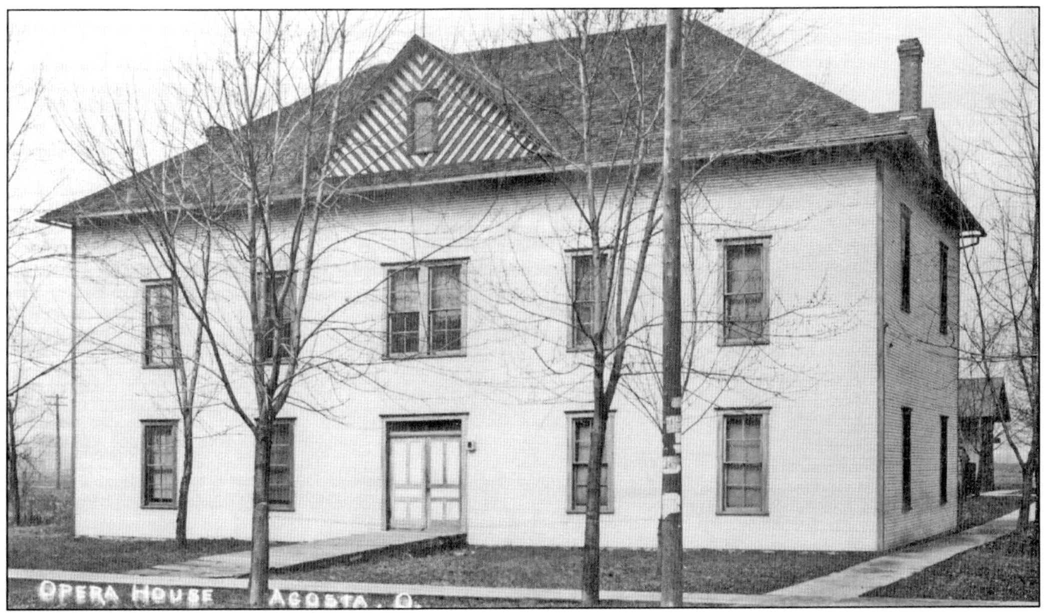

Opera House. The Star Opera House was located adjacent to the Big Four Rail Depot at the corner of Washington and Buell Streets. The opera house was dedicated in 1901, with Ohio senator Warren G. Harding as the featured speaker. Throughout the years, the building also served as a community room and town hall. Basketball games were played on a small court on the second floor. (Courtesy of Ellis and Margaret Hudson.)

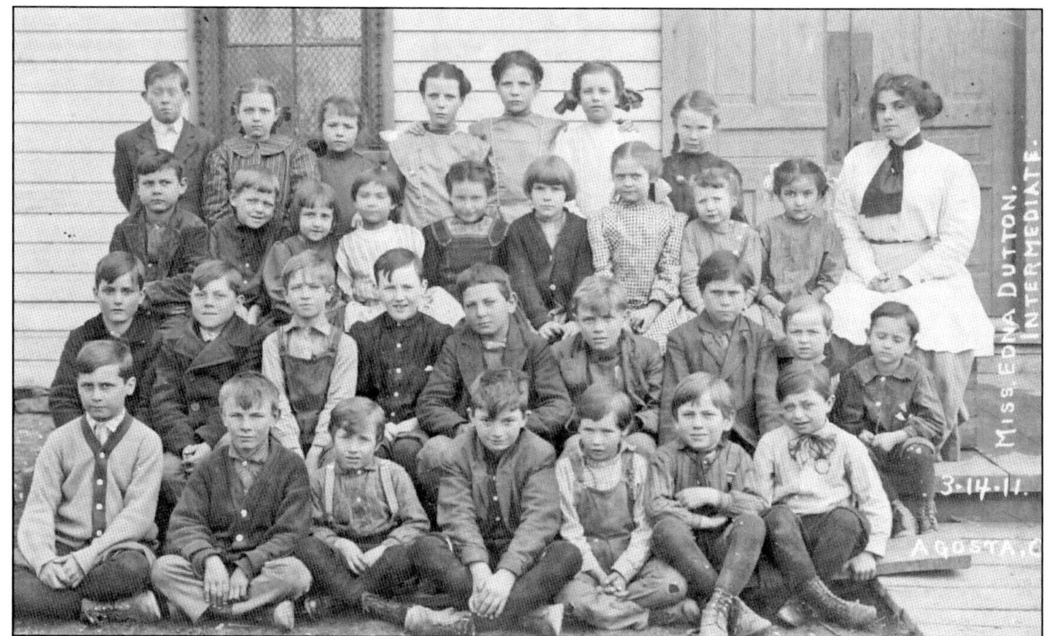

Full Class. Edna Dutton had her hands full in 1911 with more than 30 students in her intermediate class at Agosta School. The school only had two instructors, with Carlton Sinclair teaching the primary grades. E.F. Martin served as superintendent. (Author's collection.)

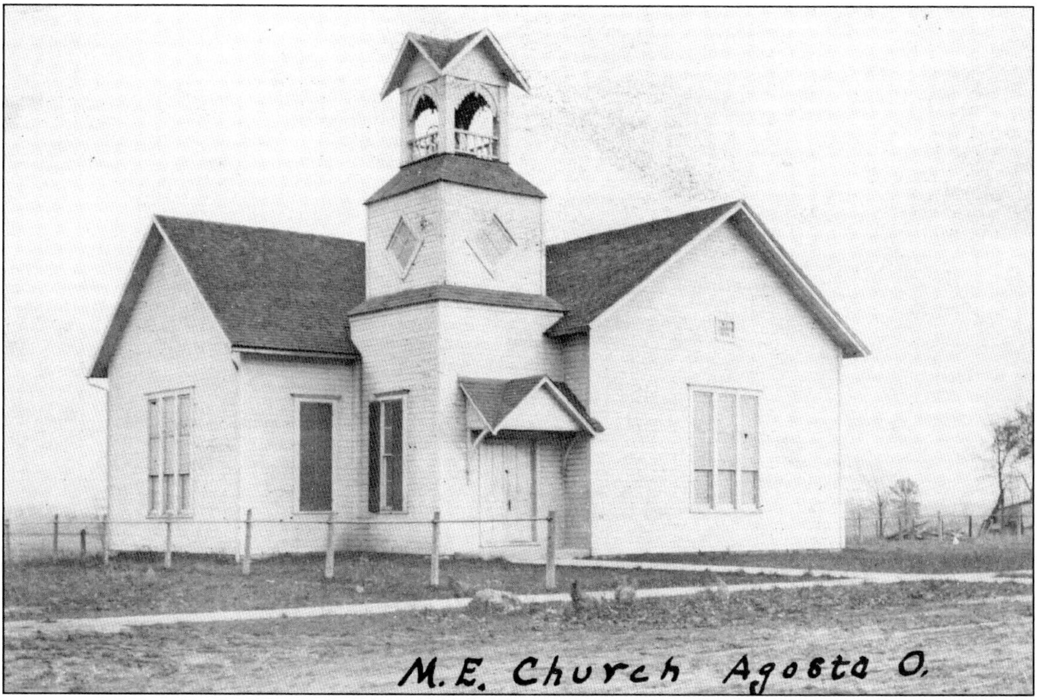

Methodist Episcopal. In 1875, Wingett Carey donated a lot as a site for the Methodist Episcopal church building. Construction was completed at a cost of $1,500. The building was significantly remodeled in 1978, more than 100 years later. It continues to serve the Methodist congregation of the New Bloomington area. (Courtesy of Richard Carey.)

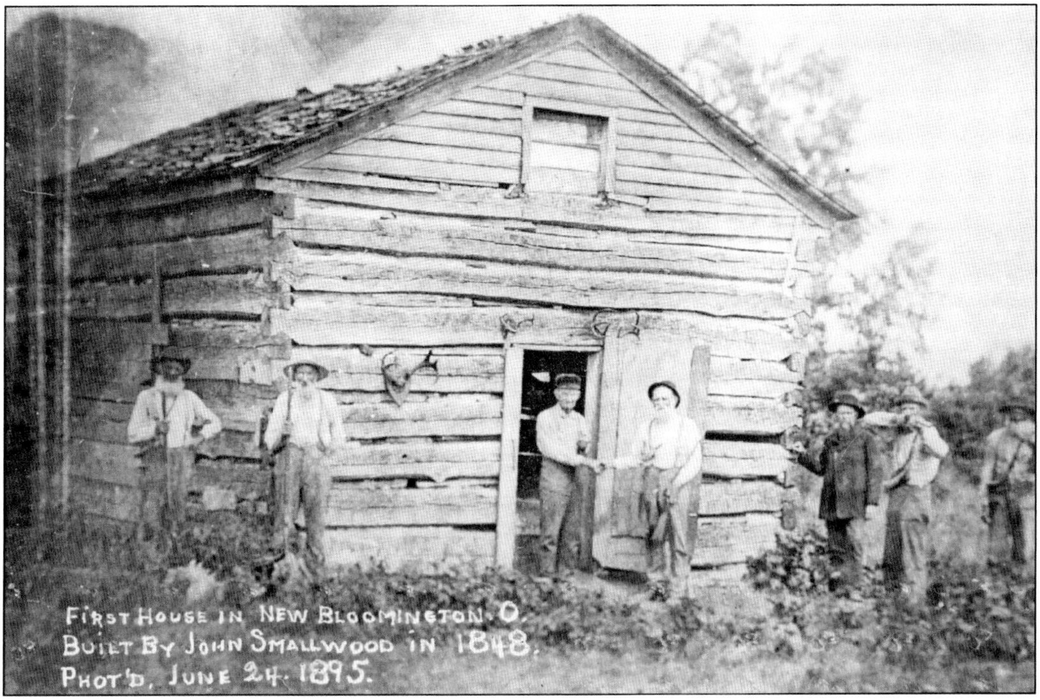

IN THE BEGINNING. John Smallwood is credited with building the first house in Agosta in 1848. The men on this postcard, which was postmarked 1912, are identified from left to right as Bob Baker, Jimmy Reading, "Grandad Carey," George W. Carey, Jacob Bentley, Silias Dickerson, and Bill Baker. Although the reason for their meeting is unknown, it may have involved hunting, as most of the men are holding rifles. (Courtesy of Ellis and Margaret Hudson.)

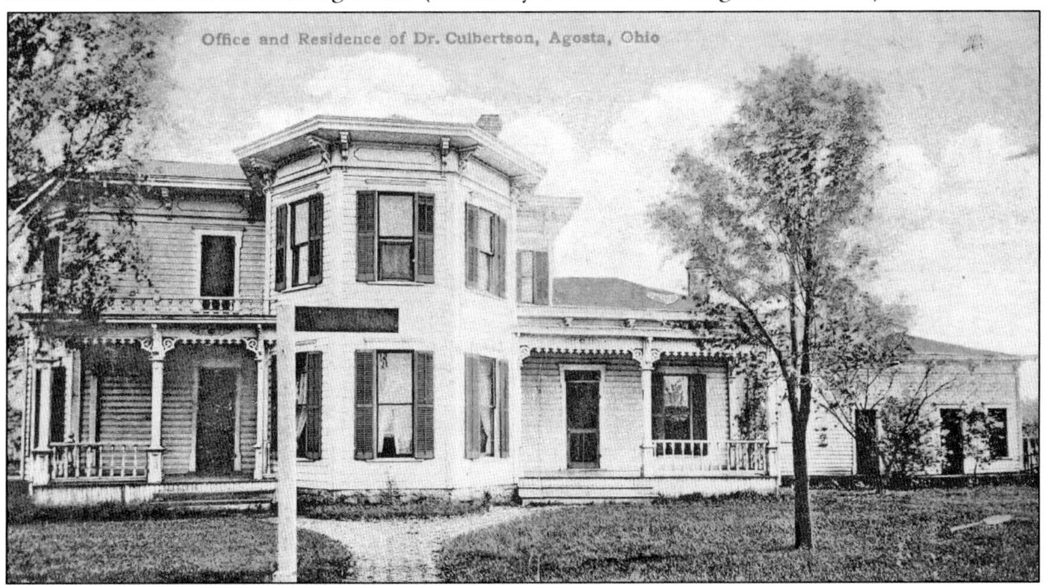

DR. CULBERTSON'S. Dr. Elihu Culbertson graduated from the Wooster Medical College in Cleveland in 1880. He started his medical practice in Huron County before moving to Marion County, where he began practicing in Agosta in 1906. He treated patients from his residence on Buell Street, which also served as his office. (Courtesy of Ralph and Erdine Eaton collection.)

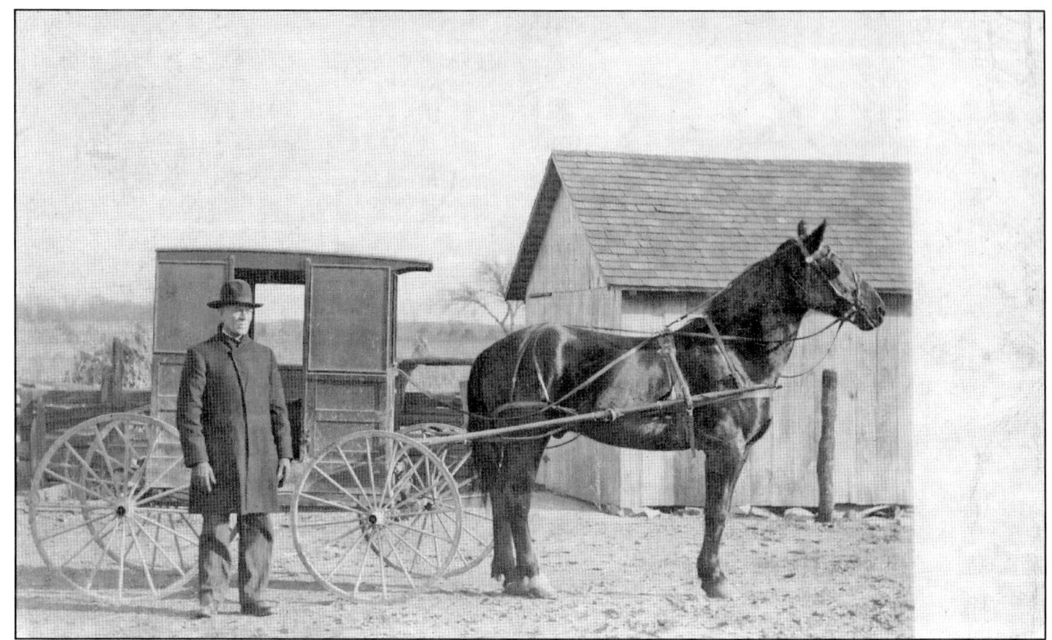

Traveling Minister. Little is known about this man, who is believed to be a traveling minister named Tom Casey. He shared in his message on the reverse of this card, which is postmarked "Agosta, 1910," that he "just closed a great meeting in Agosta with 102 conversions and 90 accessions. Go to Scott Town tomorrow to begin." (Courtesy of Richard Carey.)

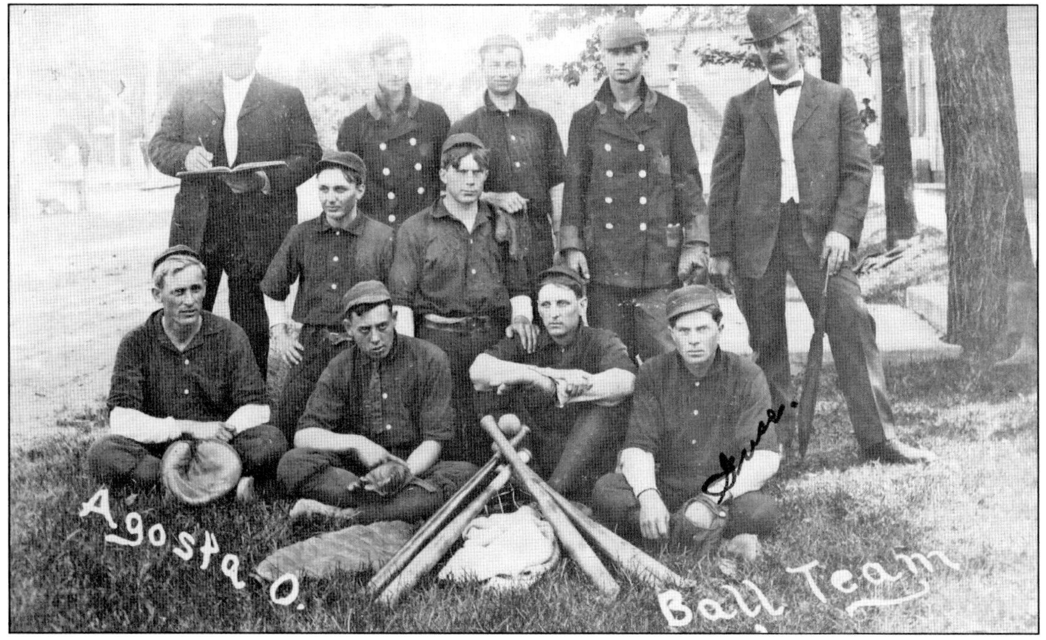

Baseball in Agosta. The Agosta baseball team posed for this picture that may include their new manager. In July 1908 (approximately around the time this picture was taken), the club elected J.E. Dutton to replace W.M. Cleveland, who had resigned. Many of the villages in Marion County had teams comprising mostly local talent, although an occasional ringer could be found. (Courtesy of Richard Carey.)

Three

Kirkpatrick and Martel Area

In 1826, the State of Ohio passed legislation granting the Columbus and Sandusky Turnpike Company the right to use more than 31,000 acres of land to build a turnpike road. The road was to run from Columbus to Sandusky through what was largely still wilderness. Col. James Kilbourne, a federal district surveyor in charge of more than 4,800 square miles of land from Delaware to Lake Erie, was assigned as chief surveyor. Work began in 1828 and was completed in 1834. The turnpike was 106 miles long and cost more than $700 per mile to build, with much of the construction done using the "corduroy" method of placing cut logs side-by-side. Toll gates were erected approximately every 10 miles. The road essentially followed the paths of the present-day State Routes 98 and 4.

Seeking to take advantage of the new roadway, Marturen Letimbra platted the settlement of Letimberville at the northern edge of Scott Township in 1833. The community, despite its location on a well-traveled road, never developed to the extent Letimbra had dreamed. It was renamed Kirkpatrick around 1910 in recognition of a local blacksmith. Kirkpatrick remains a small hamlet with a church and fewer than 200 residents.

The term "railroad town" is certainly apt for the community of Martel. Three railroads provided service through the area, which was then known as Three Locusts, before it was actually platted in 1881. The first house in the area was built by John Baker, who wanted the newly established post office named for him, but the majority of residents favored Three Locusts in reference to three locust trees that provided a favorite area of shade. The name was changed to Martel in 1883, although the reason why seems to be unknown. At the time of the official platting, three stores, a hotel, a sawmill, a blacksmith shop, a drugstore, and a millinery shop were already in operation. Dr. George T. Harding, father of future president Warren G. Harding, platted a settlement adjacent to Martel and named it Tully City. The new community never developed, and around 1900, it was combined with Martel.

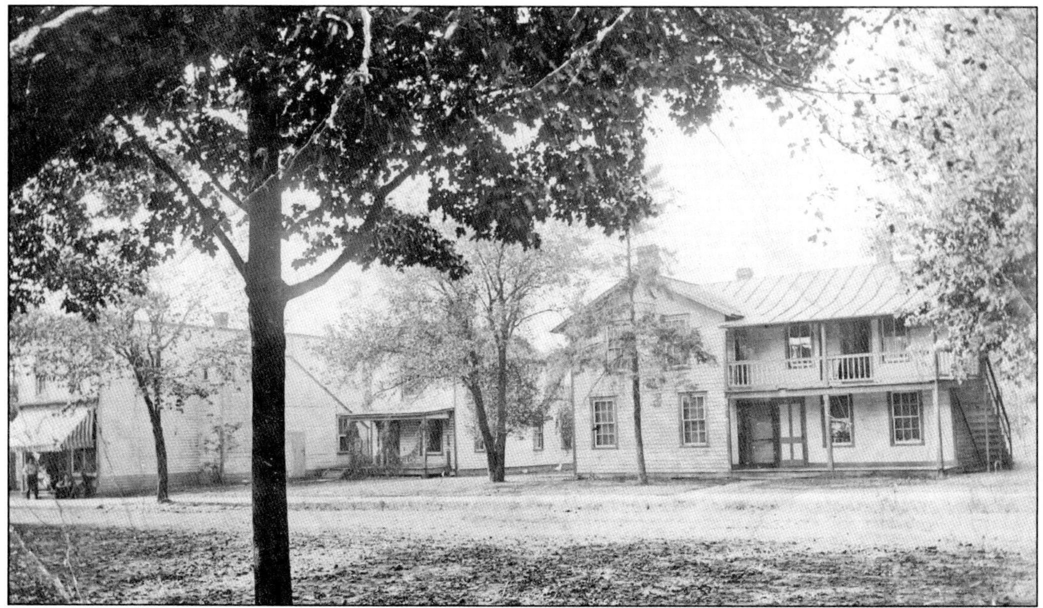

KIRKPATRICK. Travelers on the Columbus and Sandusky Turnpike passed through the tiny hamlet of Kirkpatrick. Originally platted as Letimberville in 1833, the community's growth was slow due to a lack of rail service and difficulty finding good sources of water. The temperance movement found strong support among the predominantly Methodist Episcopal residents. (Courtesy of Stuart Koblentz Haley.)

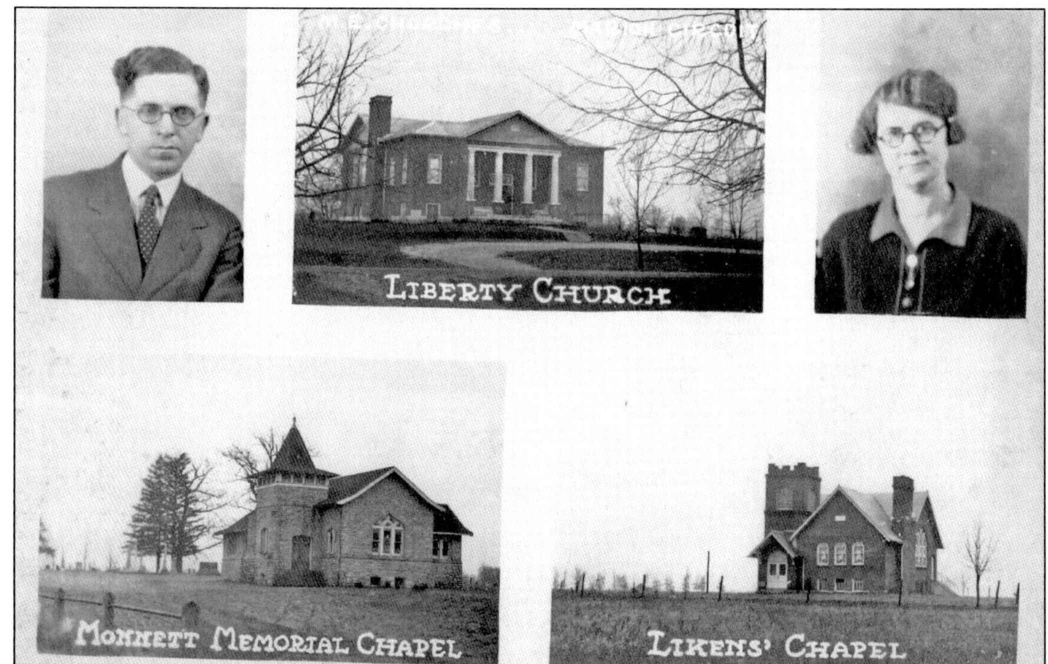

METHODIST CIRCUIT. Rev. L.S. Green and his wife, Ethel, hoped to encourage attendance on their circuit of churches in northern Marion and southern Crawford Counties when they mailed this card to area residents. The beginning of the practice of appointing clergy to a group of small churches can be traced to early frontier circuit riders. (Courtesy of Stuart Koblentz Haley.)

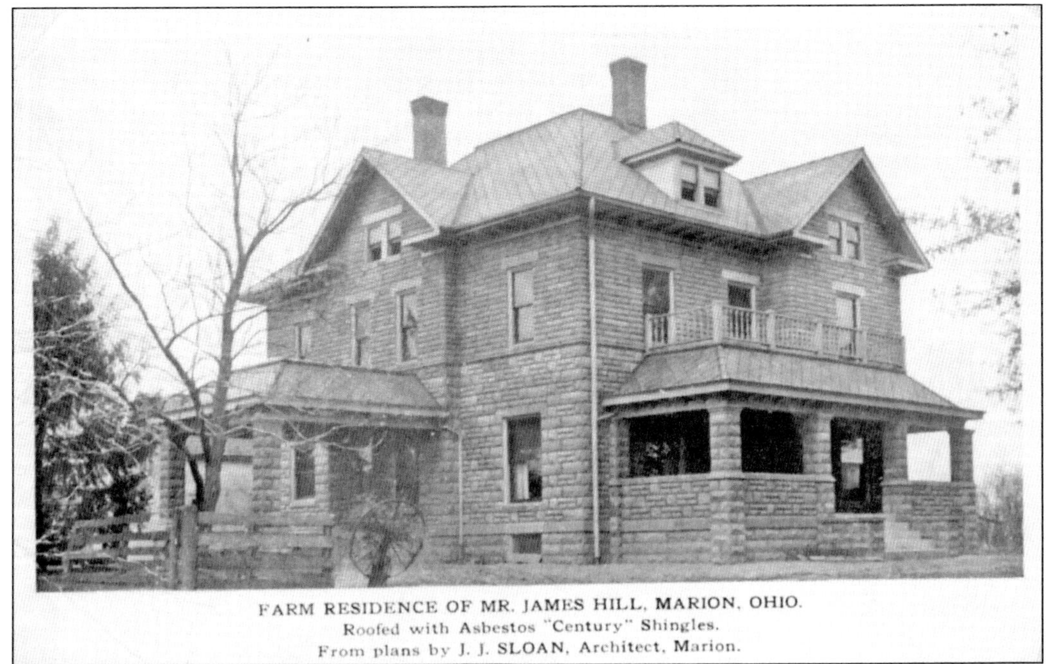

"Protect Your Home." Direct mail advertising urged homeowners to take advantage of the fire protection offered by asbestos roofing shingles such as the ones used on this residence in Scott Township. The home was built by siblings Carl and Maude Hill and featured a pressurized water system and its own generator for electricity. (Courtesy of Stuart Koblentz Haley.)

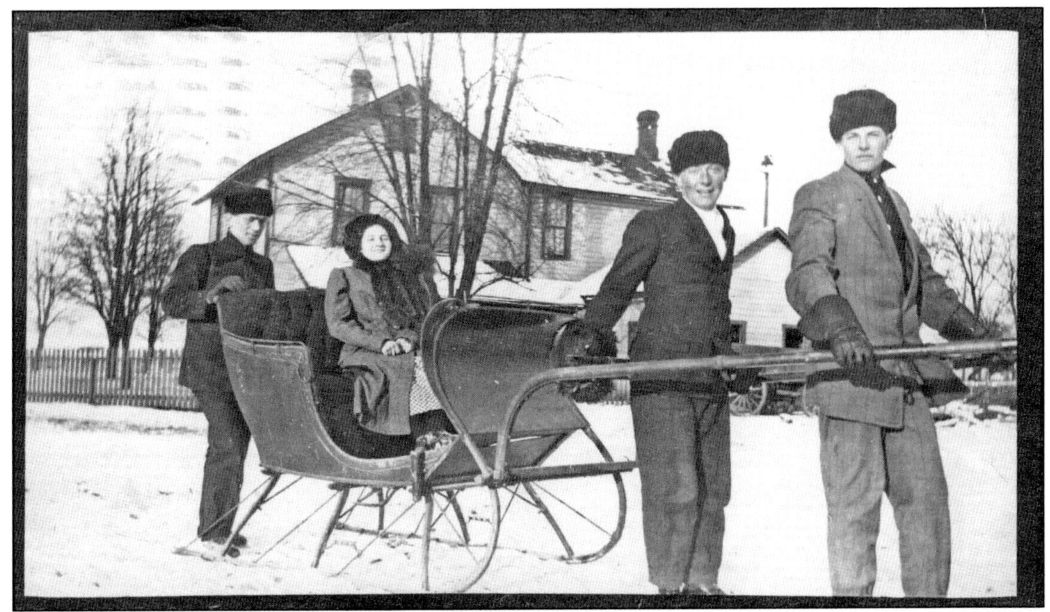

Three-Man Open Sleigh. Manpower replaced horsepower when Hazel Monnett took this ride around a farmyard on Marseilles-Galion Road in 1911. Hazel was the great-granddaughter of Abraham and Catherine Monnett. The Monnetts owned more than 11,000 acres in Marion and Crawford Counties in the late 1800s. (Courtesy of Kensel Clutter.)

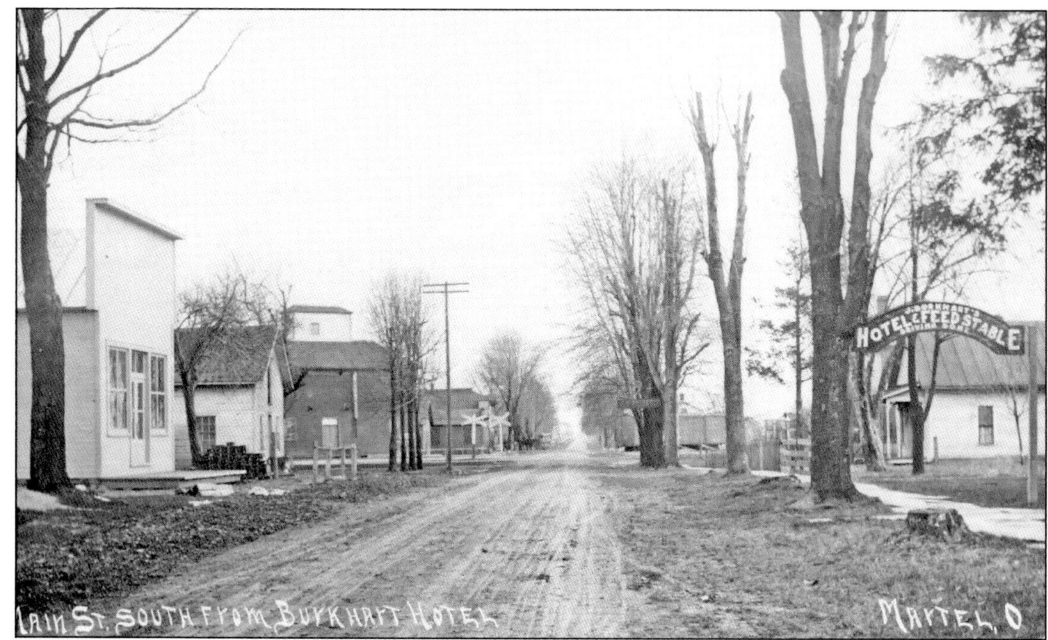

MAIN STREET. Martel started as a railroad center and grew into a thriving village. By 1883, it had three stores, a hotel, a millinery shop, a sawmill, a blacksmith shop, and a drugstore. Even with these amenities, living conditions could still be difficult, as evidenced by disease outbreaks such as a 1909 smallpox epidemic, when a number of families living south of the village were quarantined in an effort to stop the spread of the deadly disease. (Courtesy of Richard Carey.)

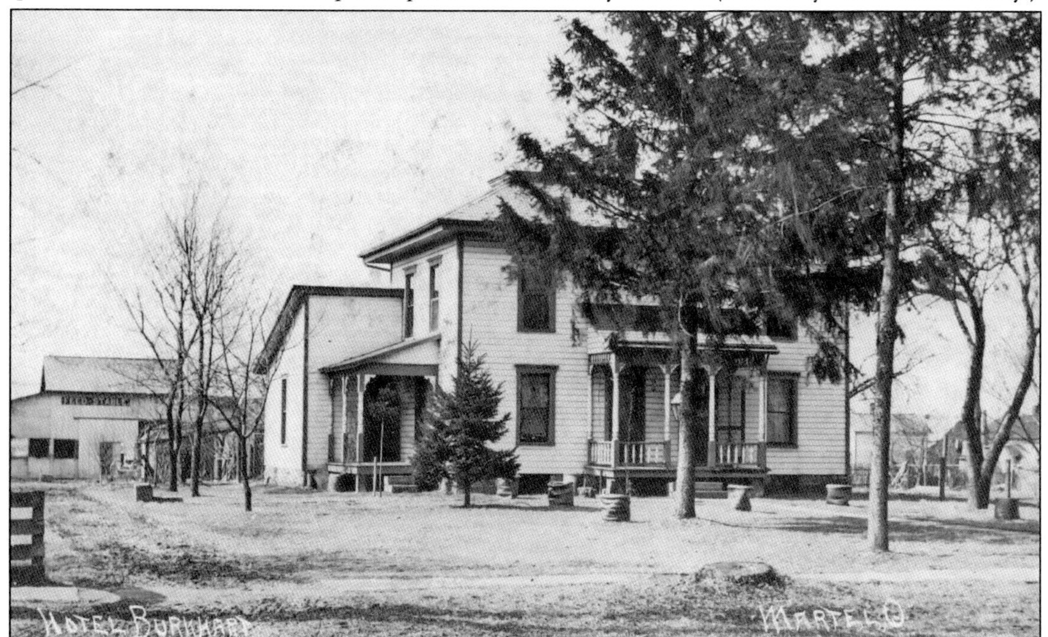

HOTEL BURKHART. Lodging was available for man and beast at the Burkhart Hotel on Main Street in Martel. It was located just down the street from the train depot, which made it a convenient lodging place for transient passengers. The practice of converting a home and barn to a hotel and stable was commonplace as villages grew. (Courtesy of Richard Carey.)

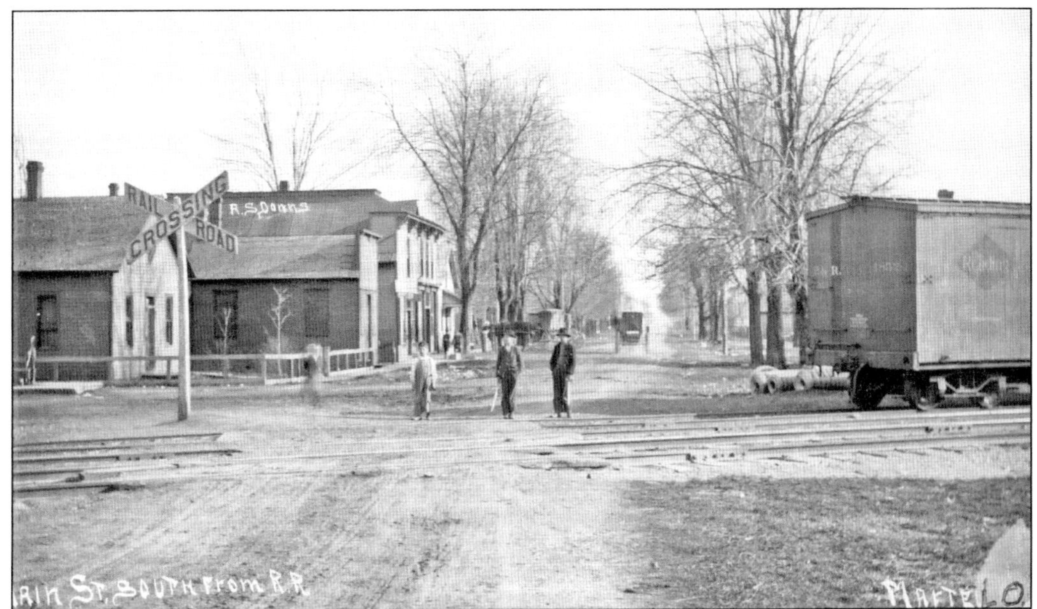

BY THE TRACKS. These young men are ready for battle with their wooden swords. Hopefully, they were not going to challenge one of the numerous "iron horses" that passed through the village each day. A popular activity at the time was train-hopping, which often had deadly results. One such example occurred in 1901, when a 25-year-old Martel resident tried to jump onto a moving train but was crushed under the wheels. (Courtesy of Richard Carey.)

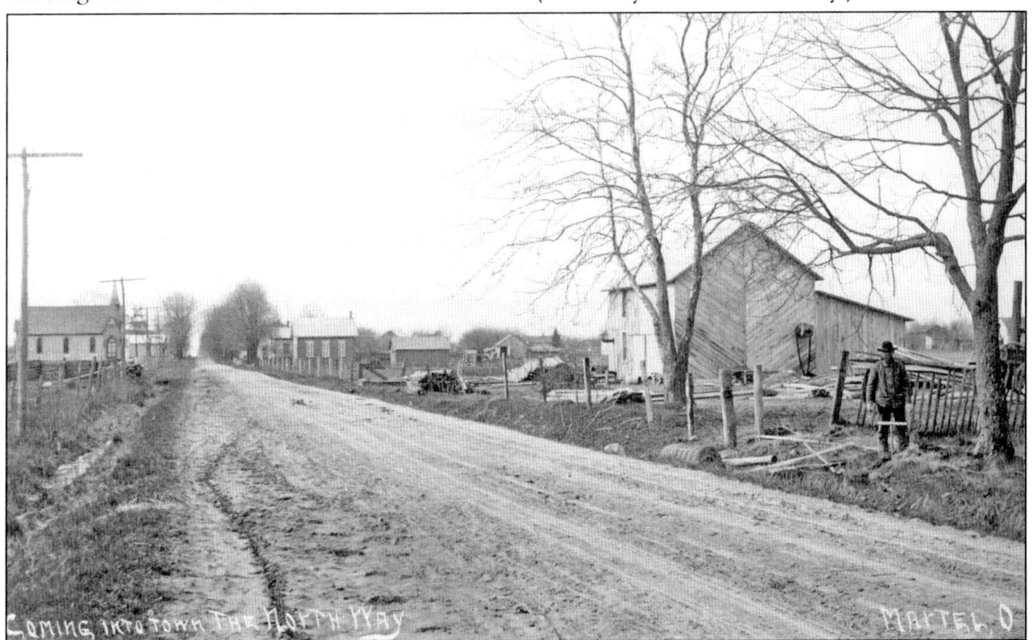

FIXING UP THE PLACE. Digging postholes for a new fence is hard work, so this man likely appreciated a short break for this 1910 photograph. Pride of ownership is evident in the intricate pattern of the wood siding on the barn in this view looking into the village from its northern edge. The Methodist church is visible at left, with the township house on the right. (Courtesy of Richard Carey.)

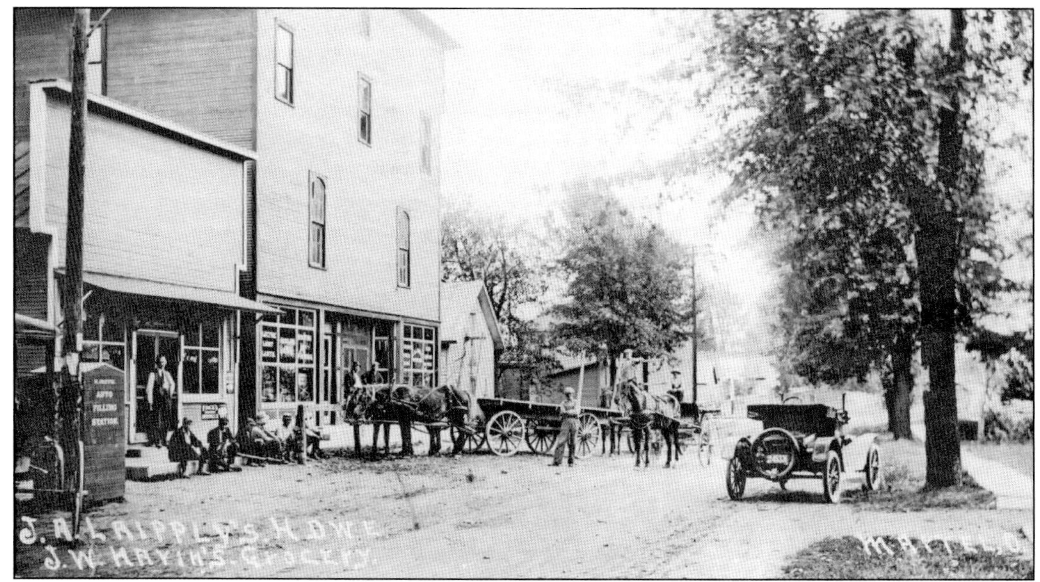

Business District. Downtown was bustling with shoppers at the J.A. Laipply Hardware Store and J.W. Havin's Grocery Store. Among the products sold at Laipply's were the Submarine brand washing machine, Fairbanks-Morse light plant, and Huber Light Four tractor. A filling station stood ready to provide fuel and other necessities for the newfangled "horseless carriages." The Martel Grange No. 2519 and the Masonic lodge met on the upper floor of the two-story building. (Courtesy of Richard Carey.)

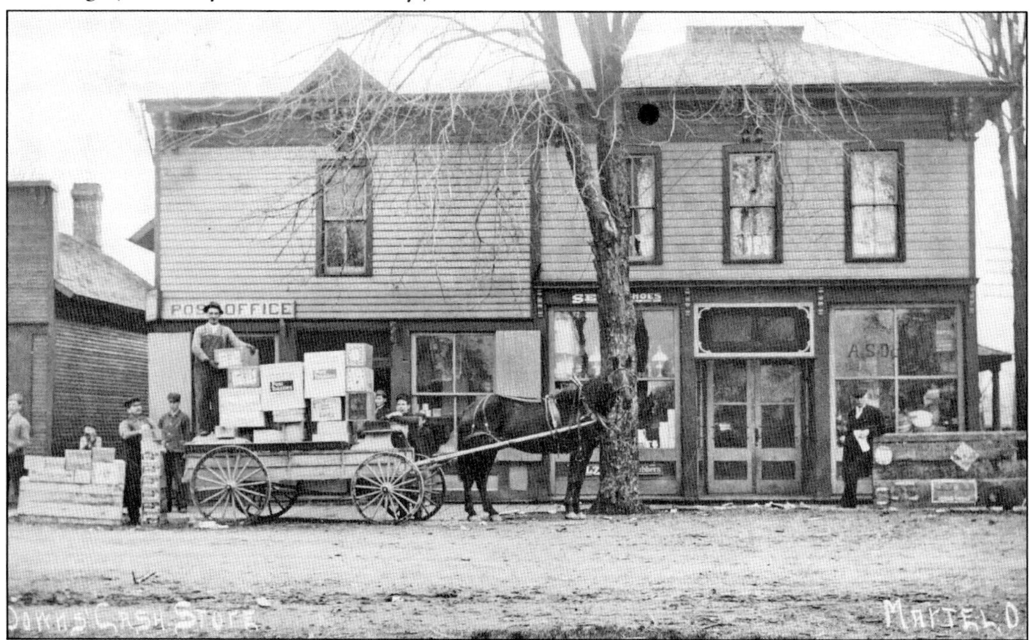

Restocking. A sizable load of supplies, including cases of Post Toasties, are being unloaded at Down's Cash Store, where "cash is king." The business was owned and operated by Andrew S. Downs from 1895 until around 1950. It provided the village with groceries, dry goods, and hardware and served as a post office for several years. The building was destroyed by fire in 1964. (Courtesy of Richard Carey.)

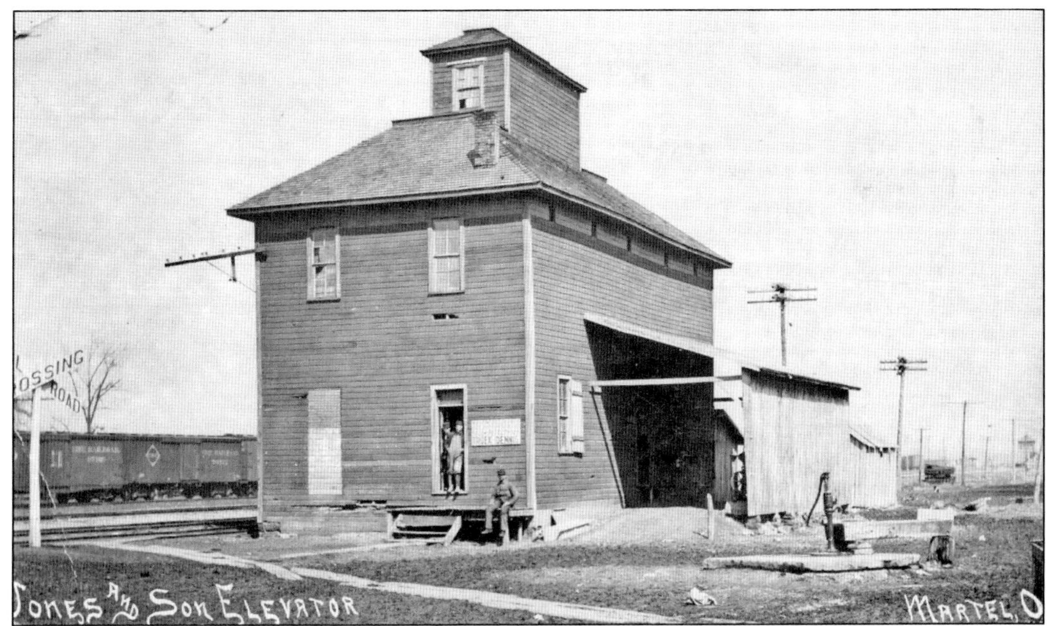

Waiting on Customers. Employees of the Jones and Son grain elevator wait to assist customers, who could use the drive-through if they wished. This hand pump was a source of sweet water for many years. Originally discovered while someone was digging a foundation for a flagpole, the water was highly valued by village residents, who often only had sulfur water available at their homes. (Courtesy of Richard Carey.)

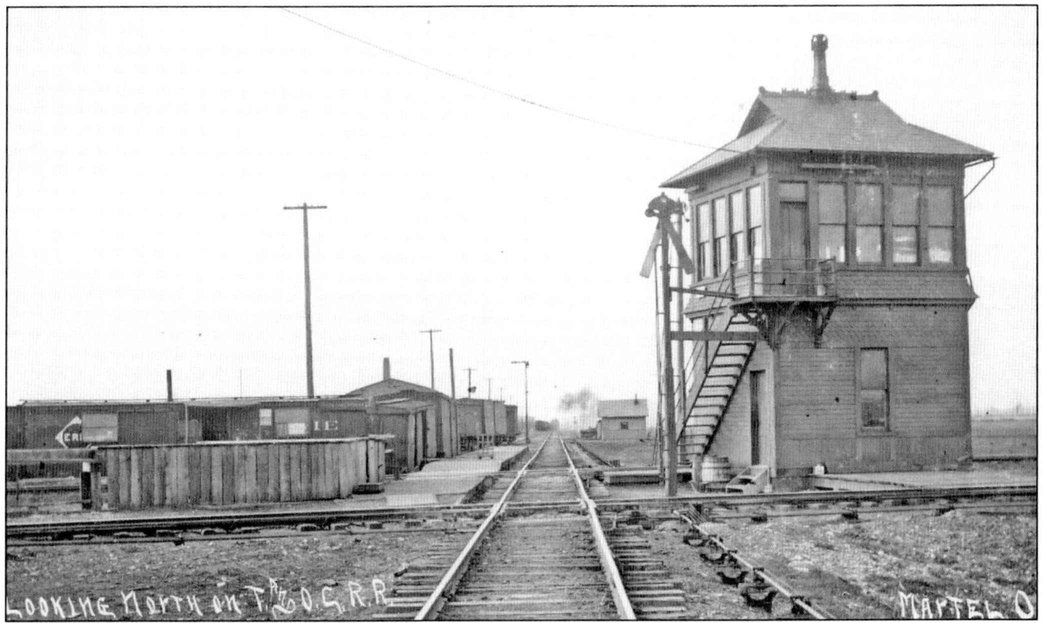

Rail Center. Although it was small, with a population of only 160 people in 1910, Martel was a significant rail center that served as an intersection for the Erie, Big Four, and Toledo & Ohio Central Railroads. The double intersecting tracks were monitored by the tower using mechanical crossing signals. A depot was built in 1909 for use by passengers and freight shippers. (Courtesy of Richard Carey.)

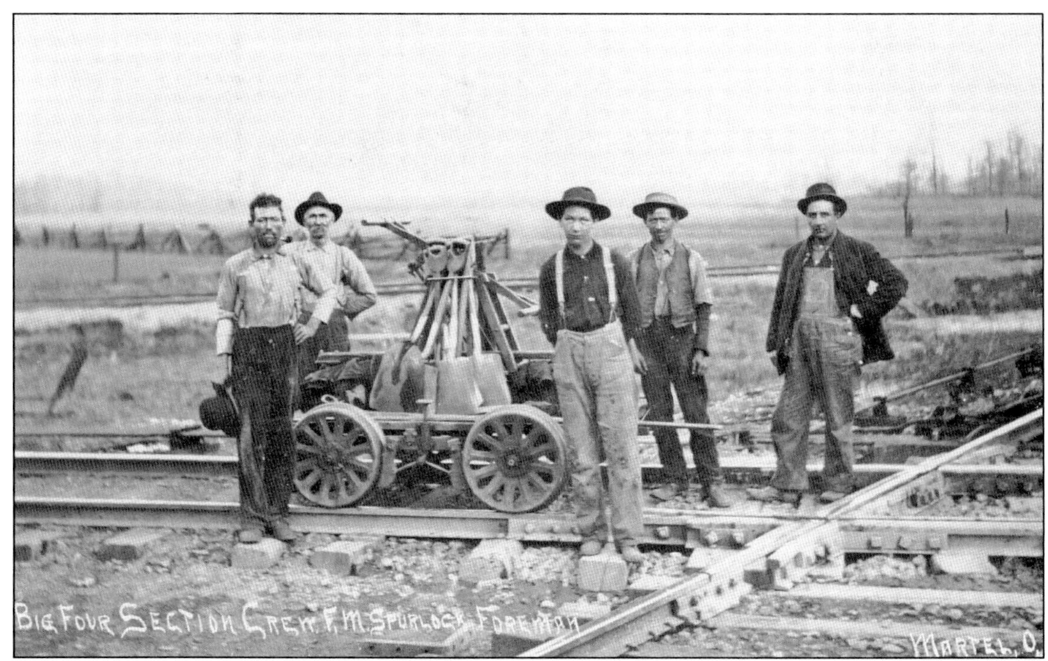

SECTION CREW. Shovels were obviously important tools for this crew under the leadership of F.M. Spurlock. Using a handcart for travel on the rails, the Big Four section crew replaced rotted ties, tamped loose spikes, replaced bolts, and repaired short sections of track. (Courtesy of Richard Carey.)

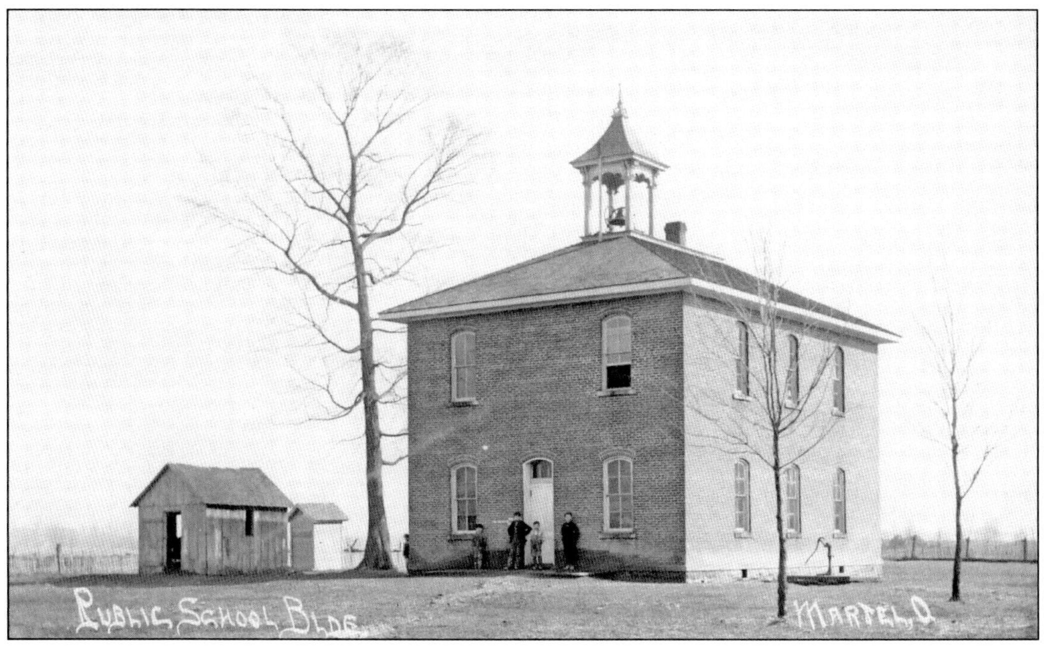

FUNCTIONAL DESIGN. The Martel Public School may not have won any awards for architectural originality, but it undoubtedly served its purpose well for many years. The water pump and outhouse were wisely located on opposite sides of the building, which stood at the east end of Ohio Street. This site is now a vacant lot. (Author's collection.)

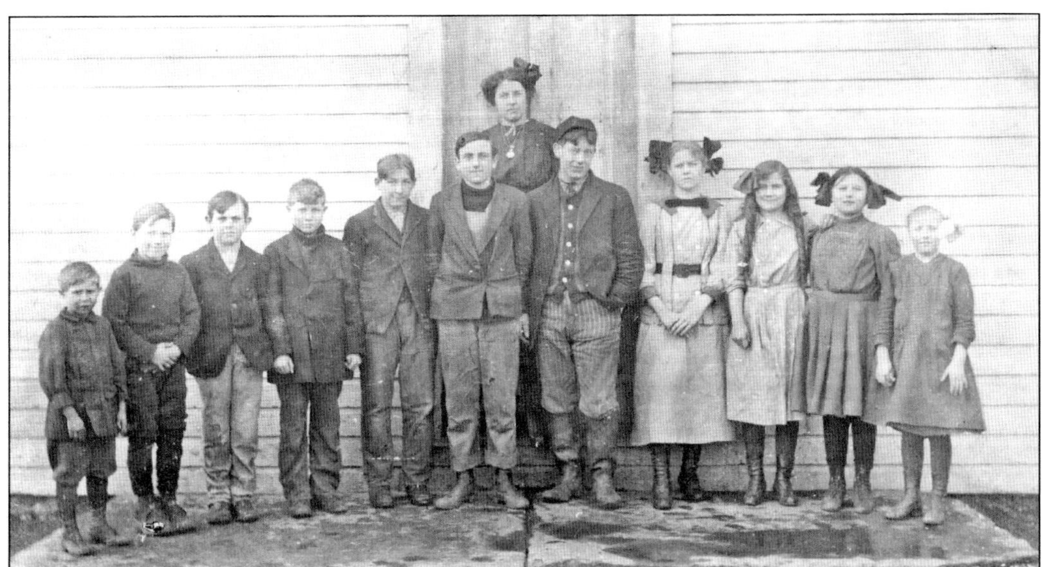

STAIR STEPS. The challenges of teaching several grades in a one-room school are illustrated by the "stair step" pose of these children standing outside the Stringtown School. Students were given individual assignments to work on at their desks, with older students sometimes helping the younger ones. A teacher would call students to her desk, or perhaps to a recitation bench, where she would quiz them on what they had learned and correct their mistakes. (Author's collection.)

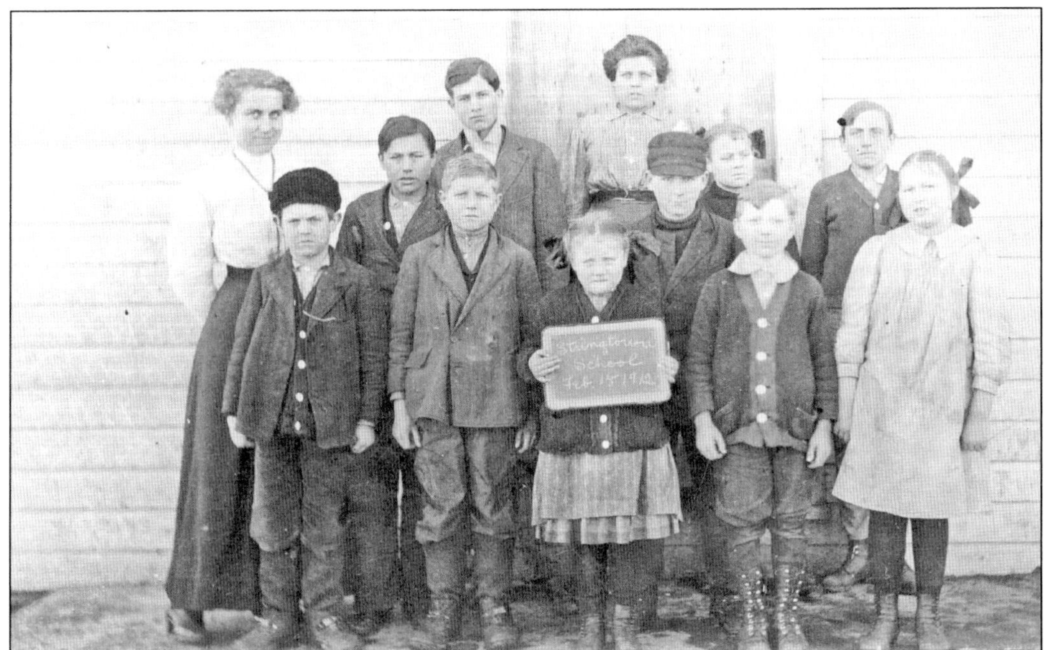

STRINGTOWN SCHOOL. While the existence of the settlement of Stringtown is verified in this 1912 photograph, little evidence of its presence exists today. Located on Lyons Road just north of Emahiser Road, it was never officially platted, although it did have a school and a community band. The school, which was built around 1892 and demolished around 1926, was the only building in the area that was not a home or barn. (Author's collection.)

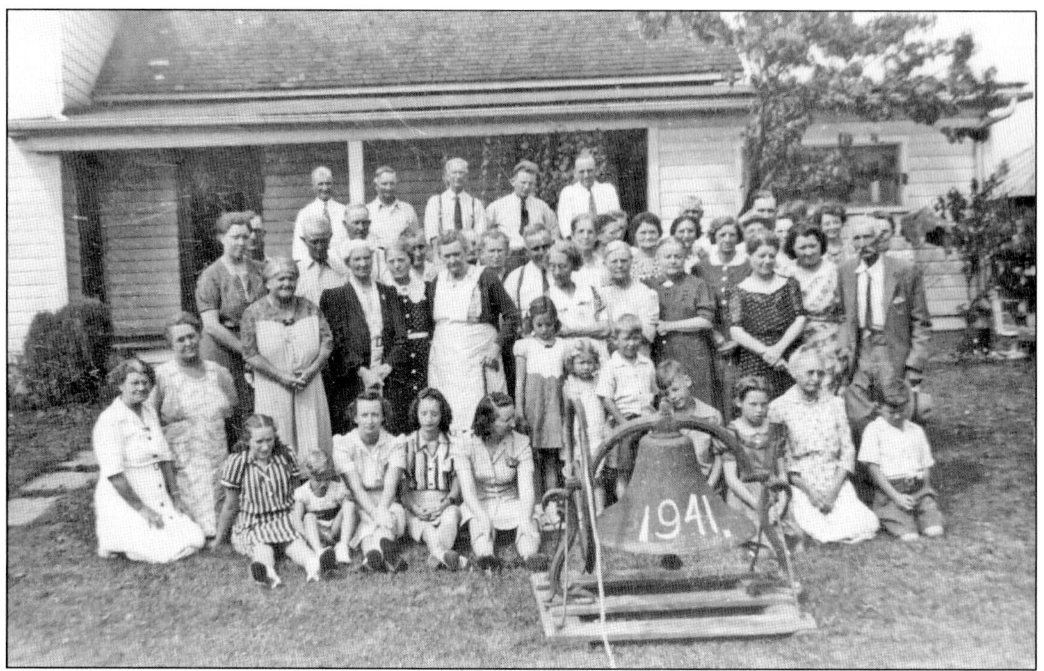

Class Reunion. Former students of the Stringtown School and their families gathered for this 1941 reunion photograph. Stringtown was one of at least 12 schools in Tully Township. Among the others were Bunker Hill, Clark, Clyde, McKinstry, Sixteen, Spies, Three Locusts, and Williamson. (Author's collection.)

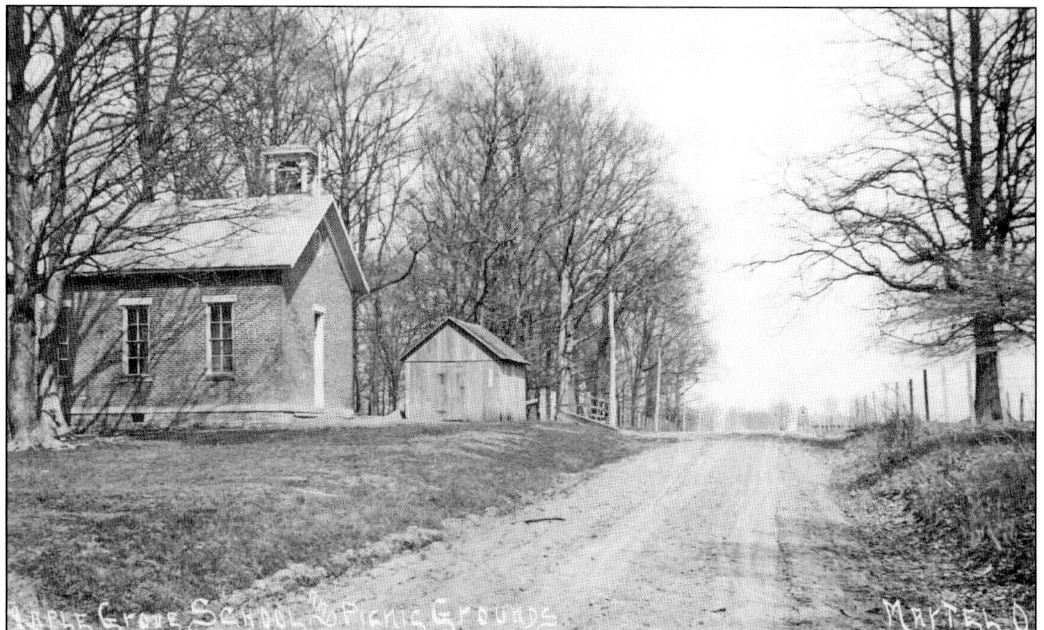

Maple Grove School. The picnic grounds at Maple Grove hosted family reunions as well as school and church functions for many years. Canoe docks on the Olentangy River provided additional entertainment. Maple Grove School sat adjacent to the picnic grounds on the north side of Morral-Kirkpatrick Road between Lyons and Timpson Roads. (Courtesy of Richard Carey.)

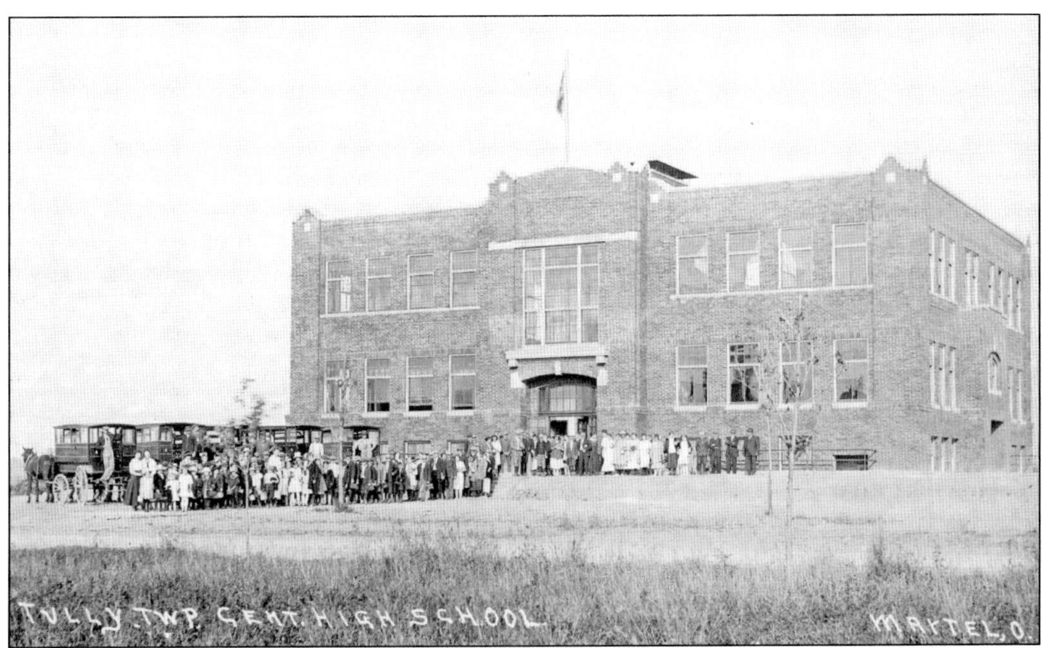

CENTRAL SCHOOL. Tully Township Central School was built starting in 1915 on a four-acre site. Shortly after it opened, the building was temporarily closed due to a diphtheria outbreak. A gymnasium, stage, and locker rooms were added in 1956. The school served all 12 grades for several years, with the last class graduating in 1960 after the River Valley Schools consolidation. (Courtesy of Ellis and Margaret Hudson.)

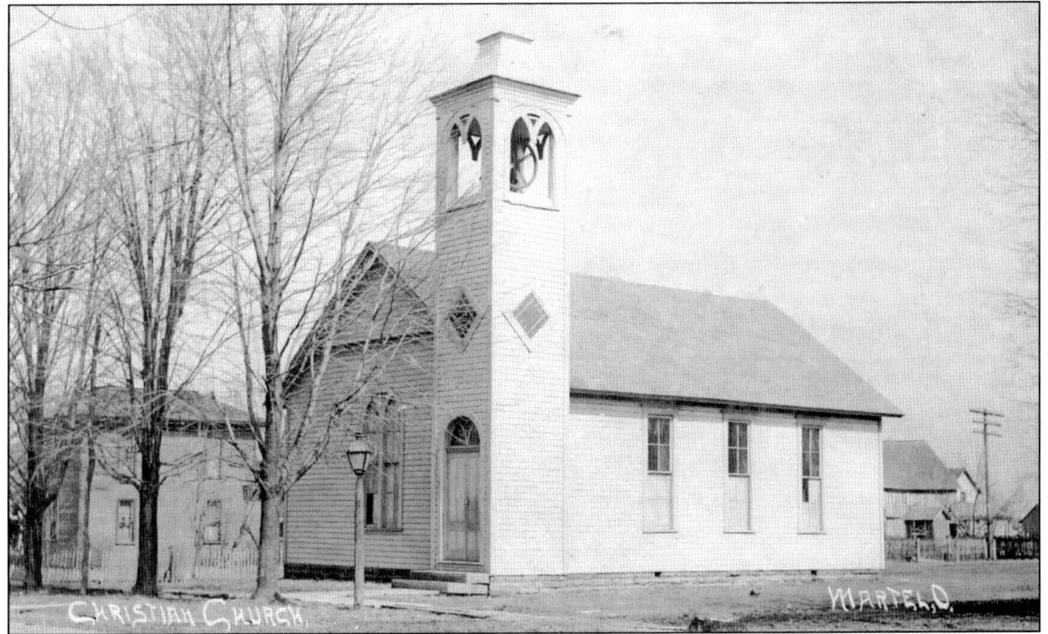

CHRISTIAN CHURCH. The Martel Christian Church focused on a return to what was believed to be the original teachings and practices of the New Testament. The church building was located east of Martel Road at the southern end of the village. After the church closed, the building was used as a grocery store and later as a storage area for many years. (Courtesy of Richard Carey.)

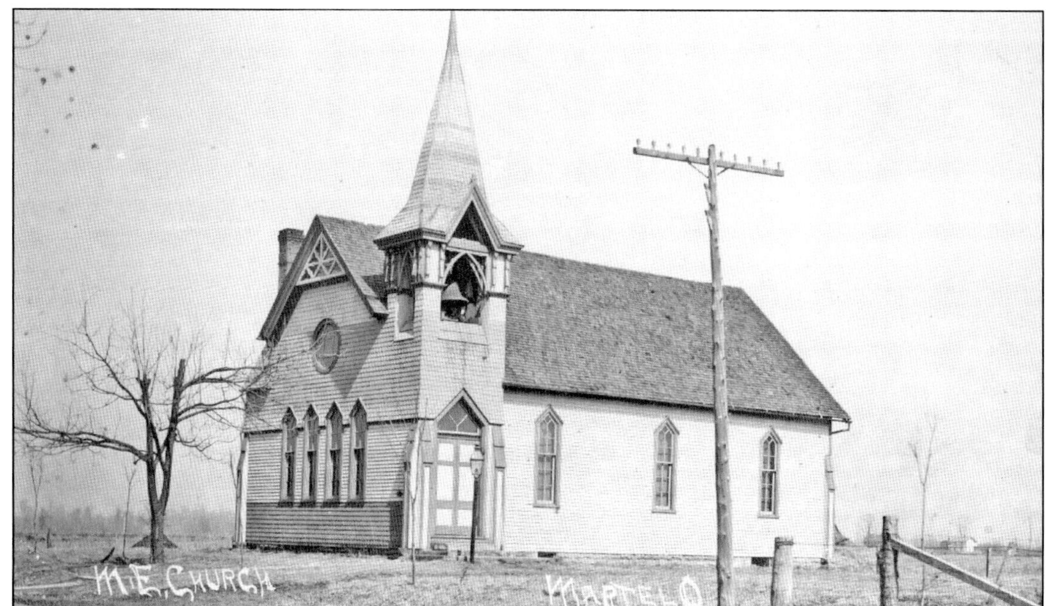

METHODIST EPISCOPAL CHURCH. Members of the Methodist Episcopal church began construction of this building in 1890. Locally grown timber was donated for most of the construction. Oak lumber was taken to Galion, where it was dried and made into pews. The congregation of the Martel United Methodist Church continues to worship in this building. (Courtesy of Richard Carey.)

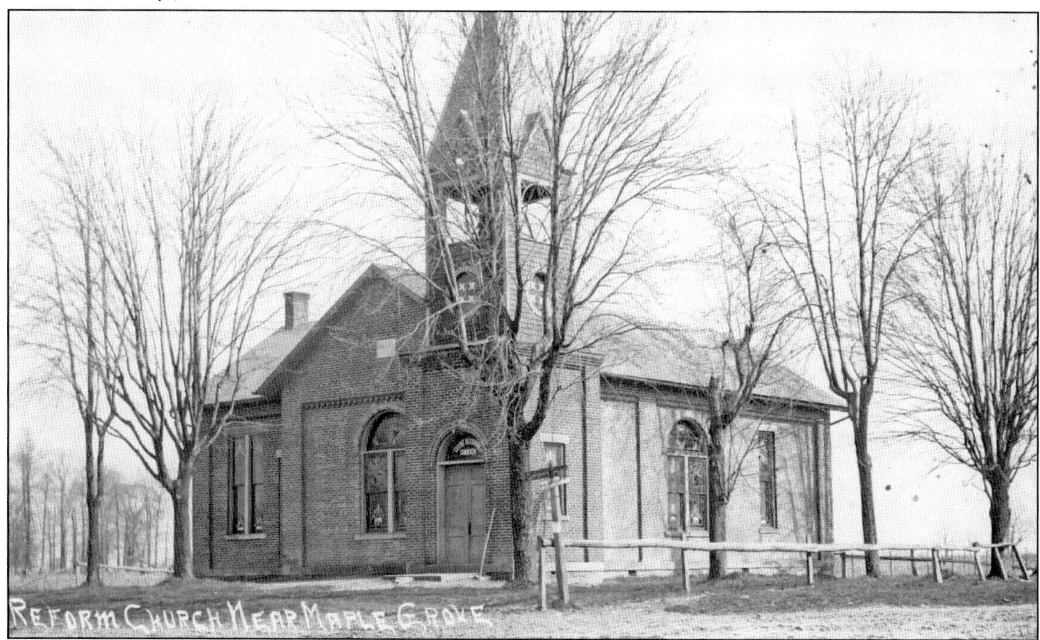

REFORMED CHURCH. Built in 1868 on the southeast corner of Timpson and Morral-Kirkpatrick Roads at a cost of $2,000, this church went by various names over the years. Among them were the German Emanuel Reformed, Maple Grove Reformed, and Clyde Reformed. Many church members are buried in the nearby German Sixteen Cemetery. The church burned to the ground in the 1970s after catching fire from burning brush on a nearby farm. (Author's collection.)

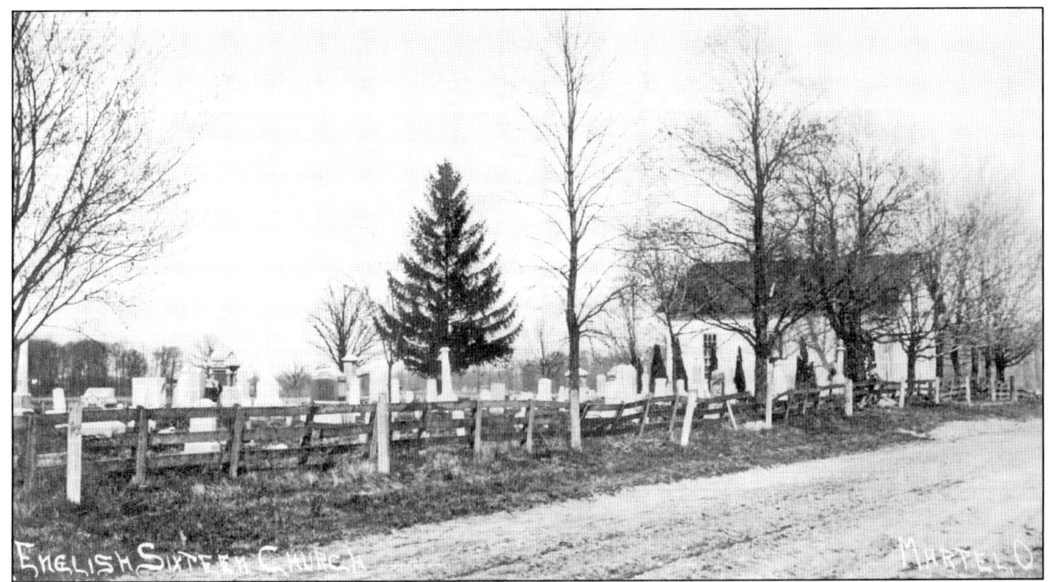

ENGLISH SIXTEEN. The English Sixteen Church was on the northwest corner of the Wyandot-Marion and Martel Roads in Section 16 of Tully Township. When it was first built around 1860 by a United Brethren congregation, it stood in Marion County, but it later became part of Crawford County as a result of county boundary changes. The church closed around 1919, and the lumber from the building was used to construct a storage building on a nearby farm. (Courtesy of Ralph and Erdine Eaton collection.)

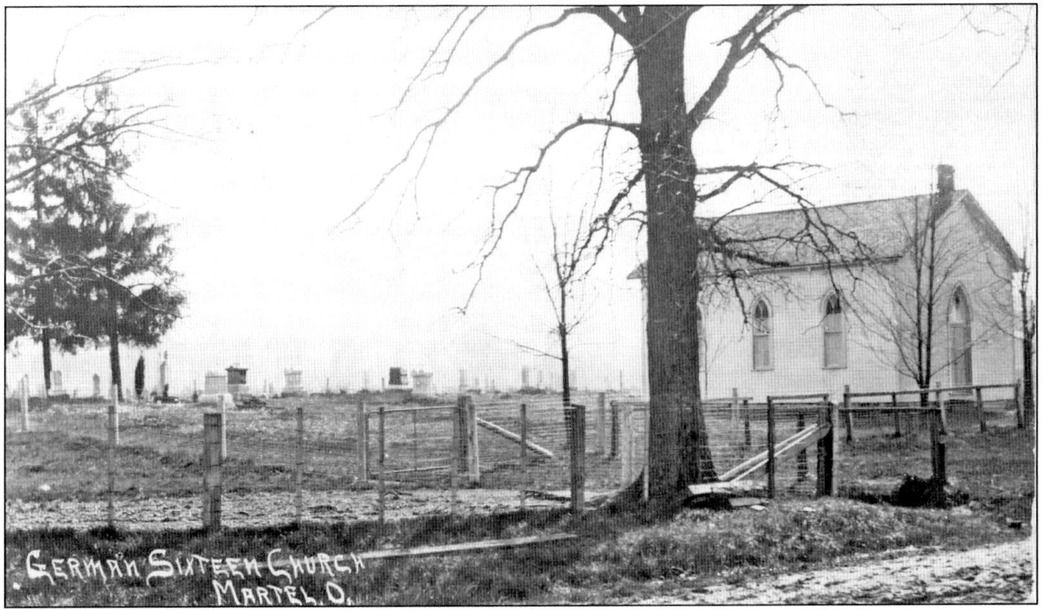

GERMAN SIXTEEN. The German Sixteen Church traces its origins to around 1858, when a German Reformed congregation erected a frame building church at a cost of $700 on Morral-Kirkpatrick Road just west of Martel Road on a one-acre lot purchased for $10. The first sermon was delivered by Rev. Jacob Rothweiler. The first wedding ever held in the church took place in 1964, more than 106 years after it was built. The congregation, now known as Sixteen United Methodist Church, continues to worship here. (Author's collection.)

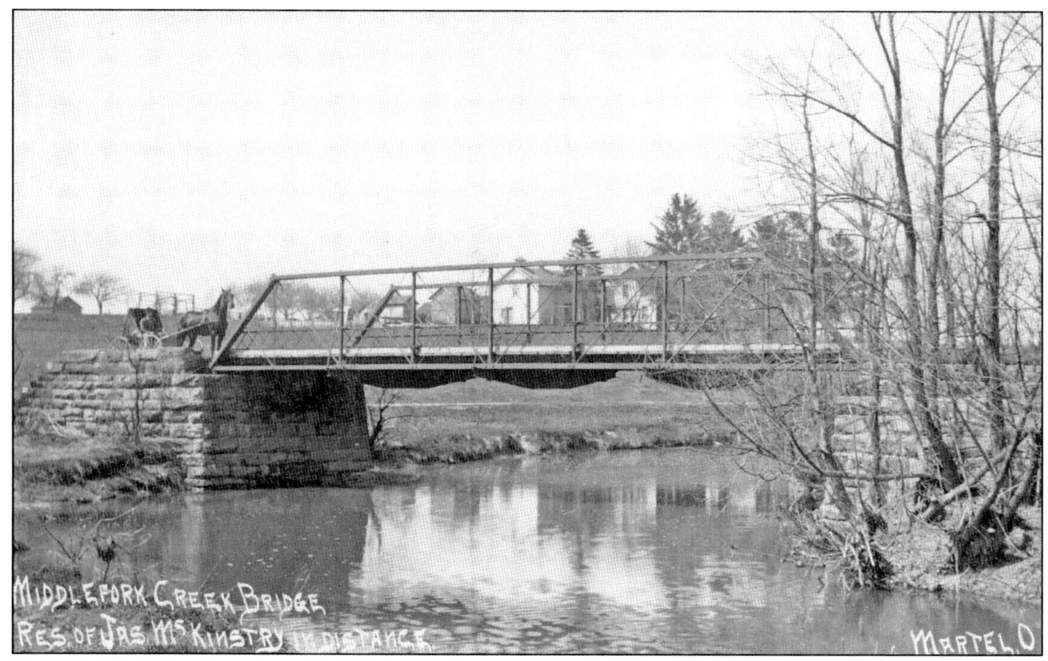

RIVER CROSSING. This traveler in a convertible-top carriage paused for a photograph before crossing the Middlefork Creek (also known as Whetstone Creek or Flat Run) on Linn-Hipsher Road. The farm of James McKinstry is visible in the background. The McKinstrys, one of the first families to settle in Tully Township, came to the area around 1833, when John McKinstry purchased 240 acres for $800. (Courtesy of Mike and Linda Perry.)

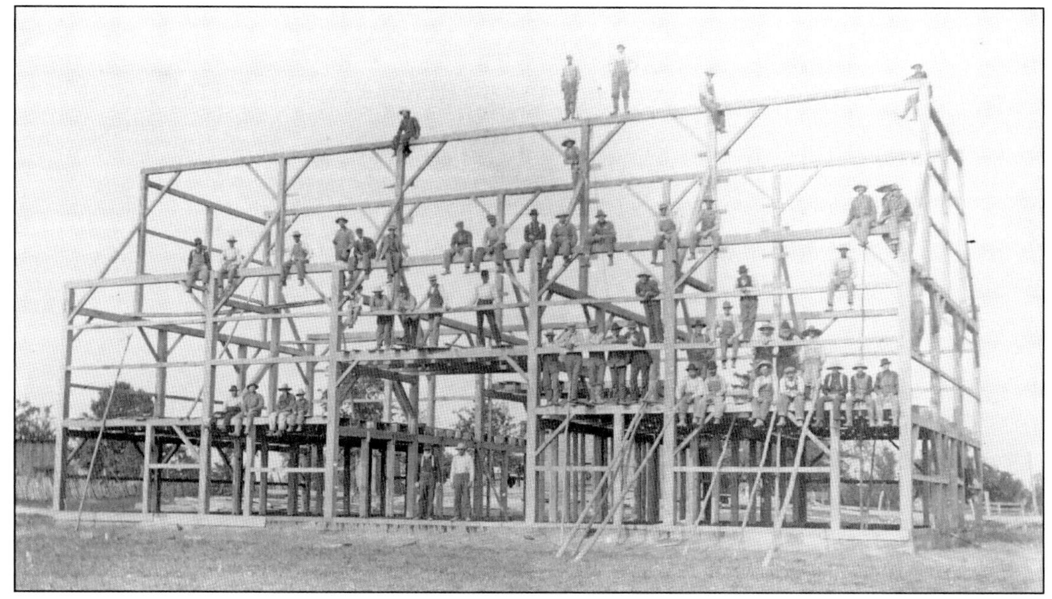

BARN RAISING. Building a new post-and-beam barn was certainly a community affair in the Martel area, as shown by the more than 50 men and boys pictured here. The long wooden poles were used to push preassembled walls to a vertical position before they were fastened with wooden pegs. The huge meals fixed by the women of the community to fuel the men's labor were another important element of these events. (Courtesy of Mike and Linda Perry.)

Four

LaRue Area

Maj. William LaRue and his wife, Cynthia, came to Marion County in 1823 from their home in Washington County. LaRue, who was a major in the Ohio Militia, spent much of the next year exploring the land west of the newly platted village of Marion. In 1825, he moved to the area that would eventually become the village bearing his name with a goal of buying as much of the newly available land as his finances would allow. He soon purchased 70 acres on the east side of the Scioto River. The land was true wilderness, with the nearest settlers being about six miles away. An 1883 Marion County history contains LaRue's account of his first year on the property: "I chopped off five acres of timber that spring, trimmed and burned the brush, planted corn among the logs as they lay, and raised a crop of corn. There was no road and to get here, I had to cut one through the woods for about four miles."

LaRue filed for ownership of the land in 1827 and continued to develop the property while purchasing additional land. He owned a tavern, a canoe used as a ferry for crossing the river, and a store. Although the surrounding area was still largely undeveloped, other small settlements began to arise. Holmesville, later renamed Parr Town, was in neighboring Bowling Green Township and featured grocery stores, a blacksmith shop, and other businesses. Another small settlement called Winnemac was started just west of LaRue. In 1851, LaRue officially platted his community. It consisted of 90 lots, with four donated for local churches. Major LaRue's good business sense was demonstrated when he negotiated with the Bellefontaine & Indiana Railroad to run the line through his village in return for his donating the right of way and purchasing a $1,000 subscription for the construction of the rail lines. Part of the negotiations stated that every train coming through LaRue was required to stop and take on water. This led to the young village becoming a natural location for business to develop and to the eventual decline of the neighboring communities.

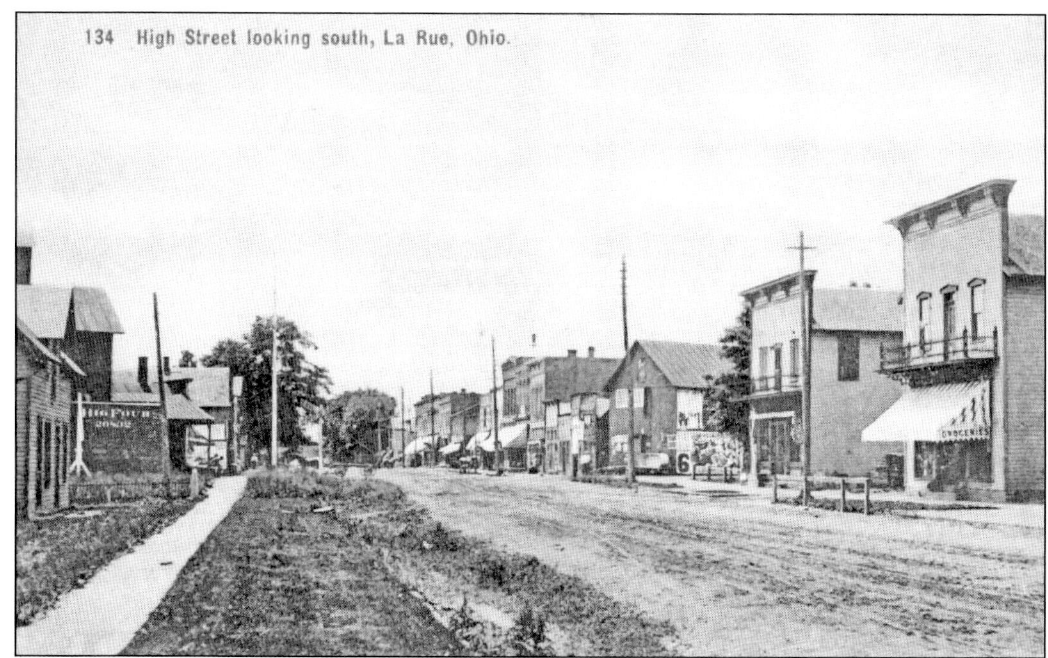

UPTOWN VIEW. Coming into the western Marion County village of LaRue, visitors found a thriving village, as evidenced by a wide variety of businesses. Among the ones shown in this view are a grocery store, a boardinghouse, a tailor, a blacksmith, and fraternal lodges. A boxcar used by the Big Four Railroad is visible on the left. The railbed had not yet been raised where it passed through the village. (Courtesy of Ralph and Erdine Eaton collection.)

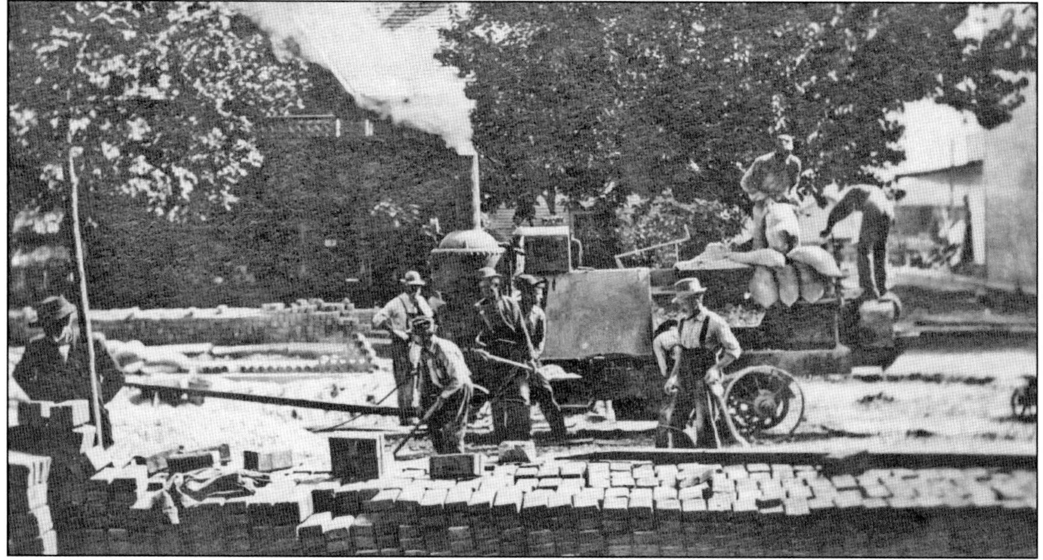

STREET IMPROVEMENTS. These men certainly had their work cut out for them when they laid brick streets throughout the village in 1910. Plank streets had been installed in many areas in 1865, requiring good oak or pine planks substantially nailed with No. 20 spikes on solid oak stringers. In 1873, the street commissioner was given authority to require all male residents between the ages of 21 and 55 (and not exempted by law) to work on the streets for a minimum of two 10-hour days. (Courtesy of Richard Carey.)

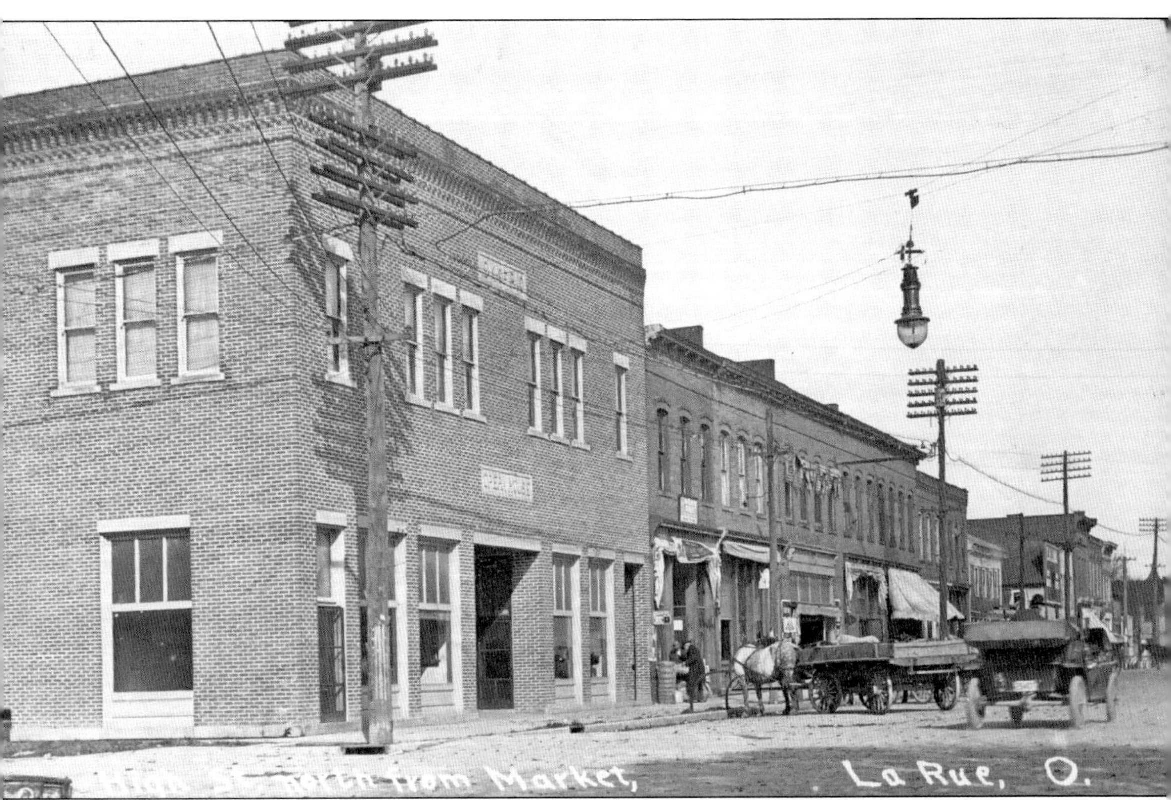

Opera Houses. Opera houses were the center of entertainment in many villages, but few could lay claim to two as did LaRue. The LaRue Opera House, built in 1910 on the northwest corner of High and Market Streets, had the Knights of Pythias lodge on the second floor. The building was later used as a fire station, city council meeting place, and library. A second opera house was located on the northeast corner of Vine and Chestnut Streets. These venues (essentially entertainment halls) rarely hosted actual operatic performances, although the name was believed to add an air of respectability. Typical events at these venues included minstrel shows, vaudeville performances, lectures, and concerts. Many of the halls were located on the upper floors of buildings in space that would perhaps have otherwise gone unused. Association with fraternal lodges was also common, with many organizations using these upper-floor spaces for lodge meetings. (Courtesy of Richard Carey.)

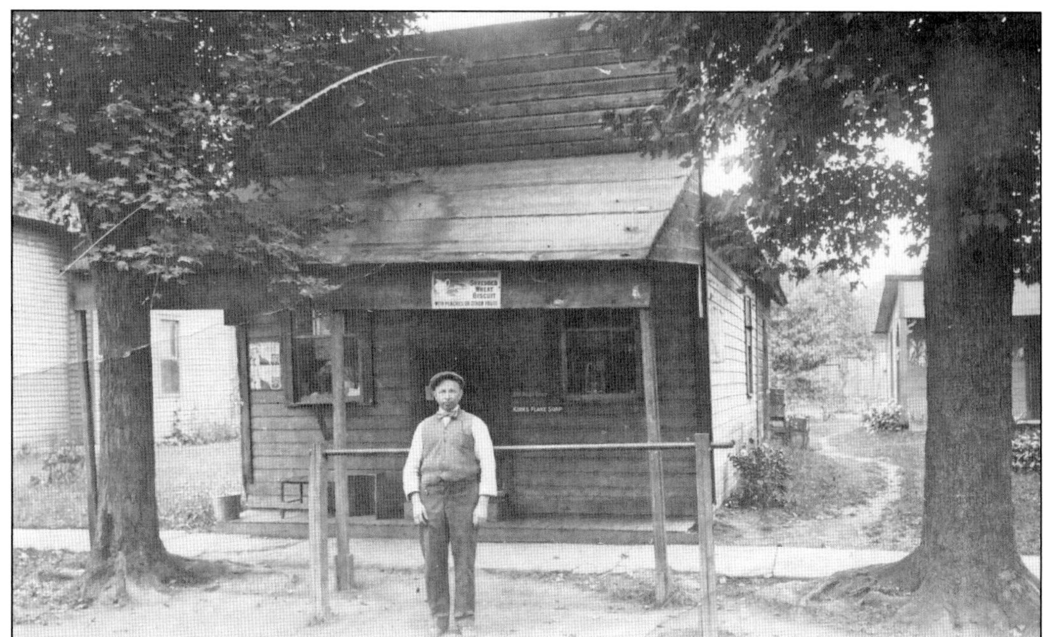

GROCERY STORE. Drake's Grocery, later known as Whitman's Grocery, was located on North Section Street. Special attention was given to the Shredded Wheat Biscuits available for purchase, as well as Kirk's Flake Soap. Many villages would have more than one small grocer, with each having its own local customers. (Courtesy of Richard Carey.)

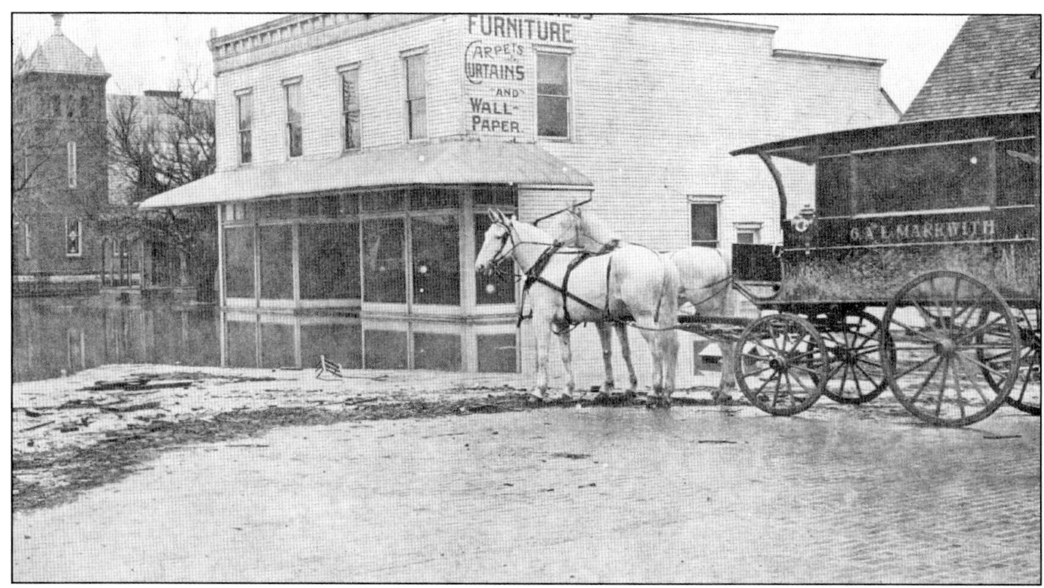

STOPPED IN THEIR TRACKS. This team of horses pulling a hearse is stopped on High Street near the receding waters of the 1913 flood. John Thombs' furniture store was one of the largest merchants in the village until it burned in 1926. George Abraham Lincoln Markwith operated a funeral service from a location on the corner of Market and High Streets. Markwith was the successor to Hiram Mills, the first undertaker in LaRue. (Courtesy of Richard Carey.)

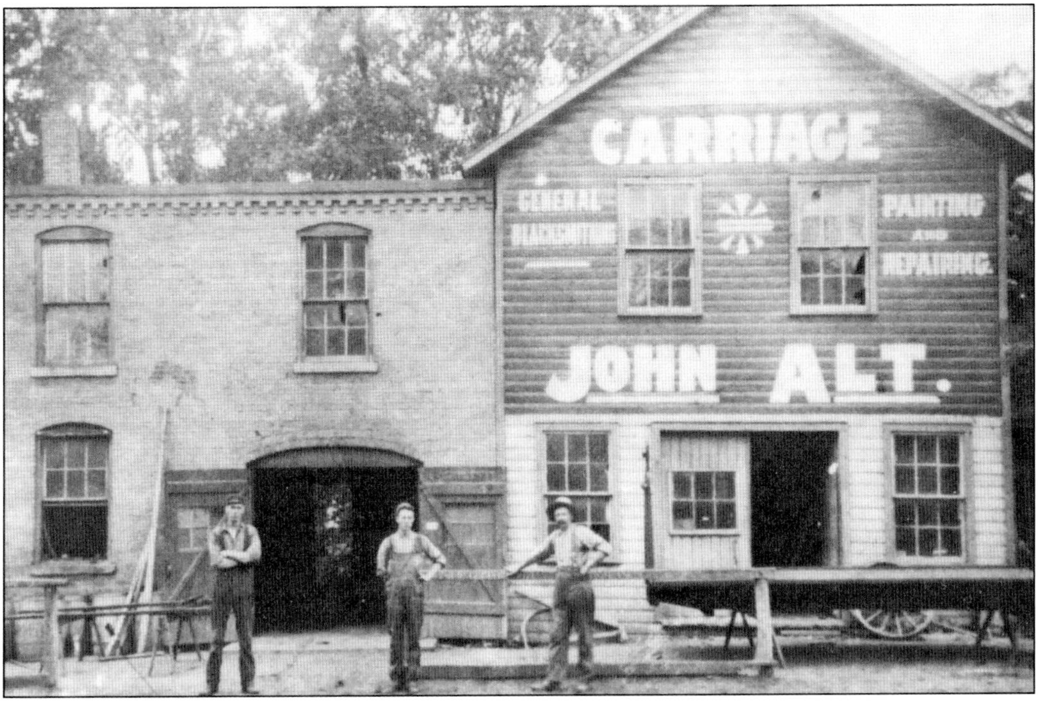

OPEN FOR BUSINESS. Employees of the John Alt Carriage Shop appear ready to help customers at their business on Front Street in LaRue. Travel over often-rutted roads required frequent maintenance on wooden carriage wheels. This building no longer stands, although the cement floor is still visible near the Scioto River bank. (Courtesy of Jim Anderson.)

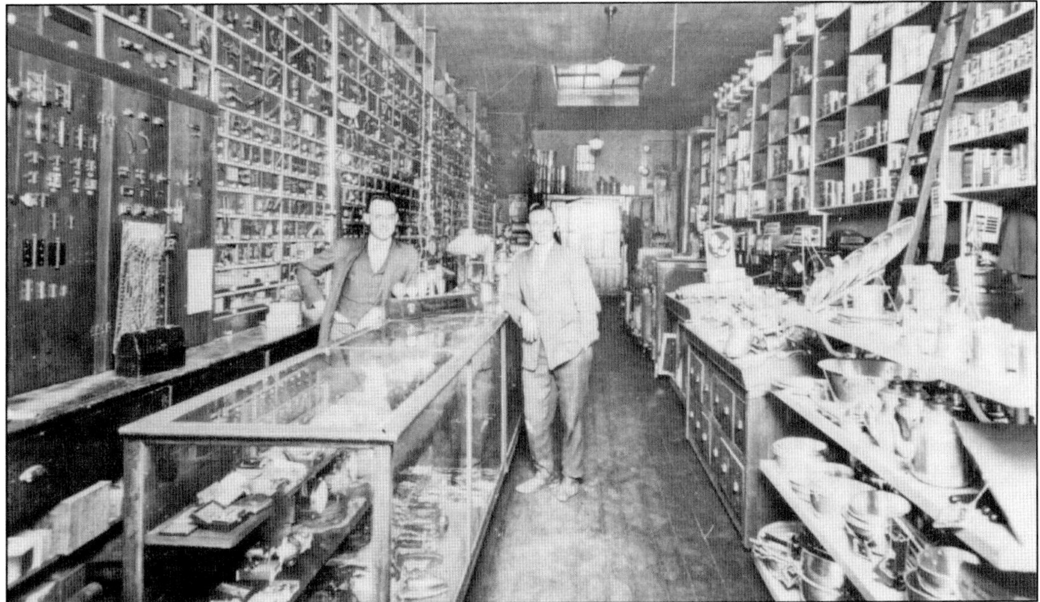

HARDWARE AND MORE. Hardware stores such as Stahl's not only carried the requisite nuts and bolts but also thousands of other often hard-to-find items. Ladders like the one visible at right often had wheels at the bottom to facilitate easy movement between shelves. (Courtesy of Jim Anderson.)

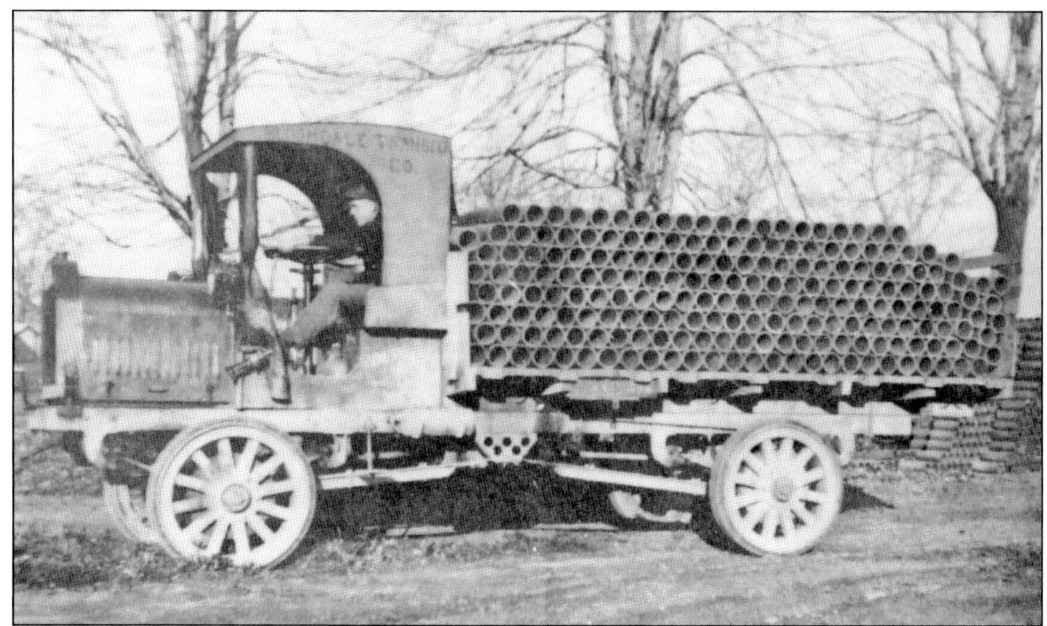

QUITE A LOAD. The four-wheel-drive power of this Bloomdale Transfer truck was certainly needed to haul the heavy load of clay tile produced at the tile works in LaRue. The company was started by Bri Miller around 1875 and sold to the LaRue Tile Company in 1910. The company continued operations for another 50 years but eventually closed due to increased competition and a diminishing supply of quality clay. The tile company's factory site was later donated for use as a community park. (Courtesy of Jim Anderson.)

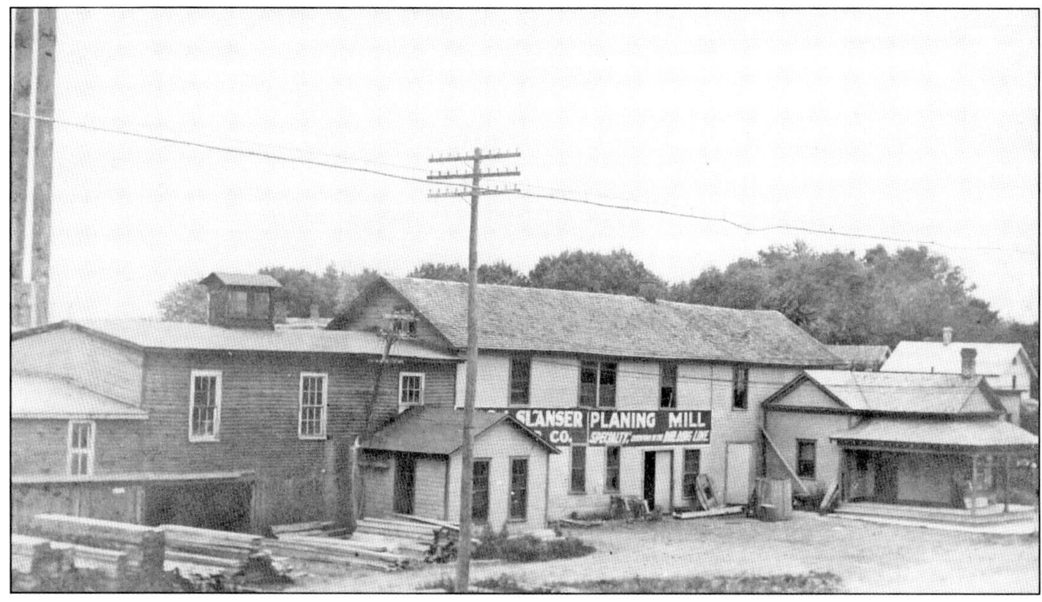

SLANSER PLANING MILL. In 1876, Joseph Slanser co-owned a patent on a wood-joining process that was used extensively in the framing of large buildings. He also owned and operated a lumber company at Market Street east of Chestnut Street that was one of the largest wood suppliers in the area. Records show that in 1901, the mill had an average stock of more than 300,000 board feet of lumber available. (Author's collection.)

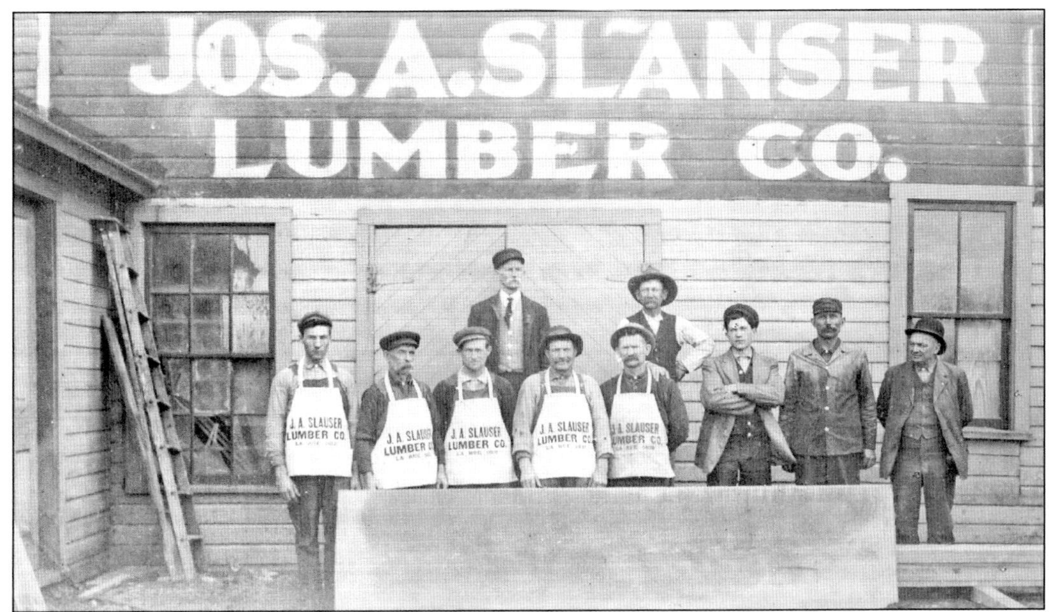

READY TO GO. Wearing their nail aprons advertising their employer, these workers may be getting ready to take the huge rough-cut board in front of them into the mill for planing. Fire was always a danger at mills due to the amount of sawdust and wood. A 1901 Sandborn-Ferris Fire Map showed that the Slanser company had a night watchman, as well as barrels of chemicals and water, to help reduce the risk of a major fire. (Courtesy of Ralph and Erdine Eaton collection.)

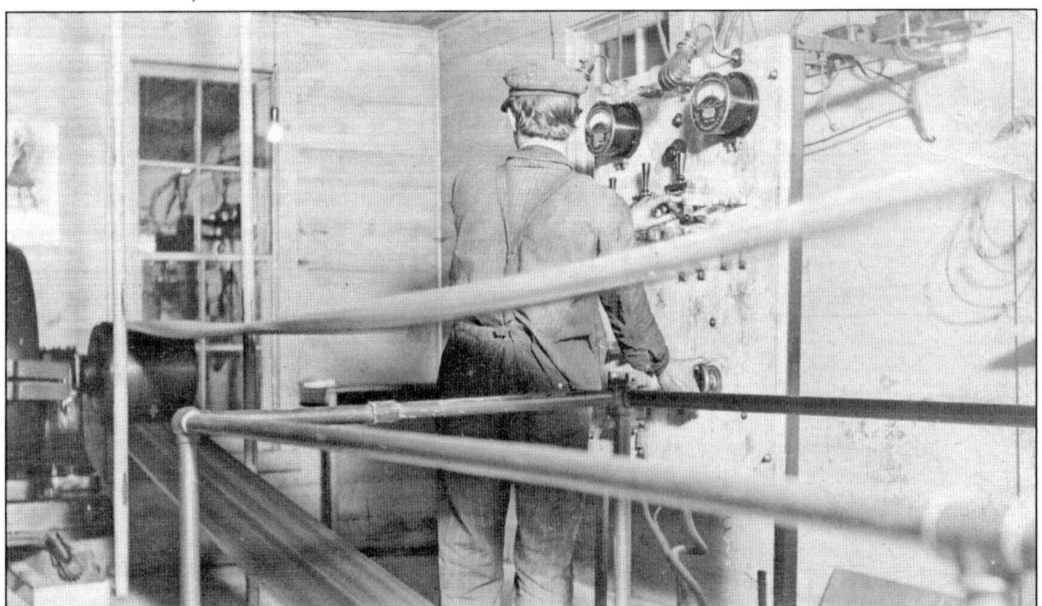

POWER SUPPLY. Slanser's mill produced more than wood products. Power generated by its steam boilers was used for many years to run both the mill's woodworking equipment and a generator that provided electricity for the village. Electricity was usually available for only a few hours each day and was shut off in the evening. Electrical service for the entire village became available in 1922. (Courtesy of Richard Carey.)

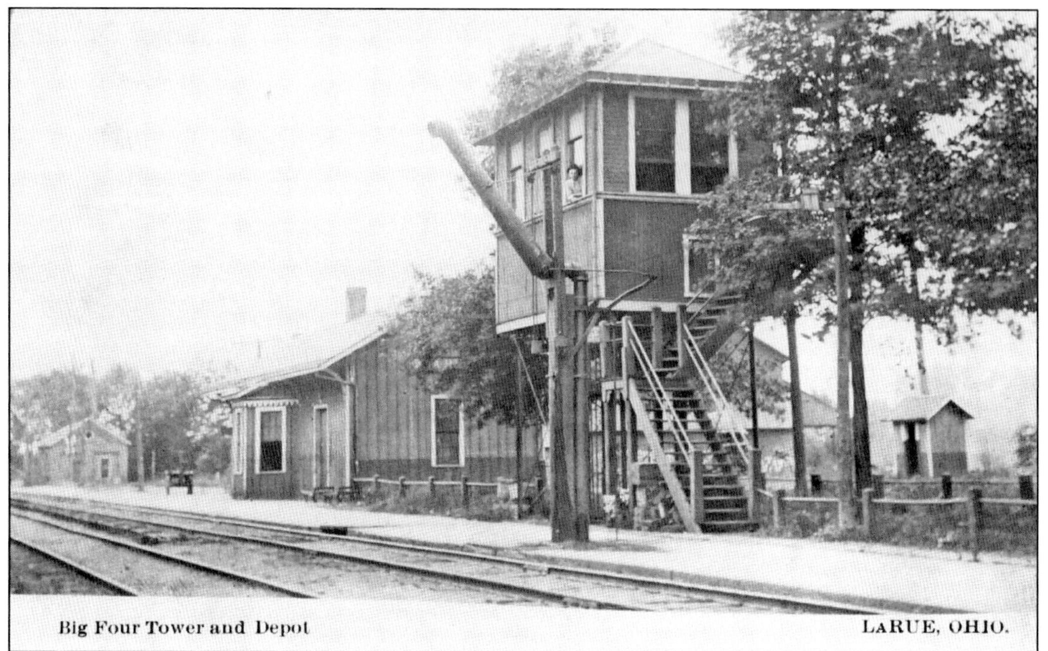

WATER STOP. Services provided for the Big Four Railroad as it passed through LaRue included a passenger and freight depot as well as a water stop. While many stops needed tanks or towers to hold water, LaRue brought it directly from the adjacent Scioto River. The track was doubled in 1918, leading to an increase in the number of trains coming through the village. At that time, the interlocking tower shown here was installed to control railroad signals. (Author's collection.)

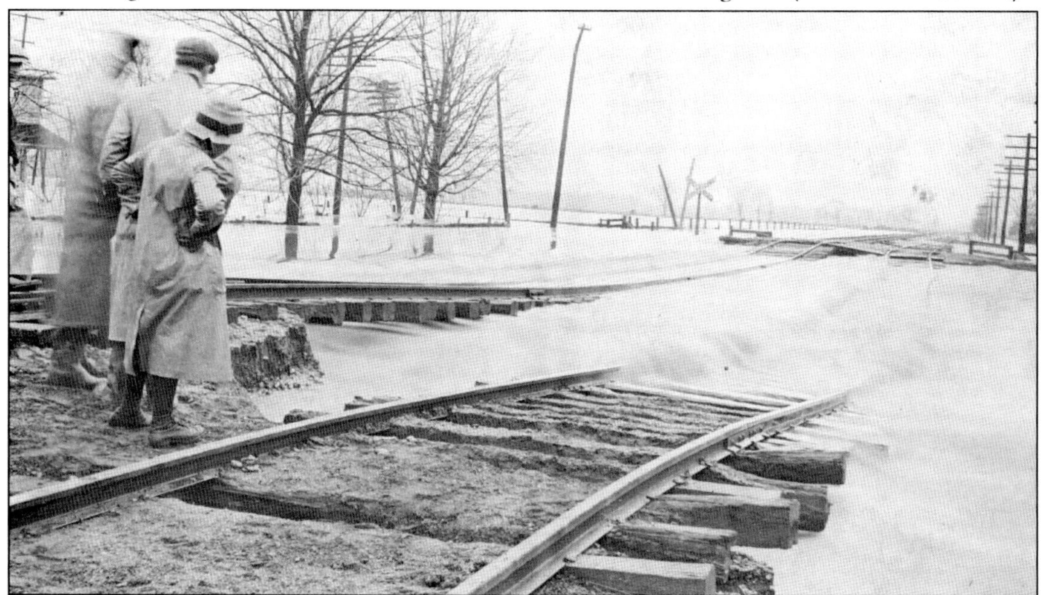

BLOWN AWAY. Problems with flooding in LaRue in 1913 were compounded when water was held back by the Big Four Railroad's bed, resulting in increased flooding on Section Street. The issue was temporarily solved when some strategically placed dynamite blasts allowed the flood waters to escape. The railroad eventually raised the railbed as much as six feet in some places and installed culverts to help resolve the issue. (Courtesy of Richard Carey.)

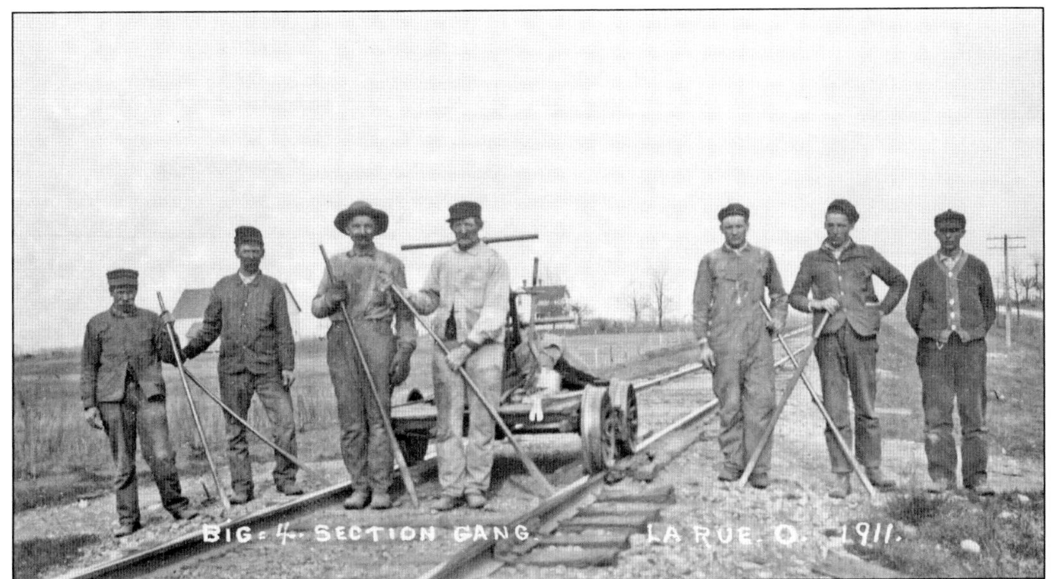

GANDY DANCERS. The workers in this Big Four section gang had their lining bars, also known as gandy bars, ready to help "dance" the rails into alignment as they maintained the tracks. The workers would often chant or sing as they pushed on the bars in unison to move the rails. Rail lines were divided into sections, with a designated gang having responsibility for each section. Travel was often done on a handcar, also known as pumper car, as shown here. (Courtesy of Ralph and Erdine Eaton collection.)

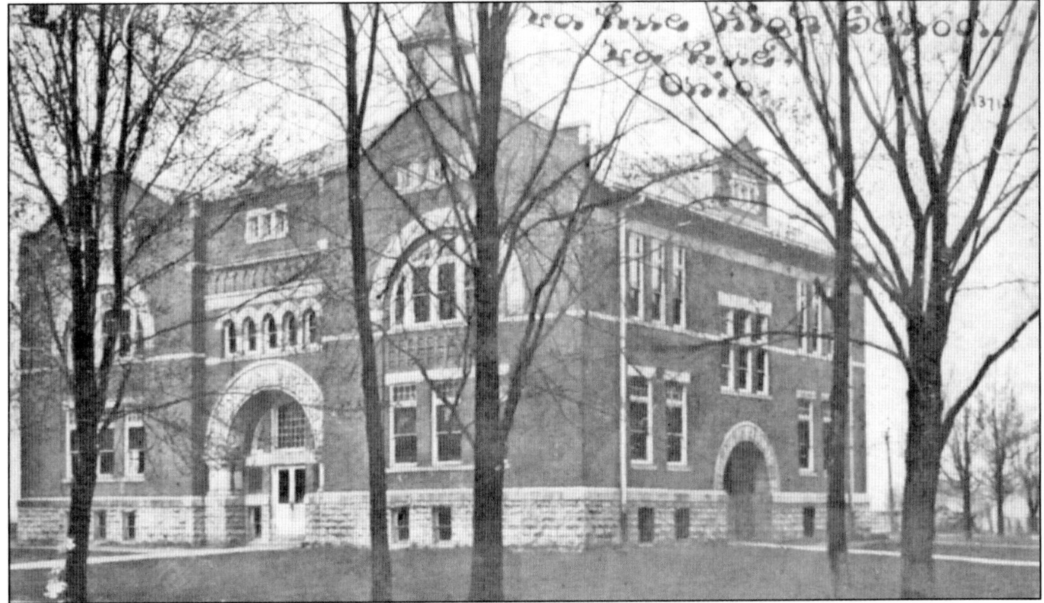

VILLAGE SCHOOL. Residents of the LaRue area were rightfully proud of this school at the northeast corner of High and School Streets. It was built in 1890 at a cost of $35,000 and featured four levels with room for more than 300 students. The bottom level was constructed of partially buried limestone, with the remainder of the building being brick. Limestone was impervious to dampness and would not dissolve as brick tended to do when exposed to the continuous moisture of the ground. (Courtesy of Richard Carey.)

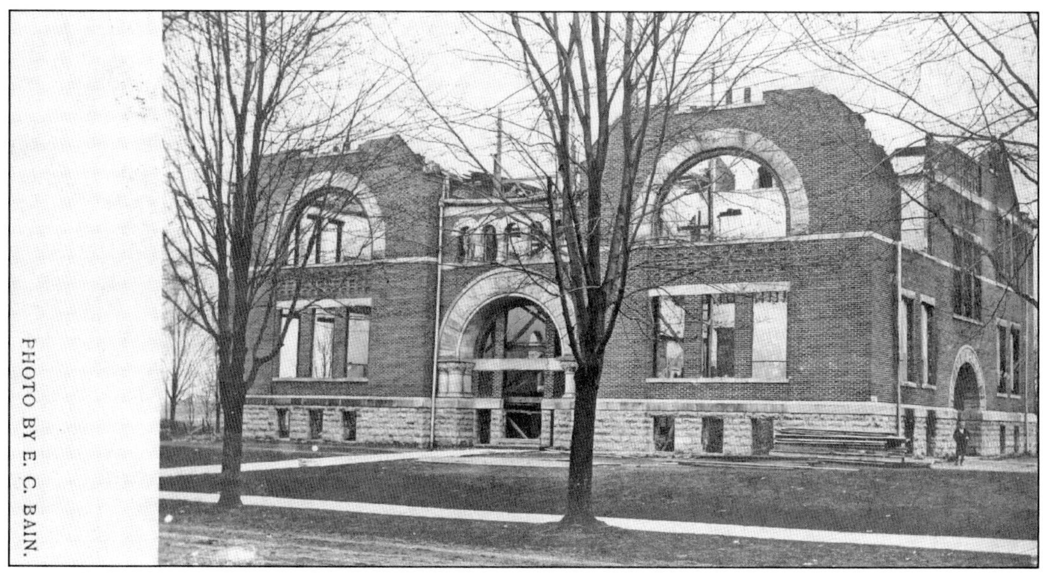

All That Remained. Tragedy struck on February 21, 1907, when fire swept through the LaRue school building, leaving only a shell. Fortunately, many of the books were saved, and classes started again in buildings around the village such as churches and the town hall. The structure was rebuilt without the third floor. It was in use until 1956, when it was razed after a new building opened. (Courtesy of Ralph and Erdine Eaton collection.)

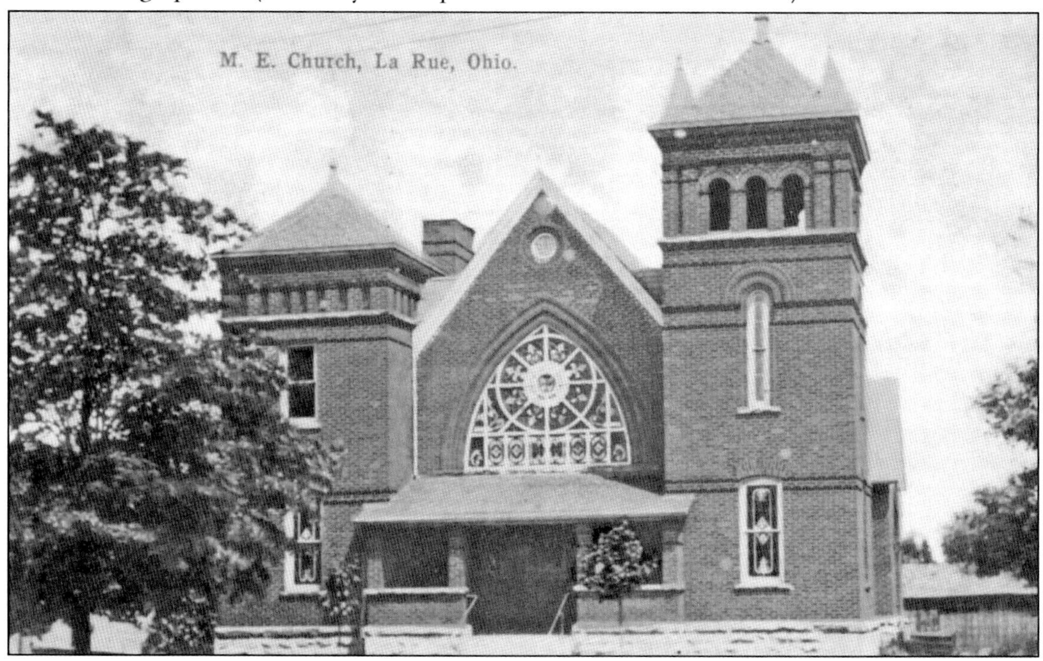

Methodist Episcopal Church. The first meetings of a Methodist congregation in the area took place in the barn of Maj. William LaRue, who helped finance the first church with a donation of cash and land in 1860. Construction on the church soon began but was delayed, and it was finally dedicated in 1870. By 1895, a larger building was needed. The congregation quickly raised the necessary funds, and the cornerstone of this beautiful building was laid on August 10, 1895. (Courtesy of Richard Carey.)

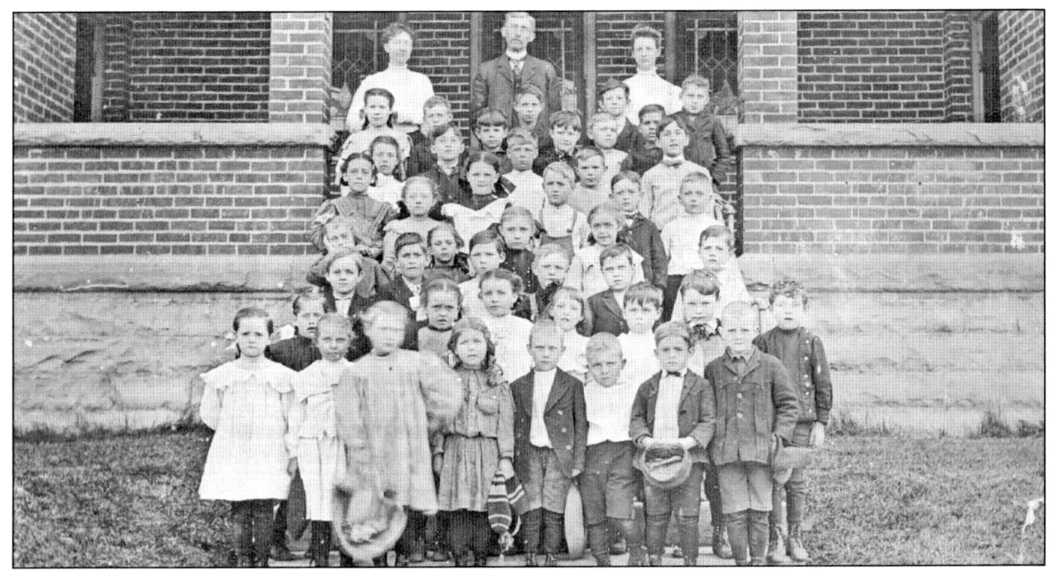

School Class. While the location featured in this picture of children and their teachers is most likely the steps of the Methodist Episcopal church, it is not known what type of school the children were attending. They may have been students whose classes were moved from the burned-out LaRue school to the church, or perhaps they were attending Sunday school. At any rate, many of them appear to be dressed in their Sunday best. (Courtesy of Richard Carey.)

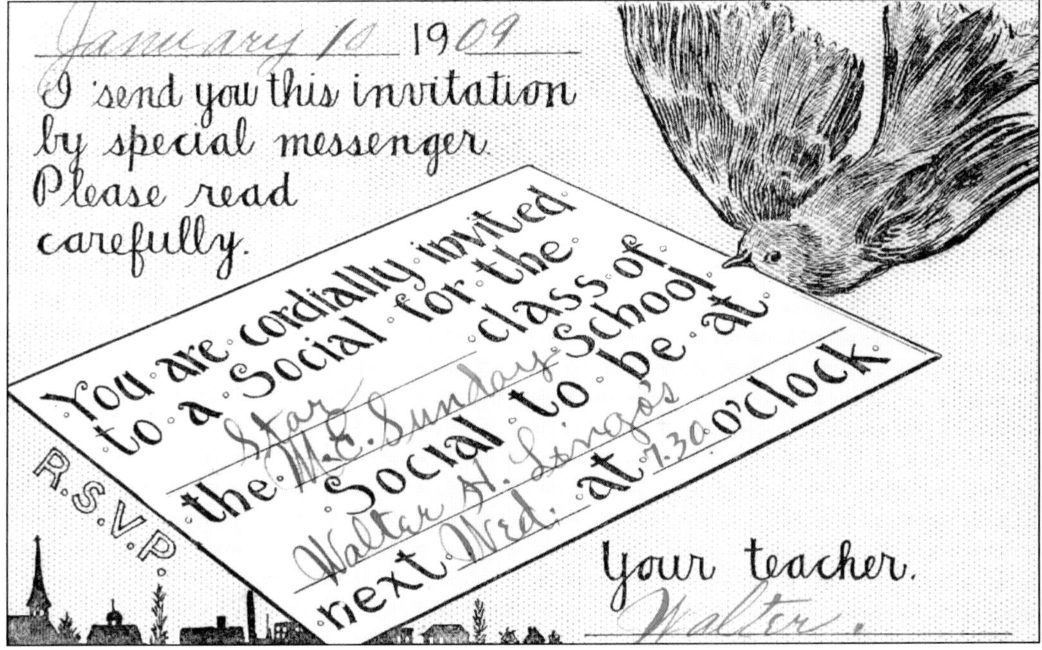

January 10 1909

I send you this invitation by special messenger. Please read carefully.

You are cordially invited to a Social for the Star class of the M.E. Sunday School. Social to be at Walter H. Lingo's next Wed. at 7.30 o'clock

R.S.V.P.

Your teacher.
Walter.

Air Mail Invitation. This invitation, with its "air mail" delivery theme, was sent to members of the Star Class of the Methodist Episcopal church to invite them to a social at the home of Walter Lingo. The 1909 date is before Lingo became well-known as the sponsor of the Oorang Indians National Football League team. The team featured all Native American players, with Jim Thorpe as its star, and was used to promote Lingo's Oorang Airedale dogs. (Courtesy of Richard Carey.)

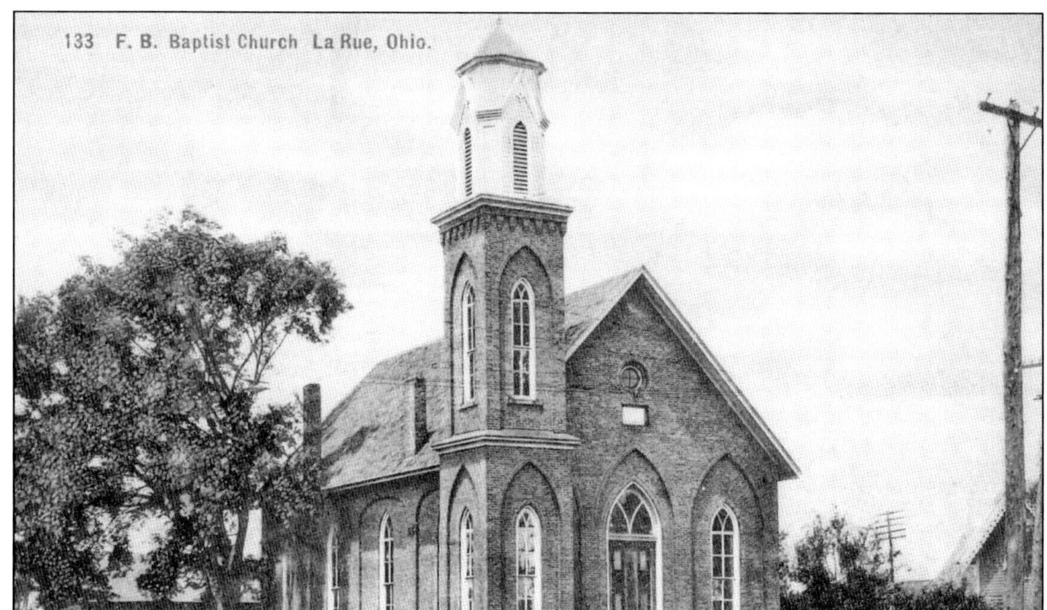

First Baptist Church. Topliff's carding mill on the bank of the Scioto River was the first site of worship for LaRue-area Baptists around 1845. After sharing a building in the village with the Methodists for several years, the congregation began constructing this building in 1877. The site was donated by Maj. William LaRue and was formerly a burial ground. The bodies were disinterred, and most were moved to the Bonner Cemetery west of LaRue. (Author's collection.)

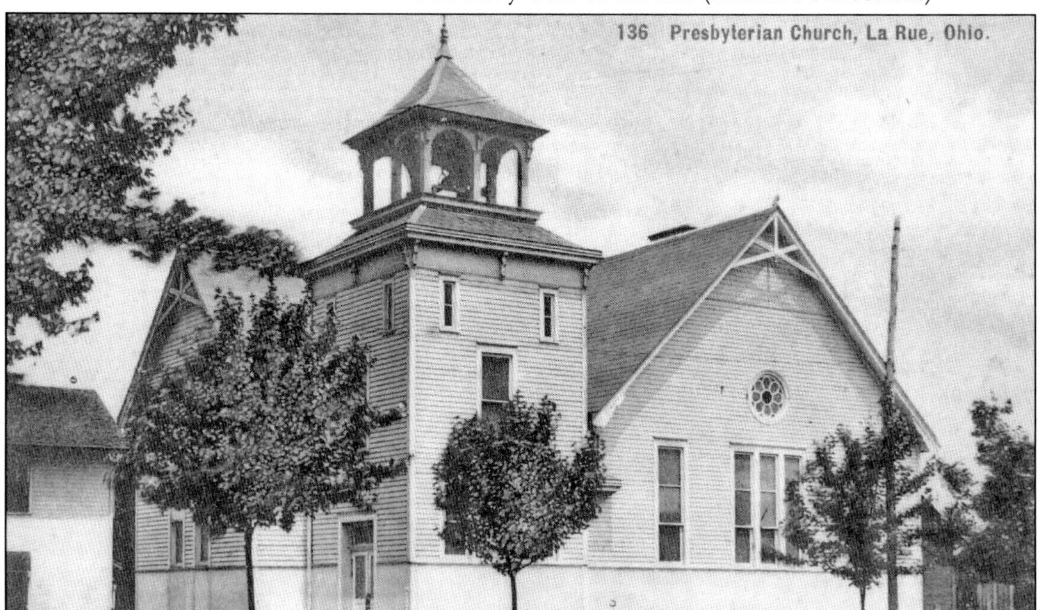

Presbyterian Church. The congregation members who founded the Presbyterian church in LaRue first worshipped together around 1843 at Parr Town on the Winnemac Pike. After building a church (the Winnemac Church) in that area in 1854, they moved to LaRue and built this worship center in 1881 at the corner of High and South Streets. Services were held here until the 1930s, when the congregation disbanded. The building was removed in 1946. (Author's collection.)

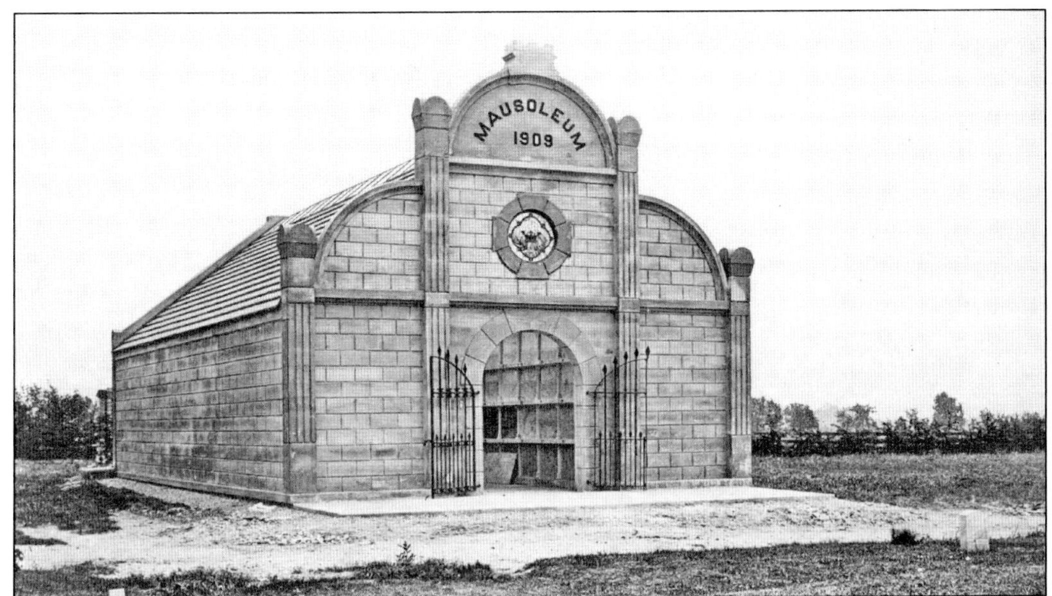

MAUSOLEUM. LaRue's mausoleum opened in 1909 with a ceremony that included speeches along with music from the LaRue male octet. The building measured 29 feet by 54 feet, featured a stained-glass window, and could hold 136 bodies. The final cost of construction was about $14,000. There are approximately 57 interments in the mausoleum today, with the last one placed in the 1960s. No additional interments are allowed due to concerns about long-term maintenance of the structure. (Courtesy of Richard Carey.)

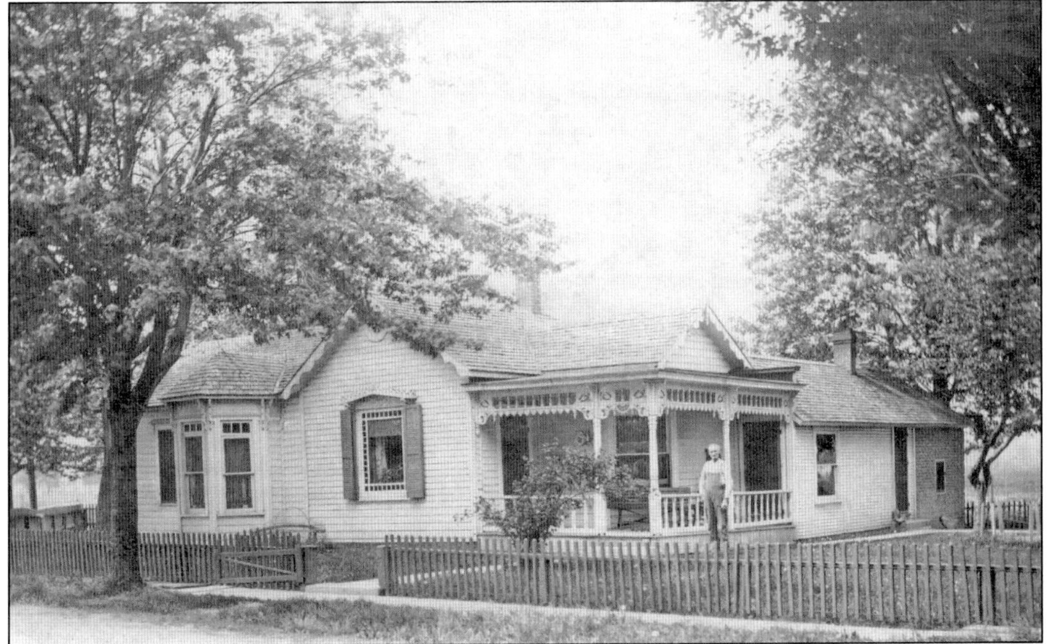

PRIDE OF OWNERSHIP. Hiram Cleveland (pictured) would have been rightfully proud of his beautiful home at River and West Streets in LaRue in this 1910 photograph. Intricate wooden fretwork on the porch and around the windows, window transoms, a bay window, and a shake shingle roof were "extras" that certainly enhanced the property. (Courtesy of Richard Carey.)

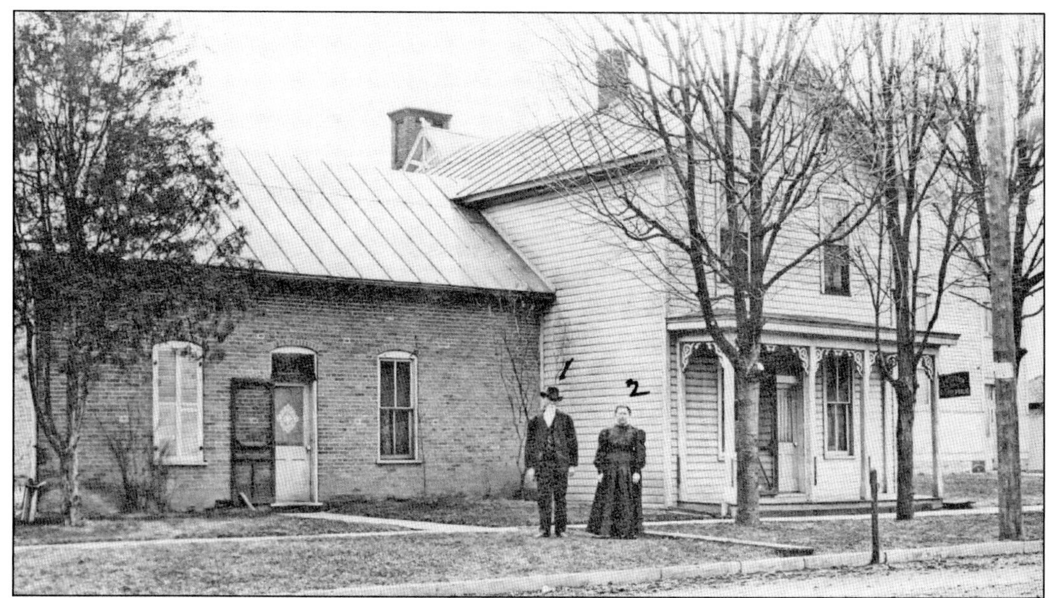

Marryin' And Buryin'. Rev. J.A. Sutton and his wife posed for this picture outside their home on South High Street. In addition to preaching the gospel, Reverend Sutton offered notary public services, as evidenced by the sign hanging on his porch. Village old-timers referred to the good reverend as the "marryin' and buryin' preacher." (Courtesy of Richard Carey.)

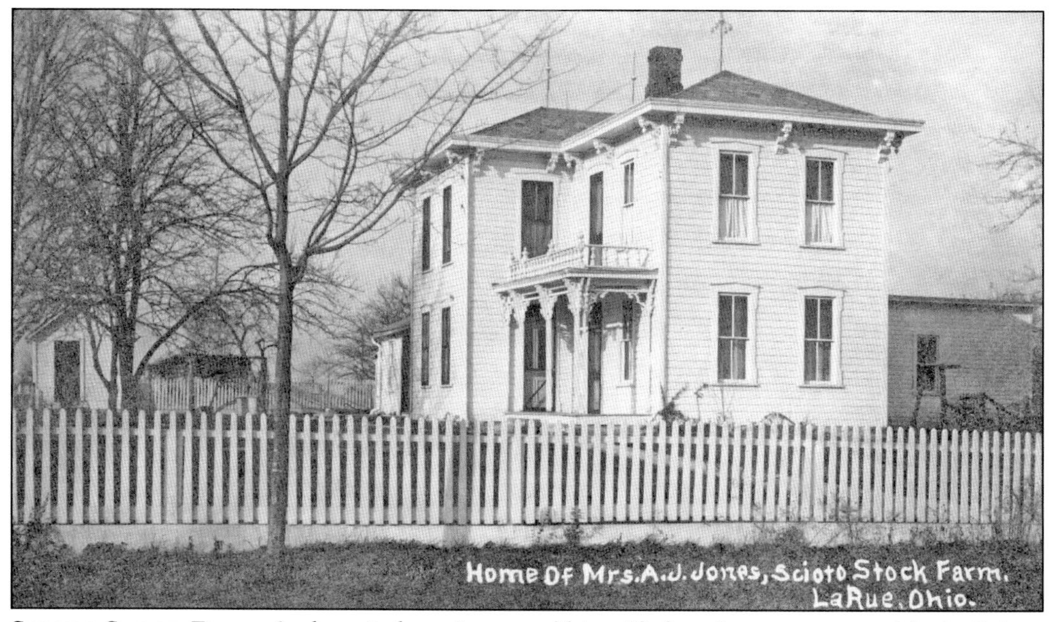

Scioto Stock Farm. Andrew Jackson Jones and his wife found great success with the Scioto Stock Farm, located about three-quarters of a mile south of the village on Essex Road (now State Route 37). Beginning around 1830, the farm grew to include several tenant houses, at least six barns, and hundreds of heads of livestock. While the farm remains in the Jones family, the home no longer stands. (Courtesy of Richard Carey.)

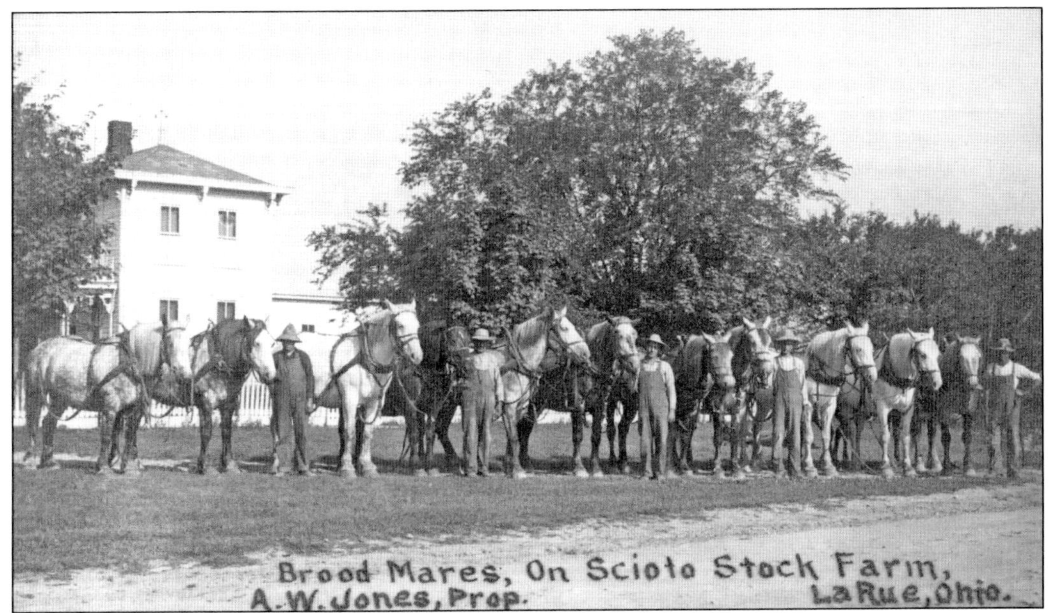

TRUE "HORSEPOWER." In the days when "horsepower" had a more literal meaning, these brood mares represented a sizable investment and source of potential income. Farming was full of risks and unexpected events, such as when A.J. Jones lost seven of his finest ewes when they were hit by a train on the Big Four tracks while being moved from one pasture to another. (Courtesy of Richard Carey.)

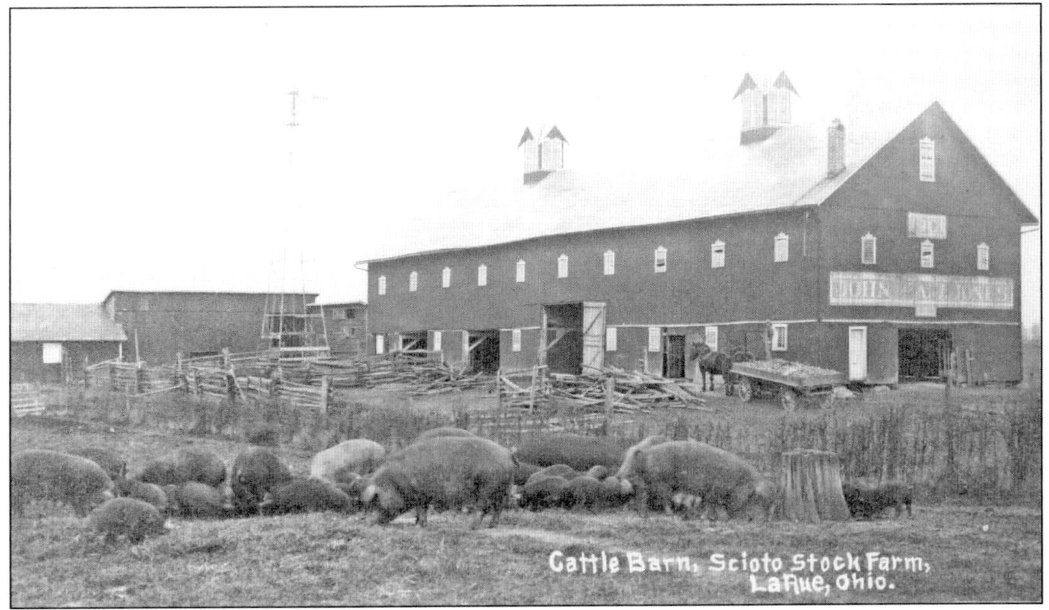

BIGGER WAS BETTER. If the size of the barn was any indication of the profitability of the farm, then John and A.J. Jones were wealthy men. Their cattle barn was undoubtedly one of the largest in the county. It was located on one of several farms they owned or rented. One significant change in livestock husbandry over the years was movement away from the huge, fat hogs that were once popular to the leaner animals marketed today. (Courtesy of Richard Carey.)

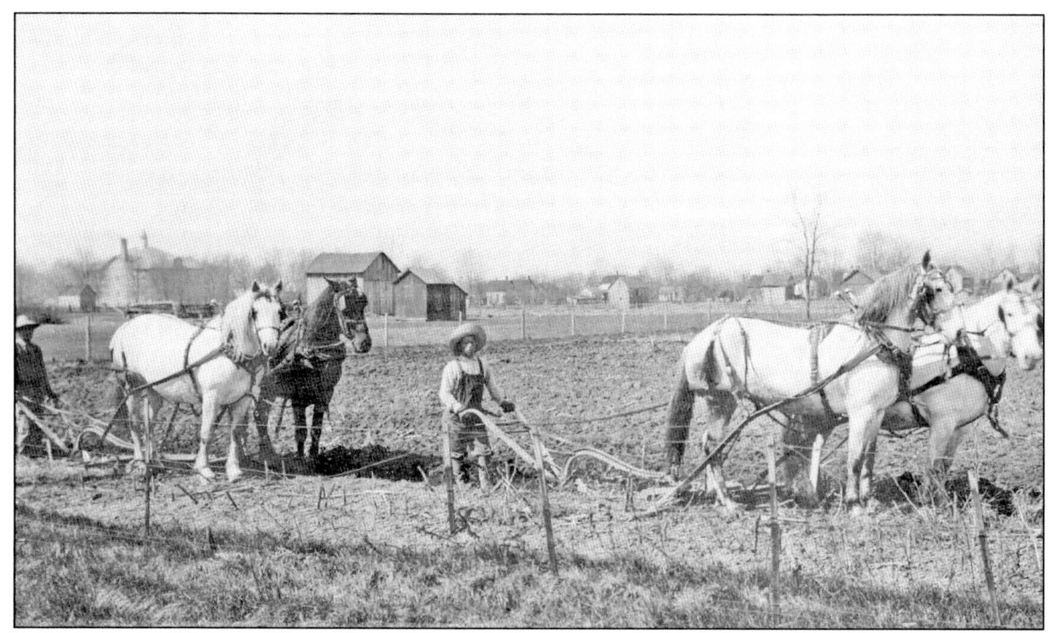

Backbreaking Work. These two farmhands took a break for the photographer while plowing a field in the area of what is now Section Street. The LaRue school is visible in the background at left. Keeping the plow moldboard at the correct soil depth while also creating a straight furrow was a skill that could only be learned via hard repetition. (Courtesy of Richard Carey.)

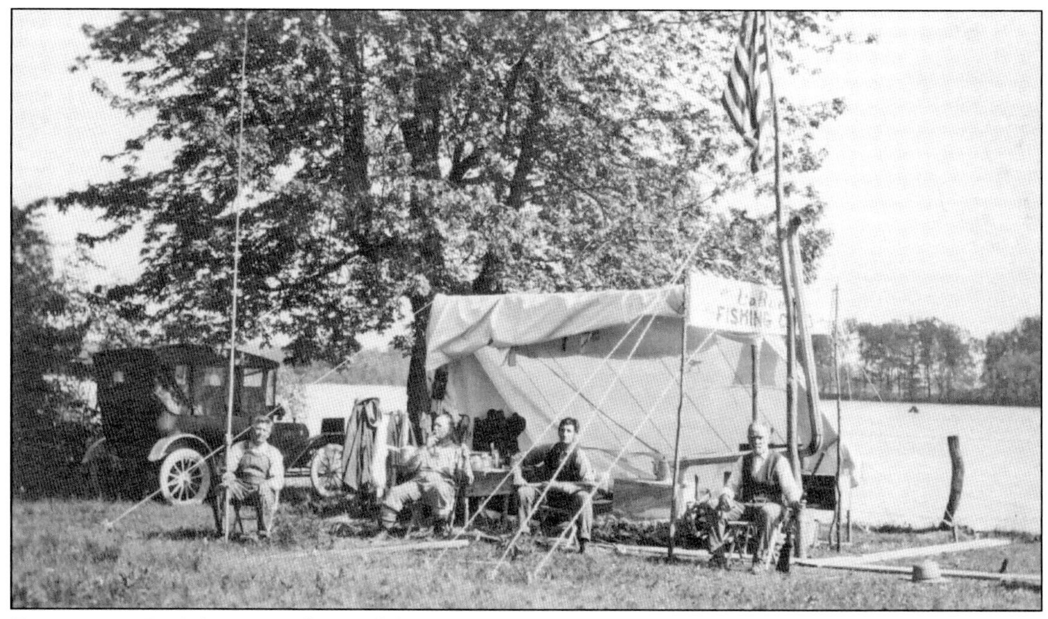

Roughing It. These members of the LaRue Fishing Club posed at their Indian Lake campsite complete with box stove and butcher-block table. The man at far left holds a fishing pole that would certainly extend his reach. Fishing clubs were the predecessors of what are now often called sportsmen's clubs. (Courtesy of Richard Carey.)

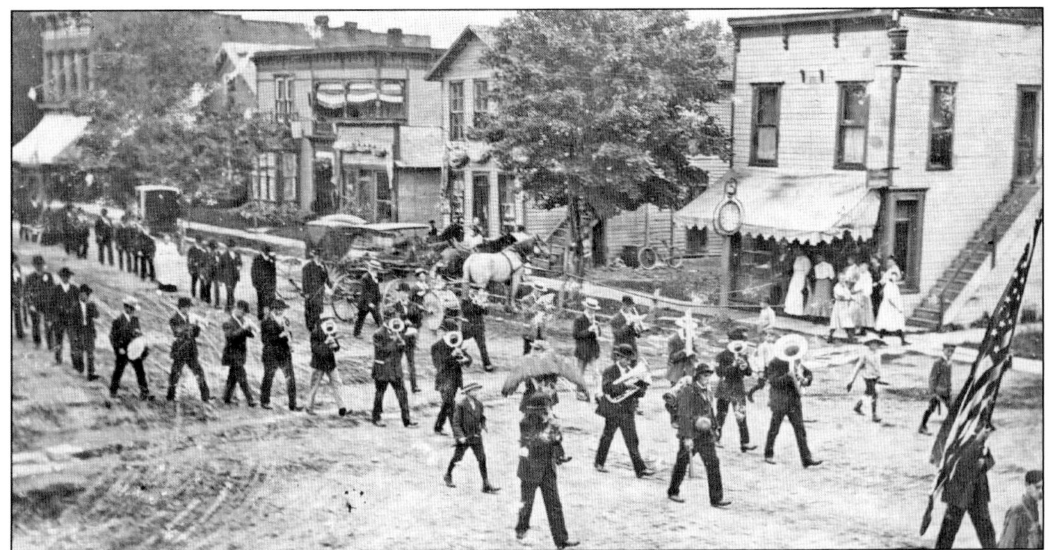

Honoring the Republic. Members of the Grand Army of the Republic march up High Street in a Decoration Day celebration around 1905. The eagle is being carried by Basil Ridgway. Perhaps many of the village residents were in the parade or waiting at another location, as few seem to be viewing the proceedings. Two small boys, carrying what appear to be toy guns, joined the procession. (Courtesy of Bob Turner.)

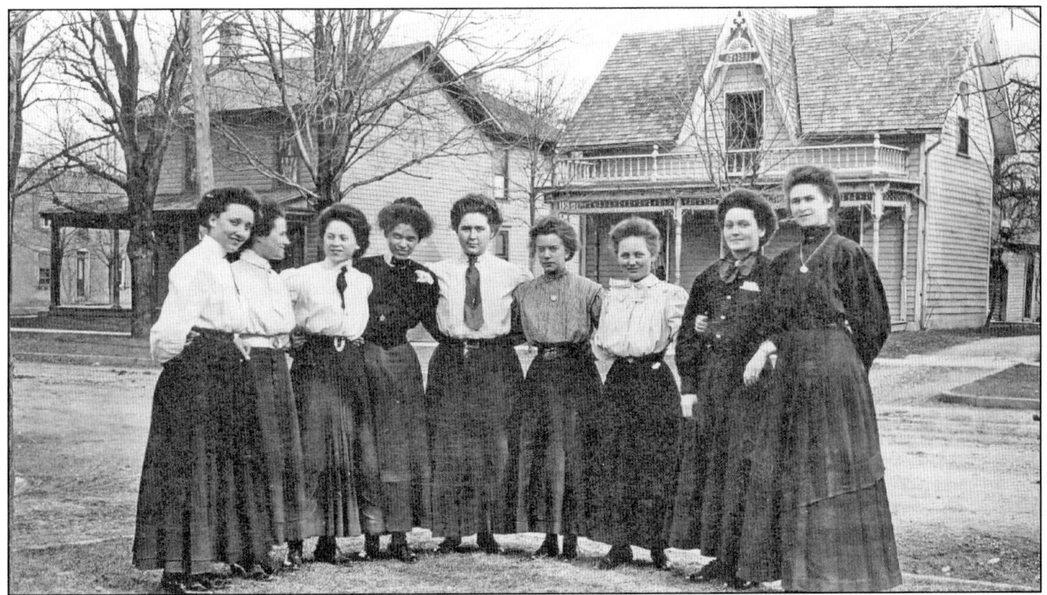

Hazel Class? This postcard presents a mystery waiting to be solved. A handwritten notation on the card reads, "The girls in Hazel class, LaRue, Ohio." It bears a LaRue postmark from 1909. There is some uncertainty as to the exact location, but the west side of South High Street may be a good possibility. (Courtesy of Ralph and Erdine Eaton collection.)

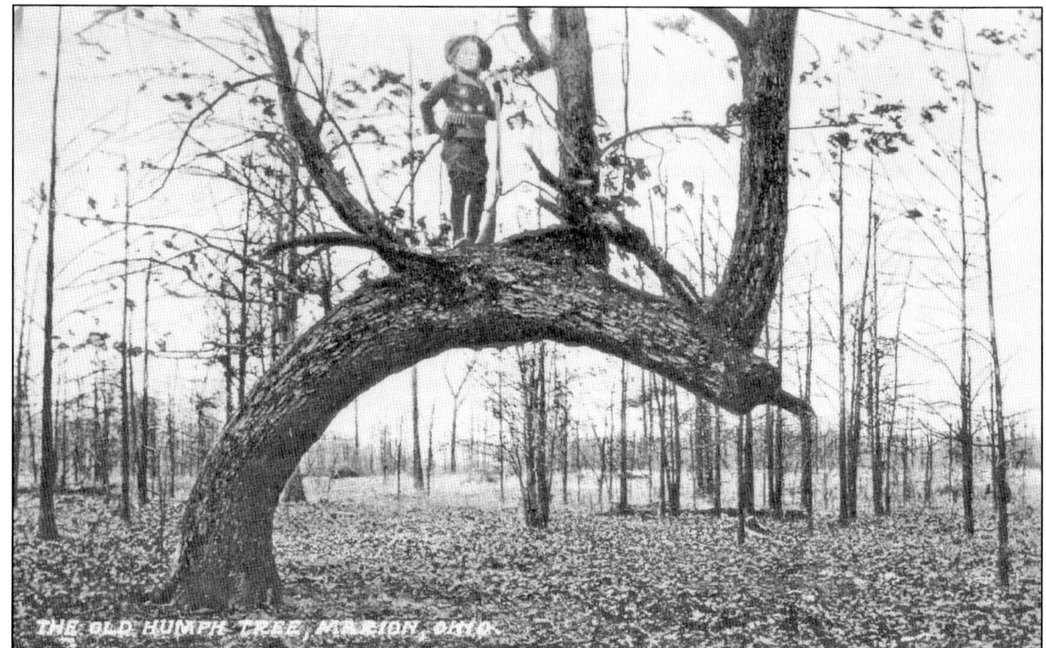

POINTING THE WAY. Native Americans used a system of marking trails that included bending trees to grow and point in a specific direction. Part of the caption on this postcard says the "Old Humph Tree" was "for upwards of a century a beacon in the forest wilderness to the savages in Western Central Ohio." The child is identified as Blanche Bain. The tree was located one mile southwest of LaRue on the Scioto River. (Author's collection.)

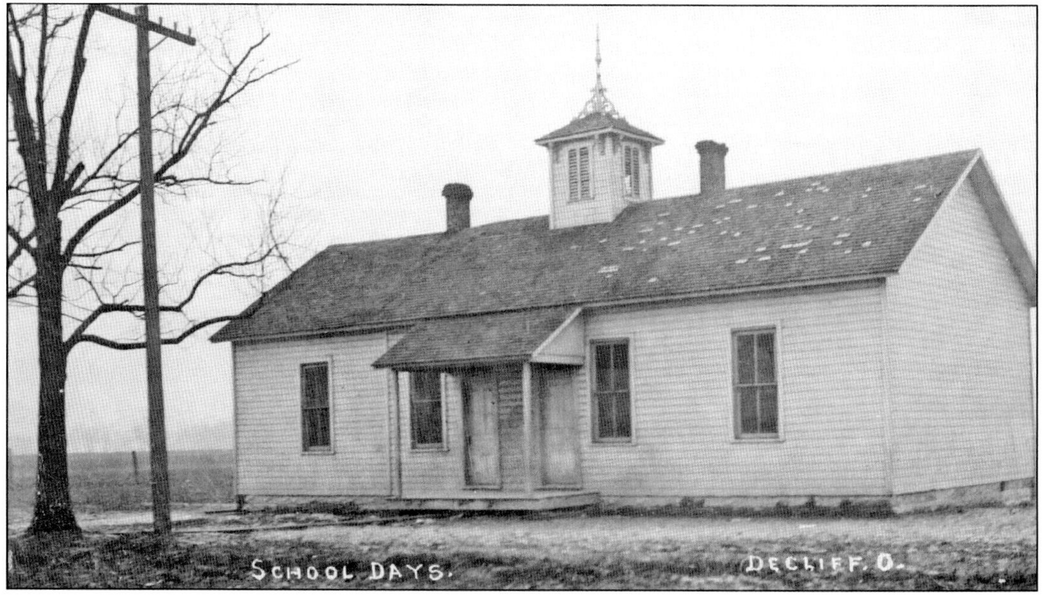

DECLIFF SCHOOL. The small frame school building in DeCliff, Montgomery Township, was well protected from lightning storms with its ornate lightning rod. The double chimneys indicate the school perhaps had two rooms as opposed to the standard one-room configuration. The building was later used for many years as a clubhouse for the Marion County Coon Hunters Association. (Courtesy of Mike and Linda Perry.)

Five

Meeker and Morral Area

In 1823, Col. William Cochran purchased a section of land containing 640 acres near what would eventually become the confluence of Big Island, Grand, Montgomery, and Salt Rock Townships. After evicting Samuel Franklin, a squatter who had settled on the land some two years prior, Cochran built a home, near which a mail route was established from Marion to Bellefontaine. Cochran's home became a post office station known as Cochran's Post or Cochranton. Heman Scott purchased 120 acres of Cochran's land in 1842 and developed a settlement that became known as Scott Town or Scottstown, although the post office remained as Cochranton. A state road from Marion to Lima was built through the village, which encouraged further development. Excitement spread through the area in 1905, when word of a proposed rail line was spread by a gentleman named Meeker. While the sequence of events is somewhat unclear, the settlement changed its name to Meeker, and although the trains never came, the name remained.

Salt Rock Township had long been known for its excellent farmland, where the rich soil of the Sandusky Plains provided for strong crop yields. Farmers prospered with both grain and animal farms but faced one significant problem when it was time to sell their products. The nearest rail lines were several miles away in Upper Sandusky or Marion. Transporting animals or crops to those depots was expensive and cut into profits. The hoped-for solution arrived in the form of a Columbus & Toledo Railroad Company proposal to build a rail line through the township. Samuel Morral and Jacob Neff, both landowners on the proposed rail line, began selling commercial and residential lots for a new village. The official documents platting the village were filed with the County Recorder on September 1, 1875, and the village of Morral was born. The railroad was completed by 1877, along with a grain elevator and stock pens. Businesses and residences soon followed, and the community prospered.

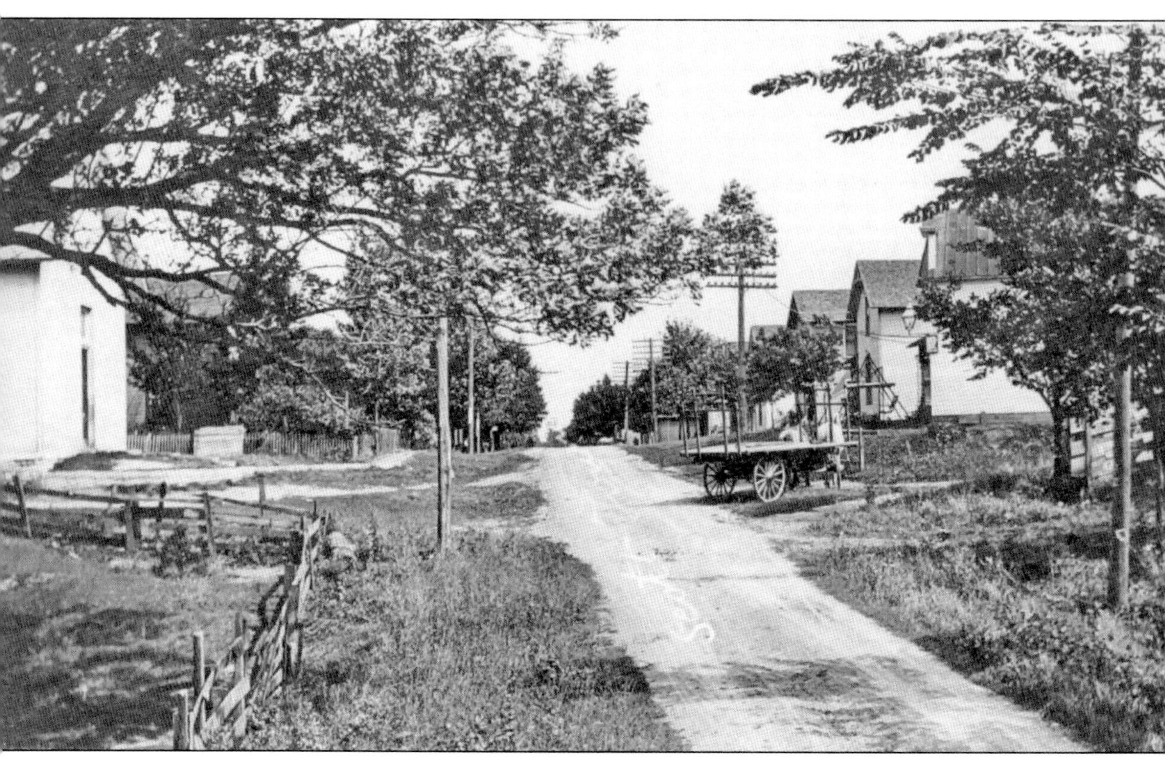

Entering the Village. A team of horses pulling a hay wagon paused near a set of weighing scales on South Main Street in Scott Town. The wooden fence at right was part of the stockyards. The Methodist Episcopal church is visible at left. Scott Town was on a state road that had been cut from Marion to Lima in 1833. The road, which later became part of the famed Lincoln Highway for a short time, helped the community grow as people traveling the road settled in the area. The highway, properly known as US Route 30, was one of the earliest transcontinental highways, stretching almost 3,400 miles from New York City to San Francisco. Conceived in 1912, the highway through Ohio had both a northern and southern route, with US 30 South passing directly through Meeker (Scott Town) on Main Street. As traffic increased, the highway was rerouted to bypass the community just to the north. US 30 South was, for a time, the better of the two routes, but it was eventually replaced by the northern route. In 1973, US 30 South was renamed Ohio State Route 309. Part of the highway also became known as Harding Highway in recognition of Pres. Warren G. Harding, who had grown up and lived on the eastern part of the road in Caledonia. (Courtesy of Richard Carey.)

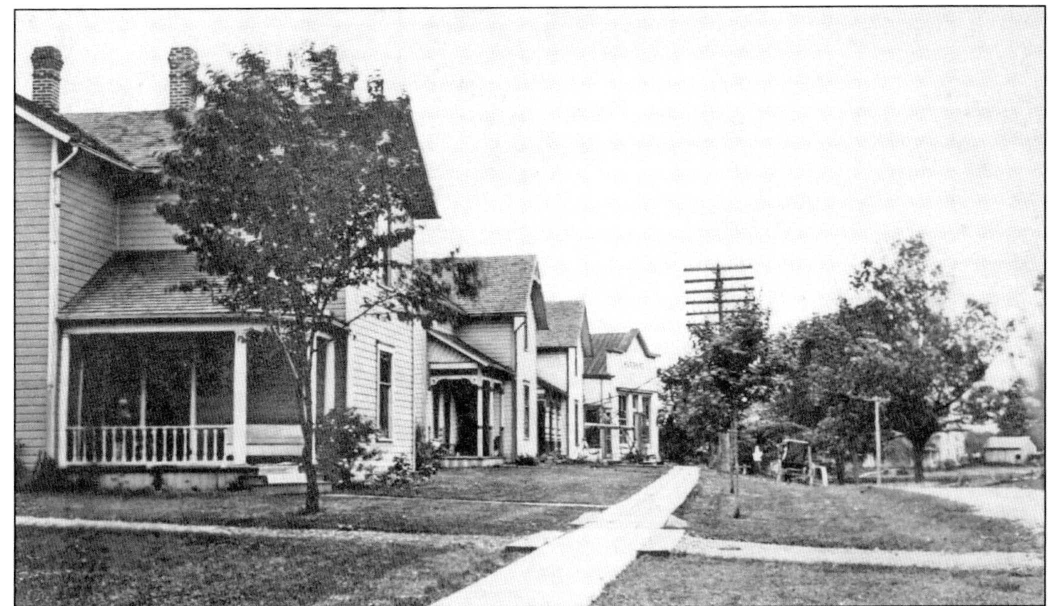

Pleasant Neighborhood. Houses and merchants shared space on Main Street, with Webb's Meat Market visible at the end of the street. A boardinghouse and livery stable were located next to the market. A row of family homes completed the street. Access to the large village green was available from the rear of the homes. The Methodist church and school were located just down the block. (Courtesy of Richard Carey.)

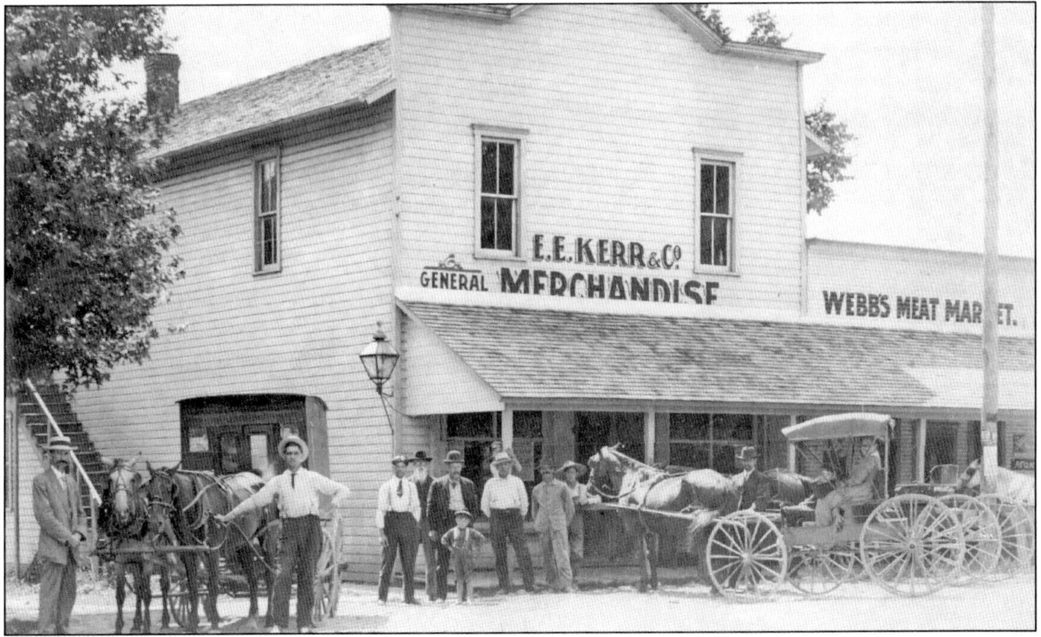

Meat and Merchandise. Residents of Meeker did not need to travel far to purchase many of their everyday staples. Elmer Kerr's grocery store was one of three in the village (along with Webb's Meat Market). Kerr's store also sold hardware and served as a post office for several years. The carriage at left made daily trips to the "big city" of Marion while transporting both freight and passengers. (Courtesy of Richard Carey.)

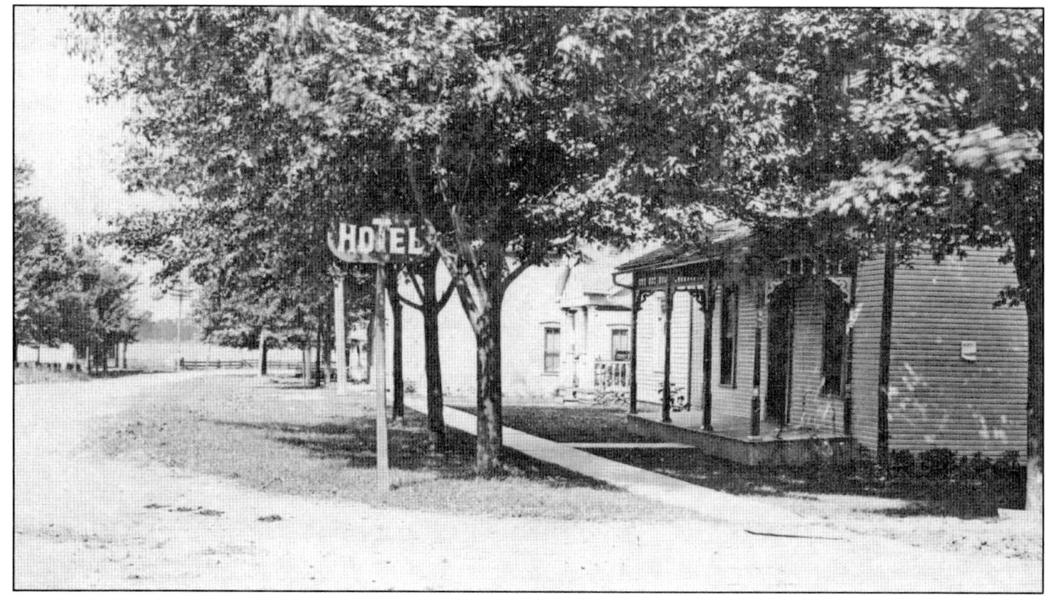

MEEKER HOTEL. Little is known about this hotel that operated in Meeker in the early 1900s. It was next to the office of Dr. Charles S. Burnside, who established his medical practice in the village around 1897. Burnside worked as a teacher in Hardin County while reading medicine at Ohio Northern University in Ada before completing his studies at the Starling Medical College in Columbus. (Author's collection.)

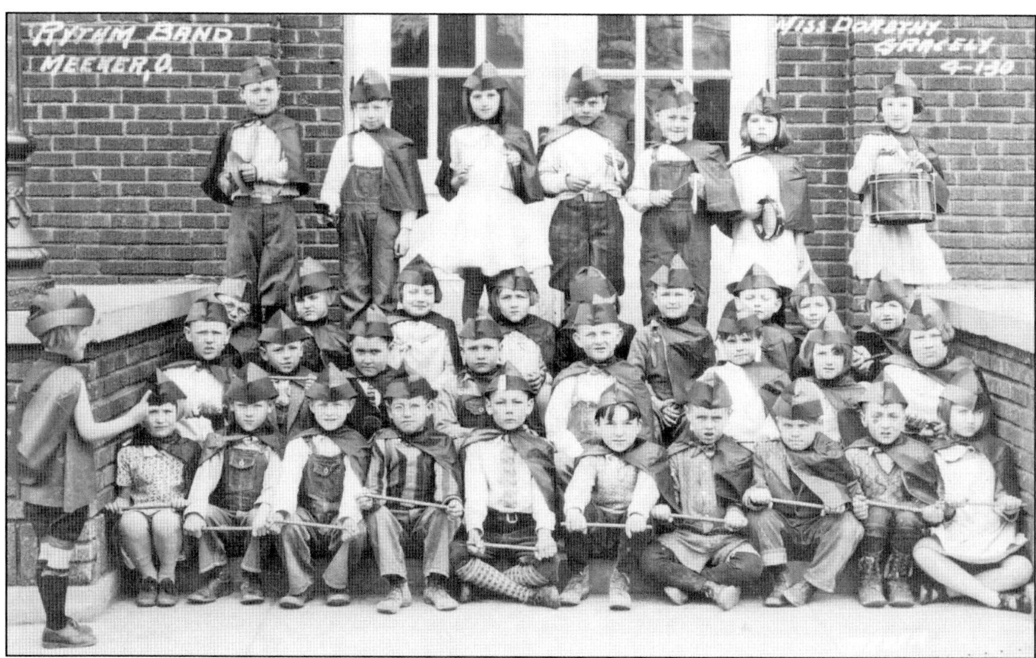

MEEKER RHYTHM BAND. In this 1930 photograph, the students in Dorothy Gracely's class are stylishly outfitted and ready to perform. Rhythm bands served as an enjoyable way to introduce students to music via simple instruments such as drums, triangles, cymbals, and wooden sticks. (Author's collection.)

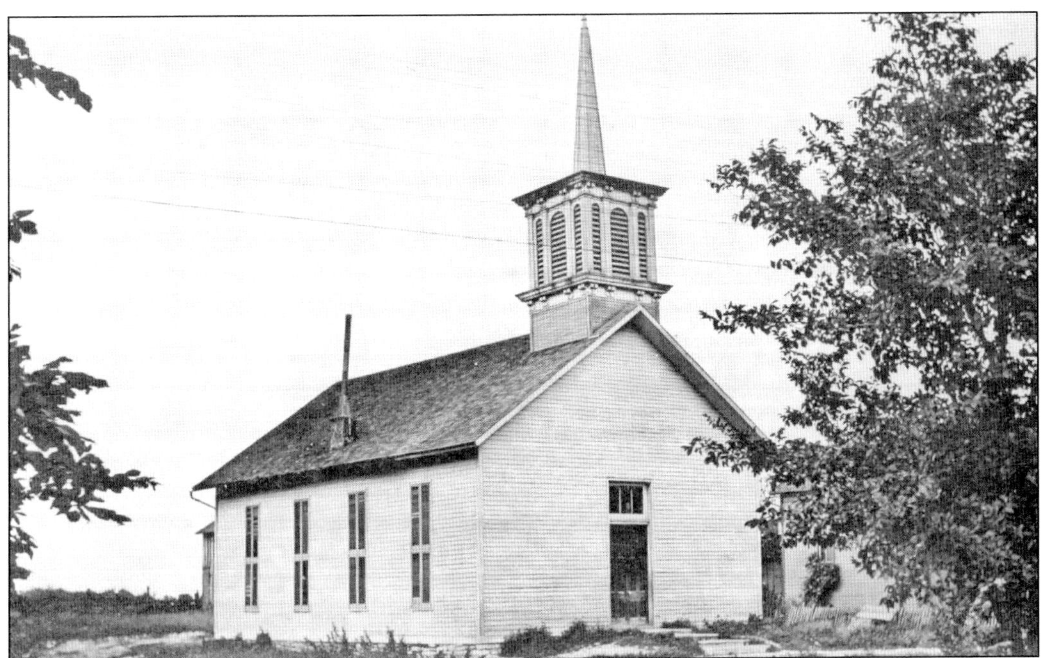

METHODIST EPISCOPAL CHURCH. The Meeker Methodist Episcopal Church was organized in 1868 and erected a church three years later at a cost of $3,000. The new structure had two wood-burning stoves, kerosene lamps, and a pump organ. A 1908 remodeling added acetylene lights, new pews, and a furnace. A large addition to the church was completed in 1948. (Author's collection.)

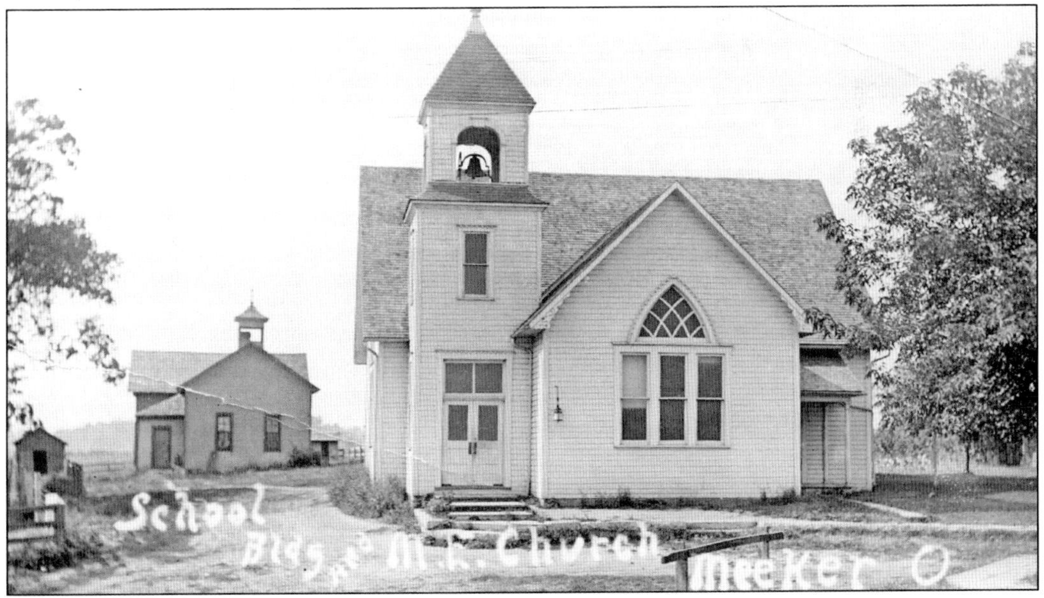

PLACES OF LEARNING. The Montgomery Township School was located adjacent to the Meeker Methodist Episcopal Church on Main Street. It closed in 1923 with the centralization of the rural schools and the construction of the Montgomery Rural School at the northeast end of the village. The building was purchased in 1925 by the Ladies Aid Society of the church for use as a community house and for Sunday school classrooms. (Courtesy of Richard Carey.)

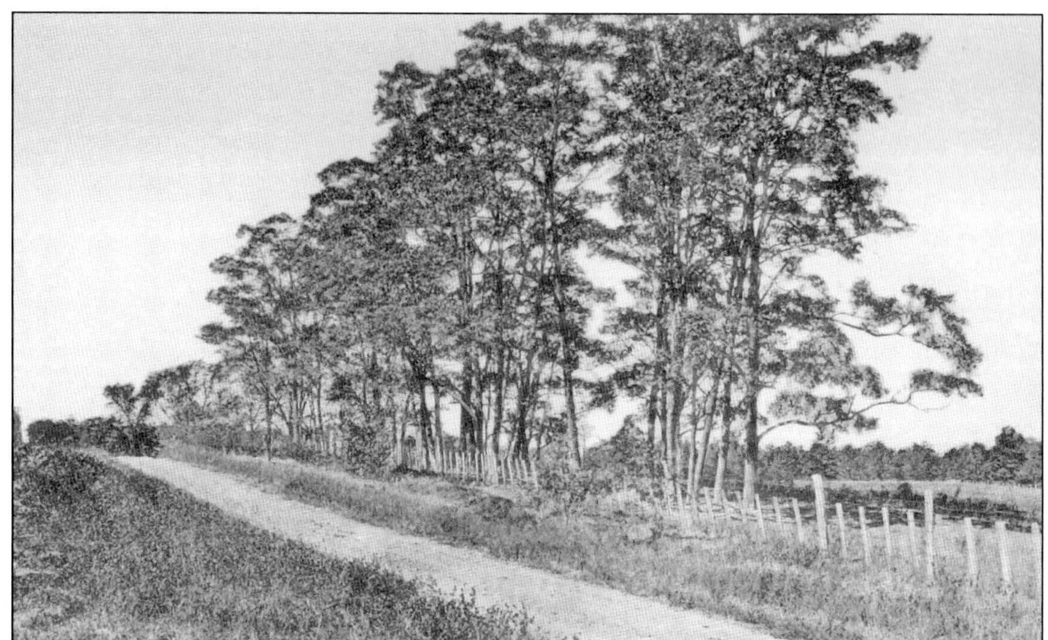

The Divide. Grand Prairie Township, located about five miles north of Marion, is home to a watershed divide delineating the line where water flows either north or south. In theory, a person standing at the divide in the rain could see water fall from each side of their umbrella to begin its journey to either the East Coast or the Gulf of Mexico. (Courtesy of Richard Carey.)

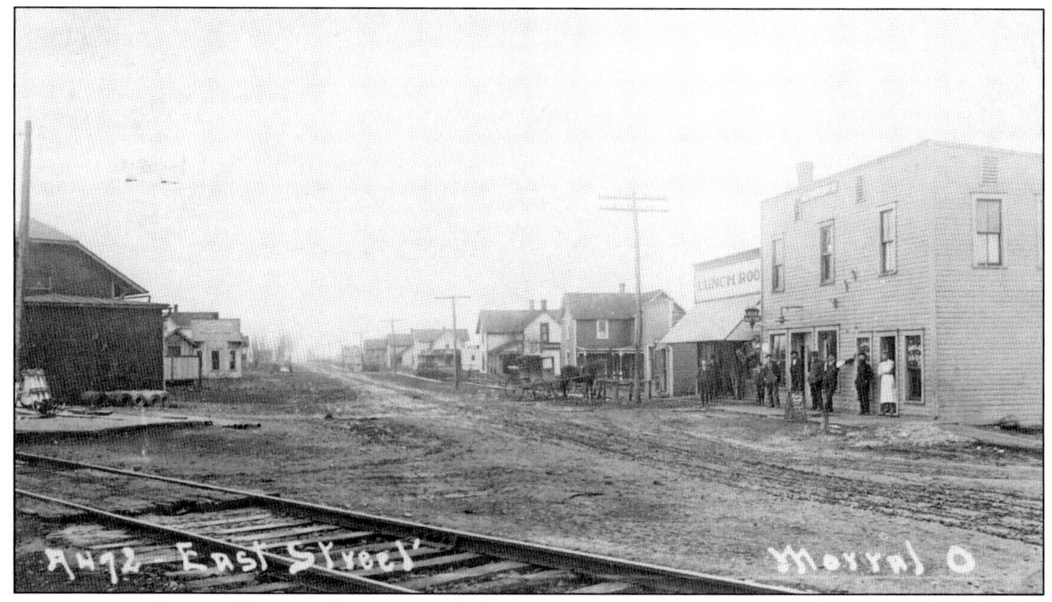

Gathering Place. The Lunch Room and the adjacent grocery store on East Street were apparently popular spots, as shown by the number of people gathered there. Being located across the street from the railroad depot made these businesses convenient stops for travelers. Several boardinghouses and small hotels were also located in this vicinity. (Courtesy of Richard Carey.)

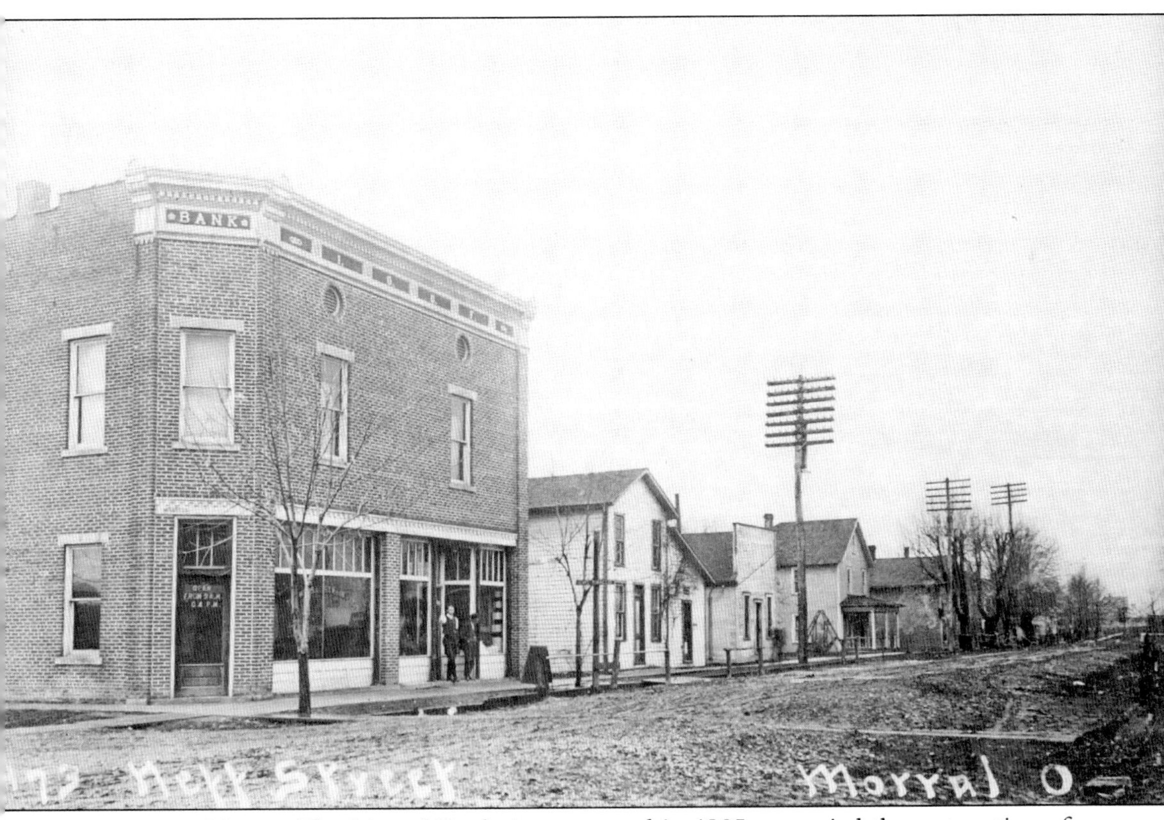

A Bank and More. The Morral Bank, incorporated in 1905, occupied the east section of this building on the corner of Neff and Green Streets. The bank's location in a small village apparently made it an attractive target, as it was robbed twice within an eight-month period. In February 1932, two armed robbers stole $2,500. A cashier and a customer were locked in the bank's tiny vault but were soon freed when a passerby heard their calls for help. The robbery was one of eight in the Marion County area over a span of eight months during the difficult years of the Great Depression. A hardware store occupied the western portion of this building for several years. Other occupants of the building included a two-lane bowling alley, a grocery store, and a laundromat. The Morral International Order of Odd Fellows had its lodge on the top floor. (Courtesy of Richard Carey.)

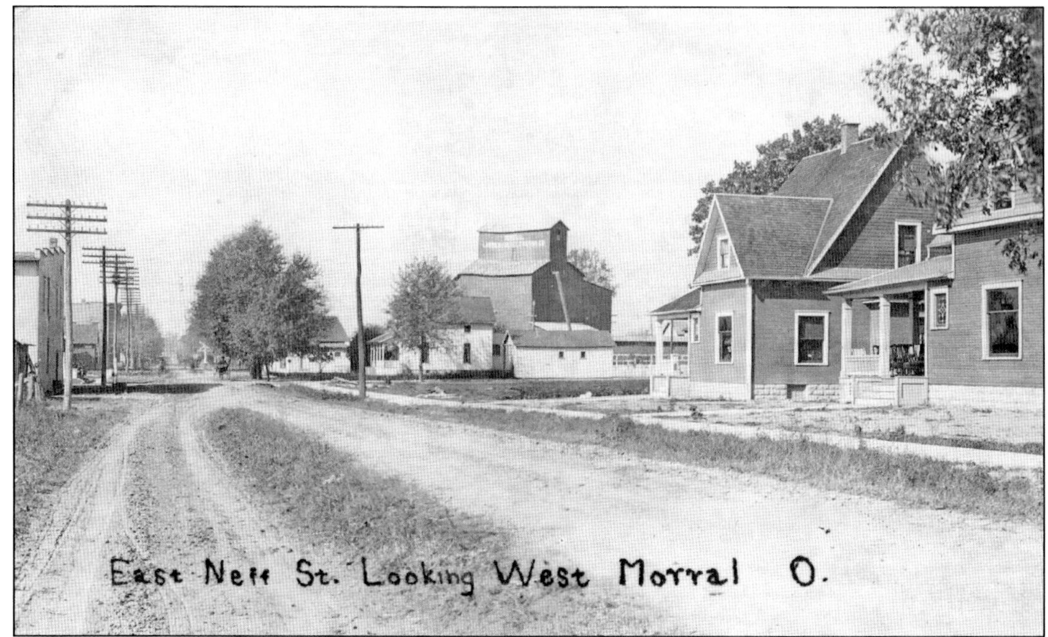

ELEVATOR AND LUMBER COMPANY. Around 1900, Ozias, John, and Howard Washburn, along with Samuel Morral, built a grain warehouse on East Neff Street next to the railroad. It was later purchased by the Morral Lumber and Elevator Company and converted to a 40,000-bushel-capacity elevator. Fire protection for grain elevators was always a top priority, with a 1918 inspection from the state fire marshal's office mandating a "thorough clean up, two pails at barrels, keep barrels filled." (Courtesy of Mike and Linda Perry.)

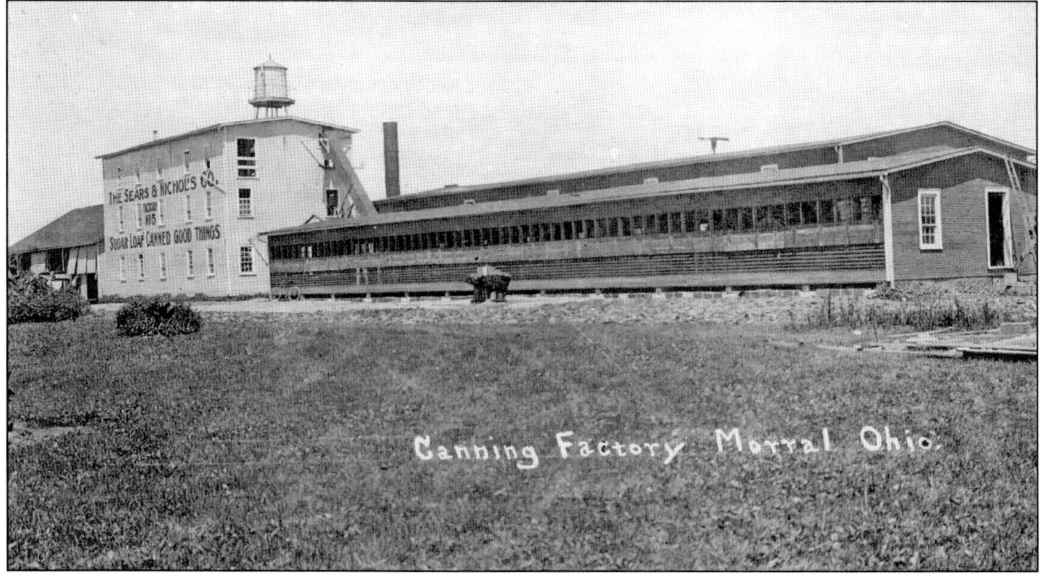

CANNING FACTORY. In 1894, John Morral began a business canning tomatoes at his tile factory. His brother, Samuel, invested in the business in 1896, at which time the brothers built a canning house and switched to canning corn and peas. The business steadily grew, and in 1907, a larger building was erected. The Morrals were mechanical innovators who invented a variety of machines to handle corn processing and canning. (Courtesy of Richard Carey.)

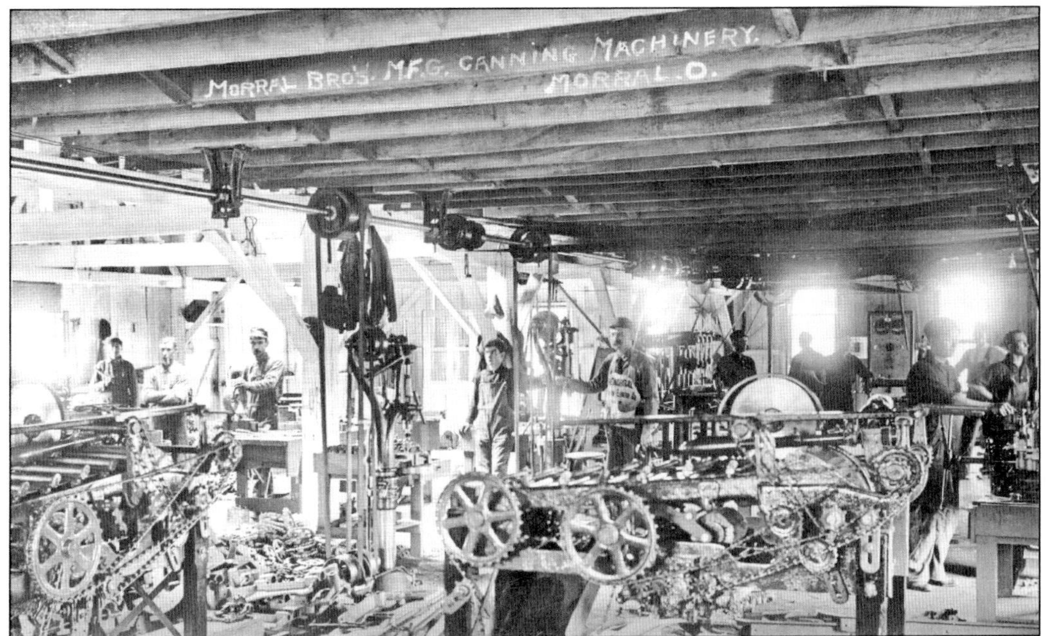

DANGEROUS WORK. Spinning blades and moving chains required the workers in the Morral Canning Company plant to pay close attention or risk serious injury. More than 40,000 cans of corn or peas could be processed during a 10-hour shift. The factory eventually employed 65 men during the peak season to handle the products derived from 600 acres of sweet corn. (Courtesy of Richard Carey.)

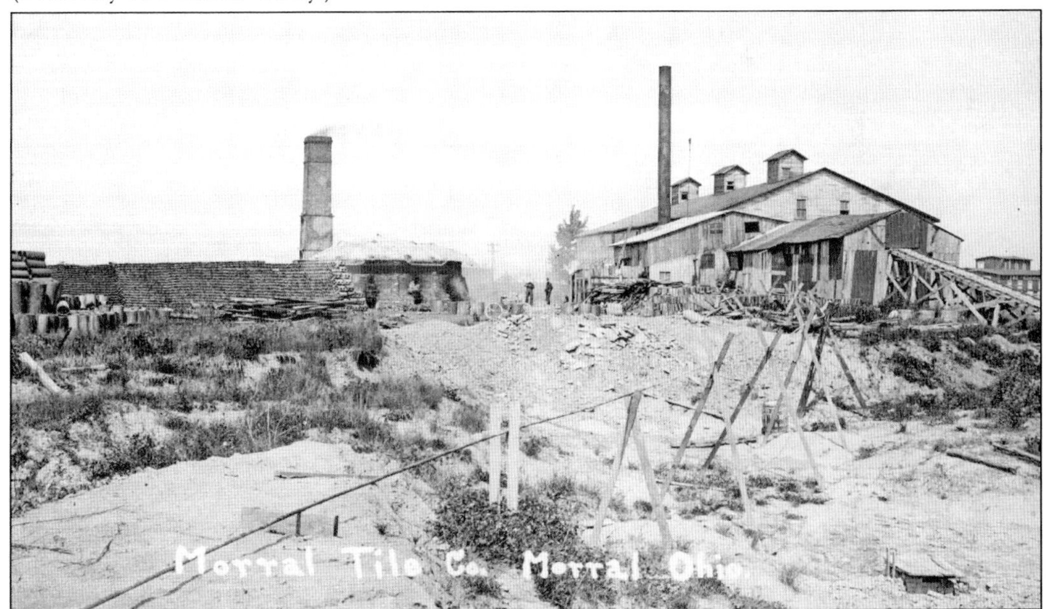

TILE COMPANY. To be effectively farmed, the flat prairie land of Salt Rock Township required the use of drainage tile. The Morral Tile Company was established to manufacture clay tiles using beehive kilns like the one shown here. With a capacity of several hundred tiles, the kiln required approximately a week to process each batch. A large stockpile of tiles is visible next to the kiln. (Courtesy of Ellis and Margaret Hudson.)

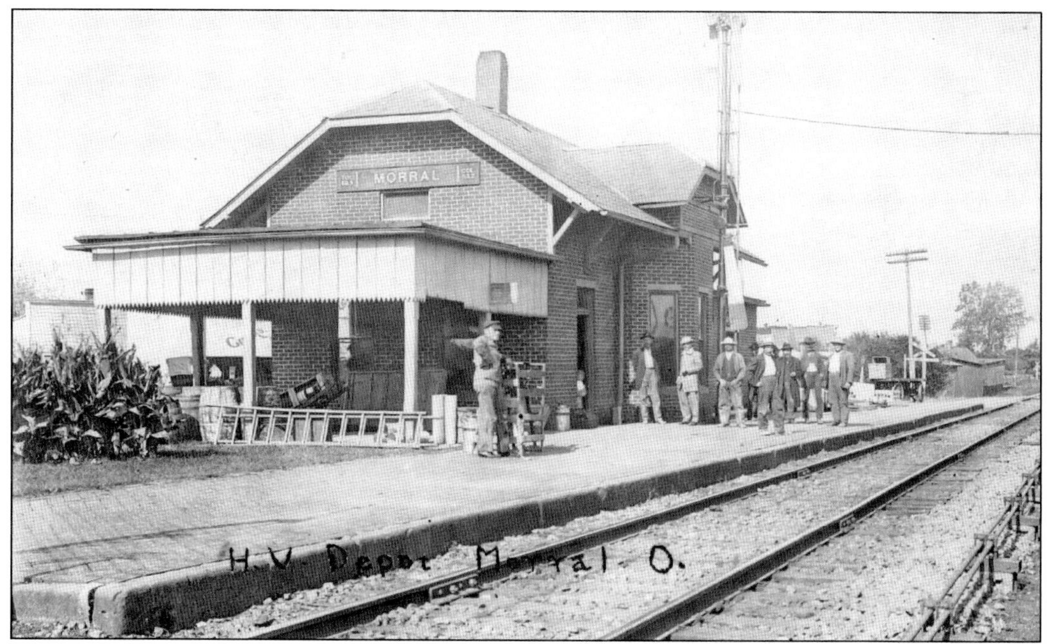

Morral Rail Depot. The Columbus, Hocking Valley & Toledo Railroad built this handsome depot with faux brick siding to provide passenger and freight service for its customers. Approximately equidistant between Toledo and Columbus, Morral was a good place for shipping commodities as well as livestock from the stockyards located east of the depot. (Courtesy of Richard Carey.)

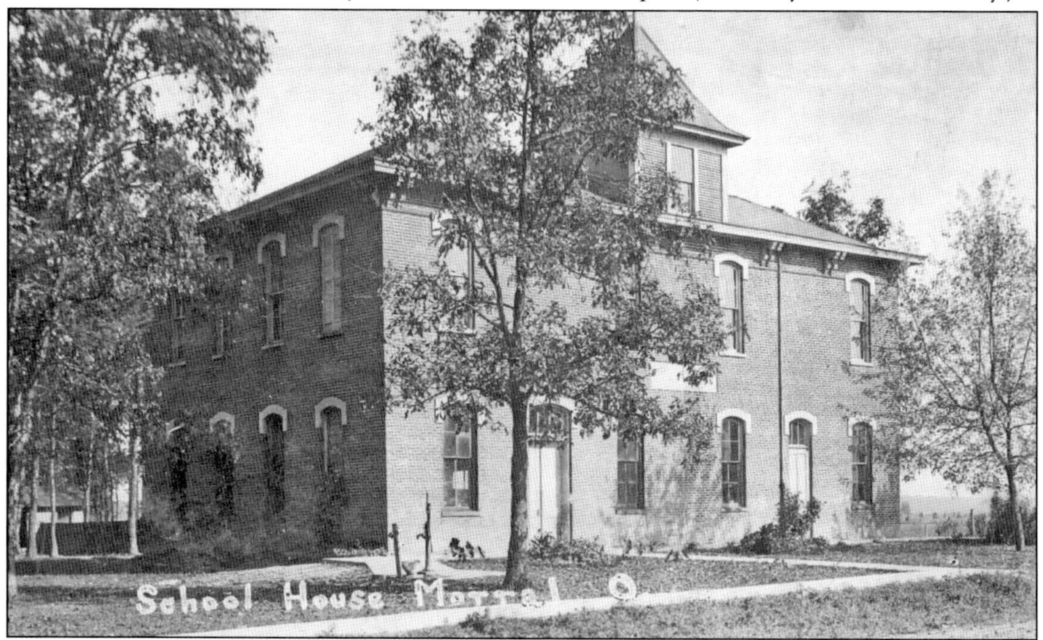

School House. The first school of record in Morral was a one-room school built before 1878. Oral histories of the school tell of hogs walking under the raised floor to scratch their backs and enjoy the shade. It was replaced in the early 1900s with this building on Neff Street at the east end of the village. Plentiful trees helped provide natural cooling for the students and instructors. (Author's collection.)

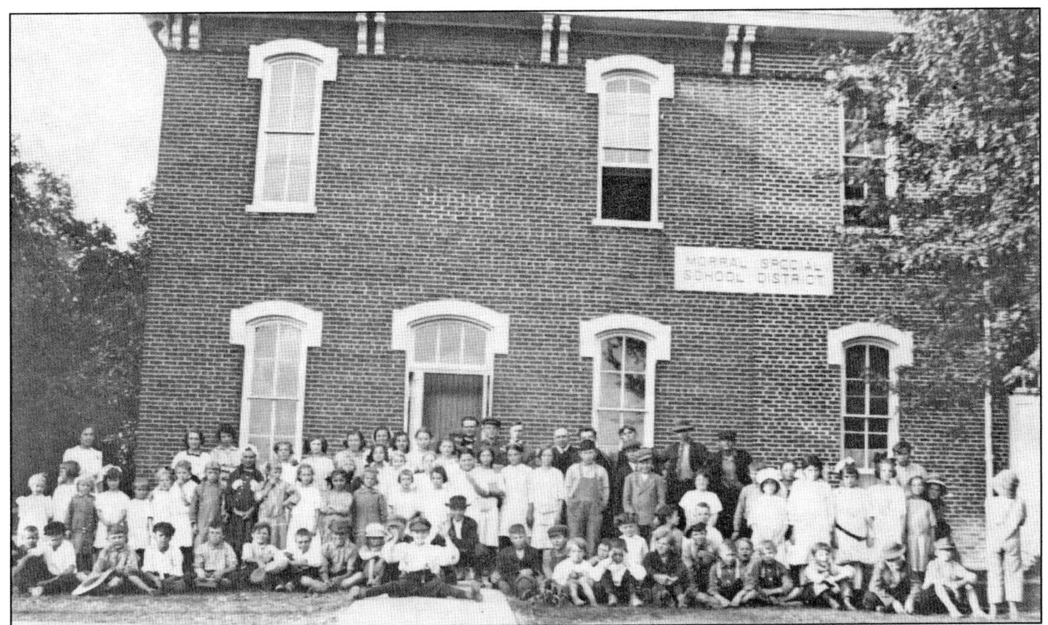

Growing Enrollment. Student enrollment in the Morral Special School District merited an addition to the building, as evidenced by the seam and variance in brick. A close inspection reveals the replacement of the original stone between the two upper windows. One youngster in front sought to be the center of attention with his unique pose, while another at the far right chose to display his "best side" to the camera. (Courtesy of John and Virginia Murphy.)

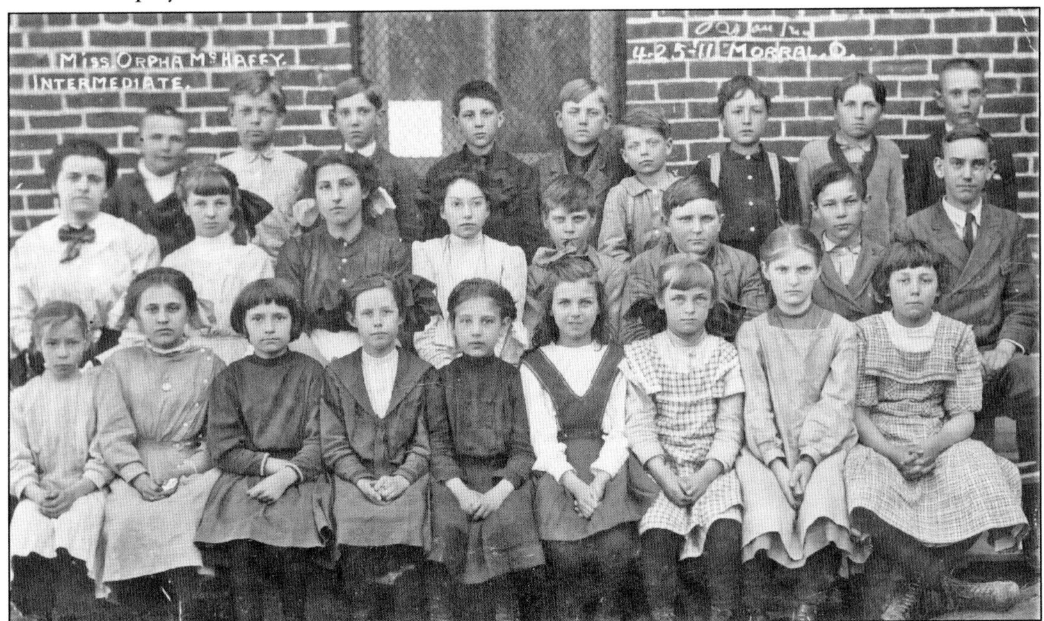

Carefully Posed. Students in the intermediate class of Orpha McHaffey maintained their poses for this 1911 photograph. School attendance was not mandatory until 1921, when Ohio's Bing Act required that children between the ages of 6 and 18 attend school. Exceptions were made for students who were not 18 but had already graduated and for those who were at least 16, had passed seventh grade, and worked on a farm. (Courtesy of Richard Carey.)

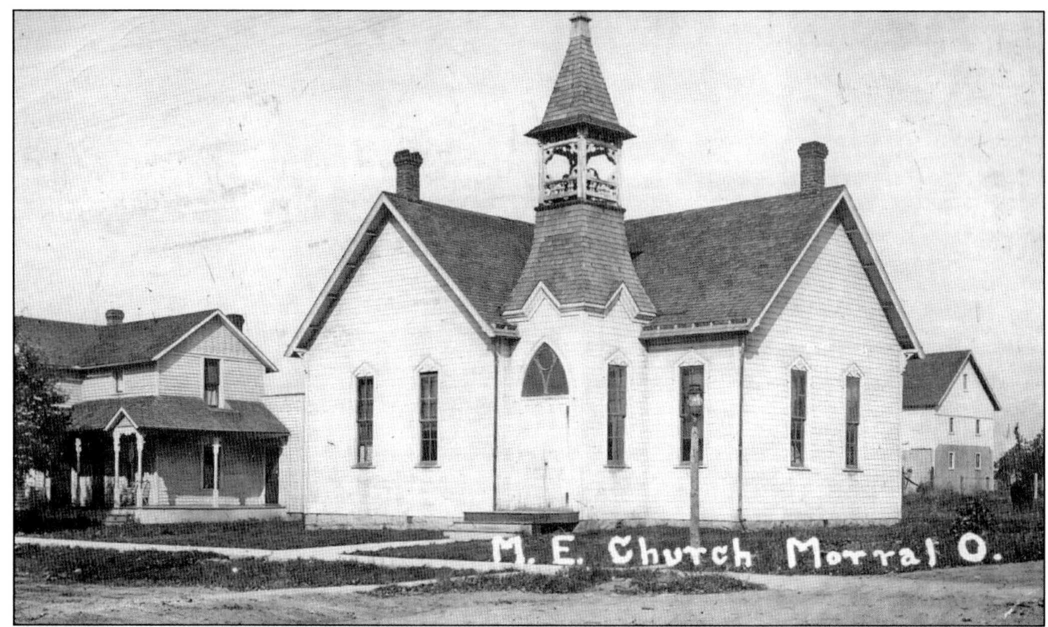

Methodist Episcopal Church. The Methodist Episcopal congregation in Morral dates from 1892, when meetings were held in the Morral schoolhouse. In 1895, Samuel Morral donated land for the church, and the members quickly raised the $2,000 necessary to build their church, which was dedicated on February 9, 1896. Significant remodeling and additions have been completed over the years. (Author's collection.)

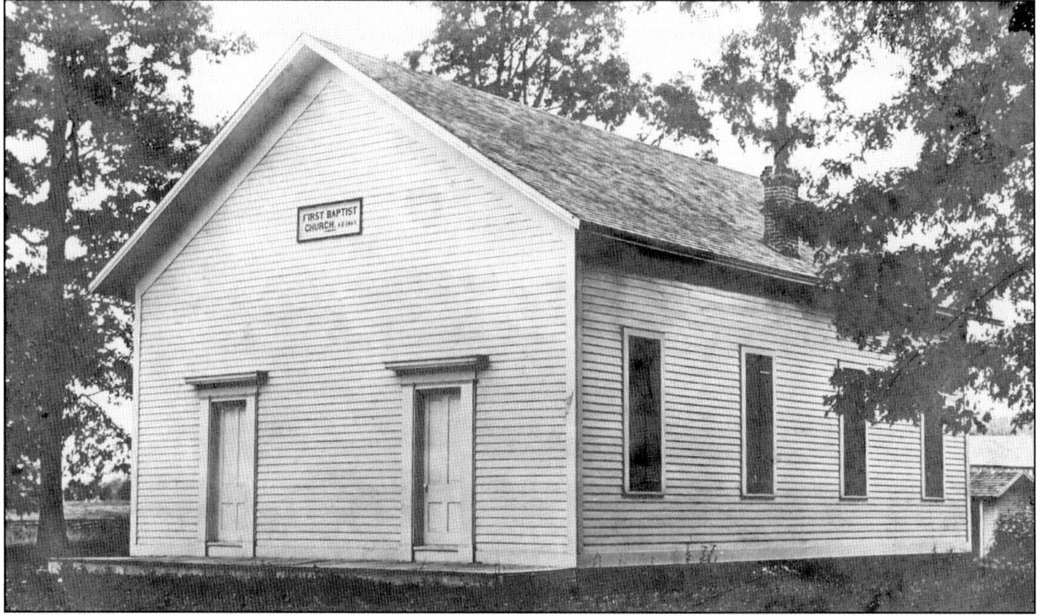

First Baptist Church. The First Baptist Church built this structure in 1867 at Brush Ridge in northern Grand Prairie Township. The separate front doors were designed for men to enter and sit on one side (usually the right side) and women on the other. The church later became known as Rocky Fork Baptist. The congregation eventually disbanded, and the building is now a private residence. (Courtesy of Ellis and Margaret Hudson.)

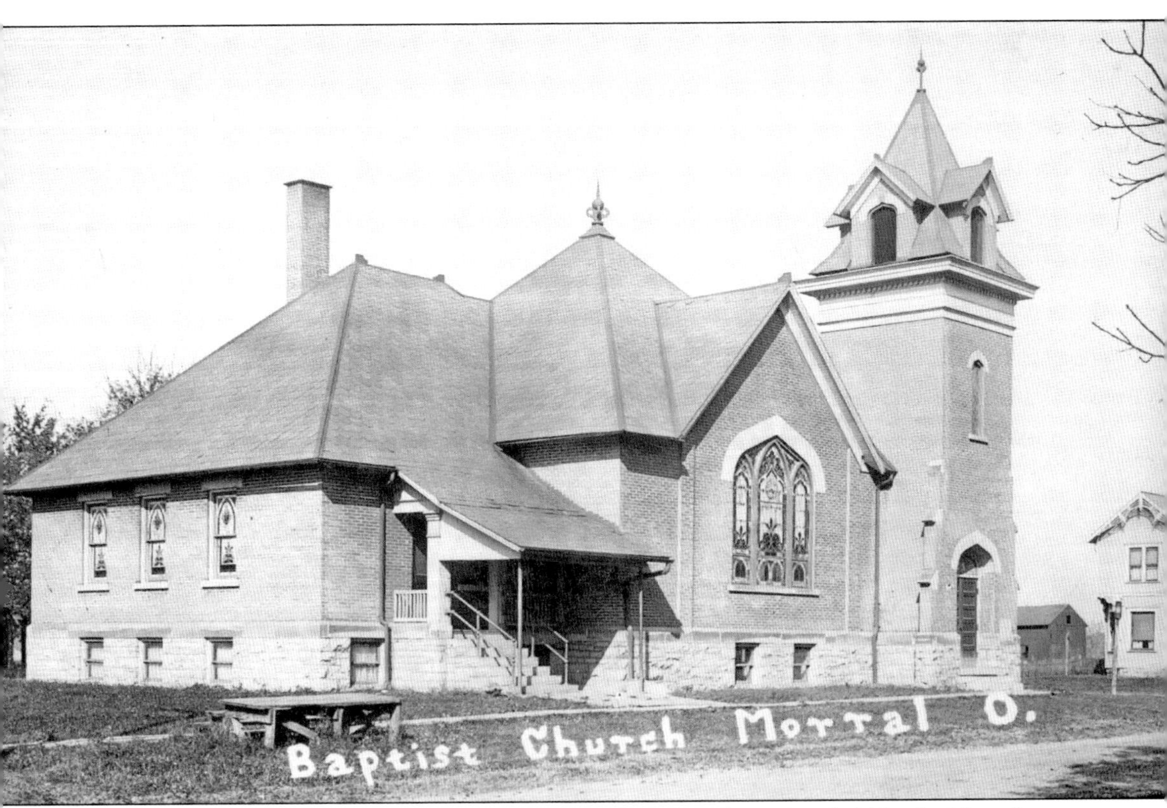

MORRAL FREEWILL BAPTIST CHURCH. Many of the first church services held in the Morral area were comprised of persons of various Christian faiths with Rev. L. Johnson leading the worship. After meeting for several years in the Morral schoolhouse, a group of worshippers formed the Morral Freewill Baptist Church and completed their "proper place of worship" in 1881 on the northeast corner of East and Center Streets. Land for the church, which cost $1,800 to build, was donated by Samuel Morral, who also served as one of the first deacons. The congregation grew and thrived for many years. However, by the late 1990s, it had significantly declined, with many members transferring to another Baptist church in nearby Brush Ridge. In 2001, the building was put up for sale by the Ohio Baptist Churches Foundation. The building, complete with its magnificent stained-glass windows that have Bible verses visible on the interior, sold for $27,000 and has since been converted to a private residence. (Courtesy of Ellis and Margaret Hudson.)

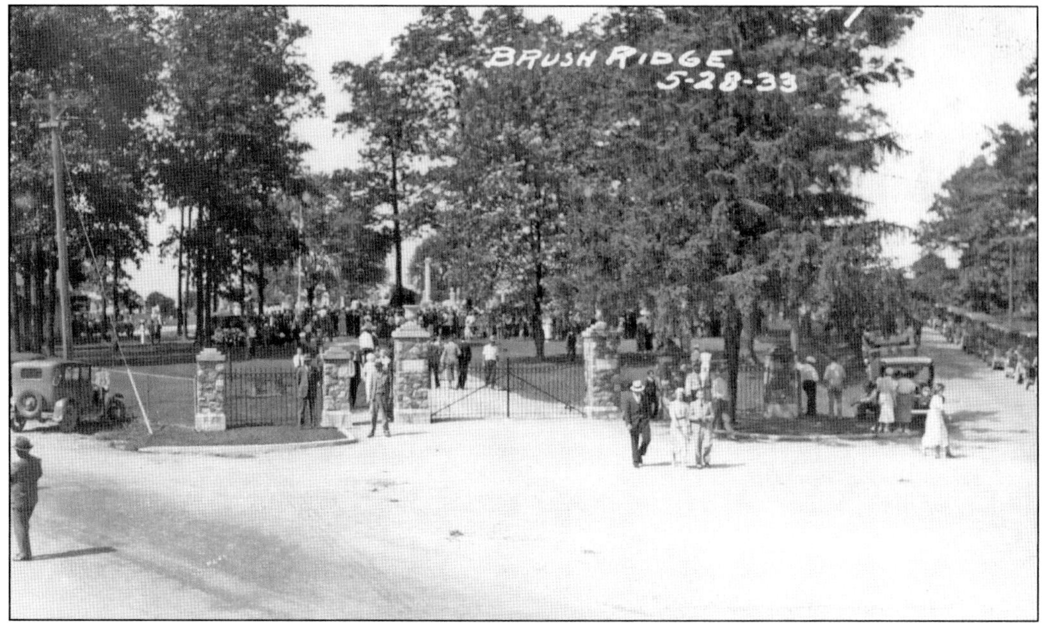

DECORATION DAY. A large crowd gathered for a Decoration Day celebration in 1933 at the Grand Prairie Cemetery in Brush Ridge. The cemetery grounds, located at the junction of Morral-Kirkpatrick and Marion–Upper Sandusky Roads, were purchased around 1881 at a cost of $65 per acre for the six and one-quarter acres. (Courtesy of Richard Carey.)

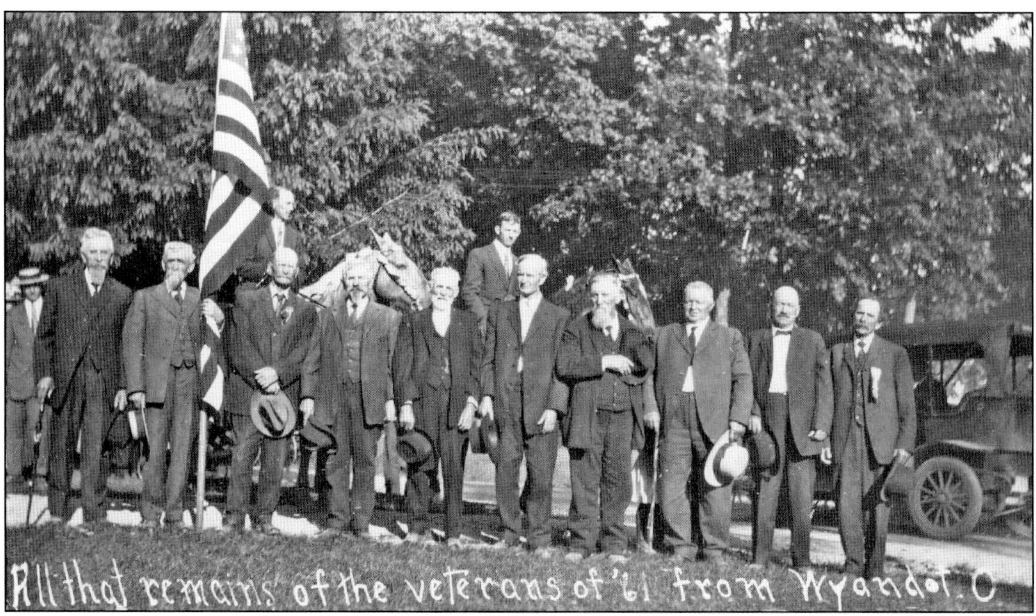

HONORED FOR SERVICE. This group of Civil War veterans received recognition at the Decoration Day parade held at the Grand Prairie Cemetery in 1914. Many of them may have been members of the Grand Army of the Republic, which was a fraternal organization composed of veterans who fought for the Union. The organization was dissolved when the last member died in Duluth, Minnesota, in 1956. (Courtesy of Ralph and Erdine Eaton collection.)

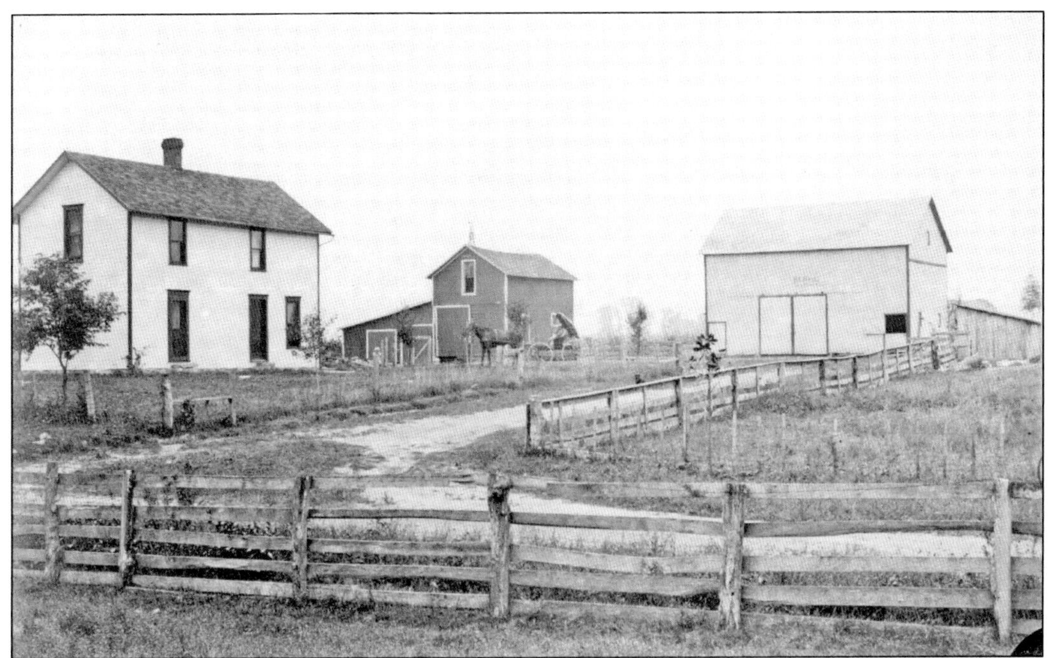

B.C. HITE FARM. Little is known about the B.C. Hite farm other than that the sender of this postcard identified it as being five miles northwest of Marion near Morral. Hite was apparently willing to do work in places other than his farm, as records show he earned $2 in 1909 for helping on a road survey crew. (Courtesy of Ellis and Margaret Hudson.)

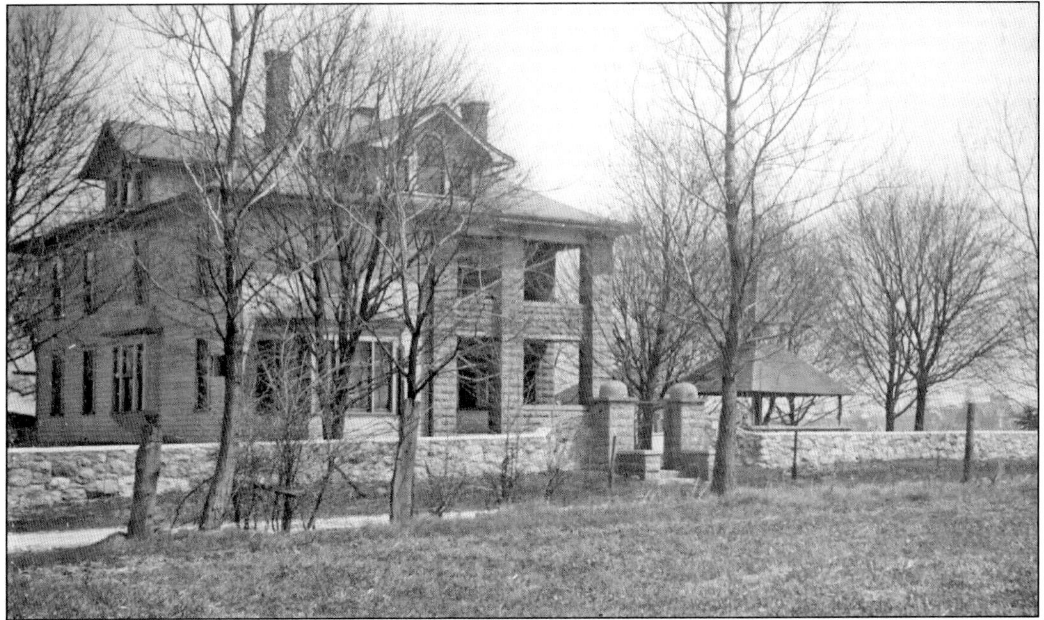

WALLED IN. This residence on Marion-Williamsport Road was enhanced by a sturdy fence made from stacked and mortared fieldstone. Cast stone was used for the gate pillars as well as the two-story front porch. Cast stone was a manufactured masonry material that was molded to look like cut stone but was more economical to make and easier to install due to the conformity of the blocks. The home and walls are still standing. (Author's collection.)

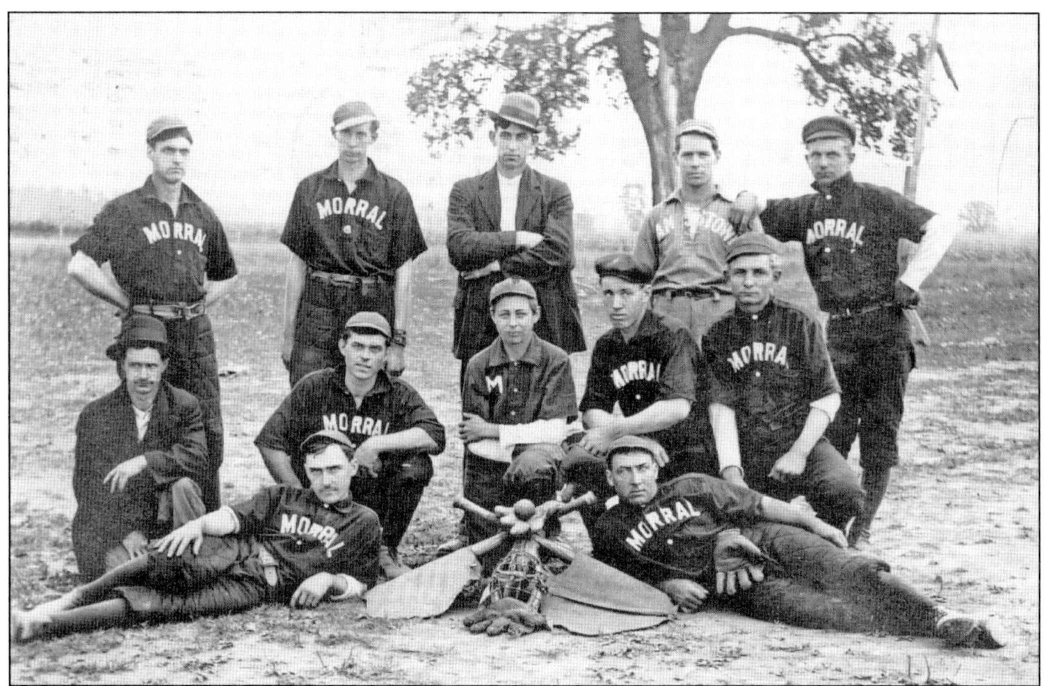

Ready for a Game. The Morral baseball team posed for a group photograph along with a player from an unknown team who perhaps had just joined the Morral squad. The photograph appears to date from the late 19th century based on some of the gloves, which have no web and were referred to as "workman-style" gloves. (Courtesy of John and Virginia Murphy.)

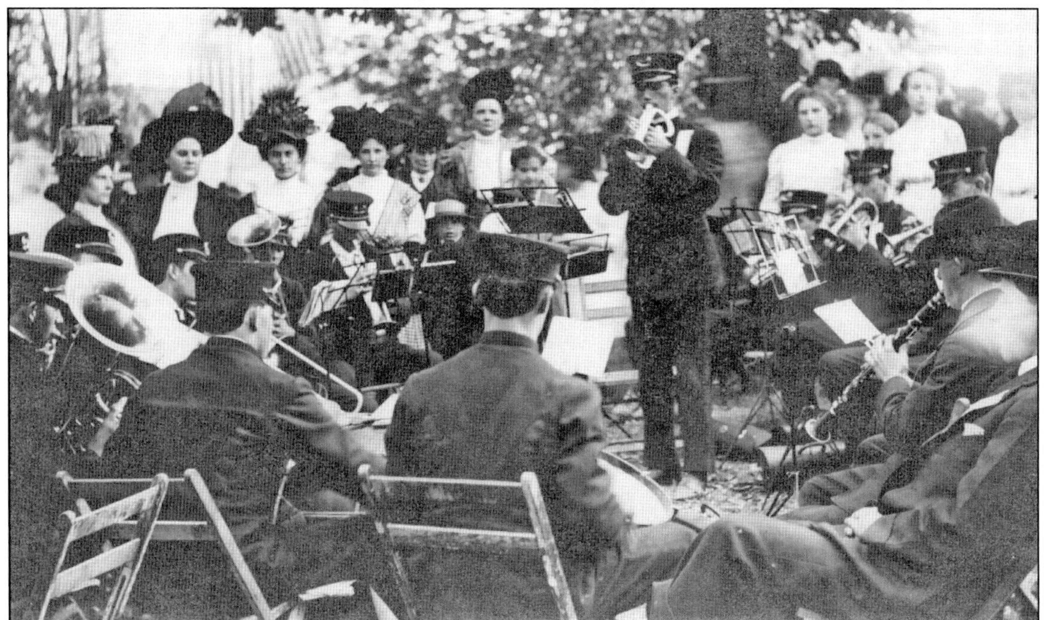

Providing Entertainment. The Morral Community Band, pictured in 1908, provided entertainment to the delight of local residents. The band was organized under the direction of J.T. Thew and provided free concerts, with a favorite location being on Green Street between Neff and South Streets. (Courtesy of Mike and Linda Perry.)

Six

Prospect Area

The village of Prospect was officially founded in 1835, when Christian Gast II entered a plat for a settlement to be named Middletown in the recorder's office in Delaware, Ohio. Middletown was chosen as the name in reference to the settlement's location, which was midway between Delaware and Marion. Gast was not the first resident of the area, as a small community had existed at the location in what was then Delaware County for several years. However, he was the first to file a village plat and thus establish a legally recognized settlement. His plat included 81 lots on land he owned on the east side of the Scioto River. Sales of the lots were brisk, with residences and businesses soon being established. Platted additions in 1837, 1839, and 1855 were required to meet the demand of potential landowners.

In 1876, Christian Gast III, following in his father's footsteps, filed a plat of 60 lots at the east edge of Middletown. The lots were split by the then-under-construction Columbus & Toledo Railroad, which Gast had helped bring to the area. The new settlement was viewed as being entirely separate from Middletown and was named Prospect by its developer.

Around this same time, many Middletown residents had grown tired of having their mail delivery and occasional legal matters being confused with other villages named Middletown throughout the state. A petition for a name change from Middletown to Prospect was filed with the Marion County Common Pleas Court in 1876 (the Marion County courts had gained jurisdiction over the area with the creation of Prospect Township as part of Marion County in 1848). The court approved the request, and the combined village of Prospect was created. The community continued to grow rapidly with the availability of both rail and water for transportation and shipping leading to its expansion. In 1883, the village was reported to have five dry goods stores, two drugstores, two hardware stores, two millinery stores, two banks, and a newspaper-printing office, among numerous other business endeavors.

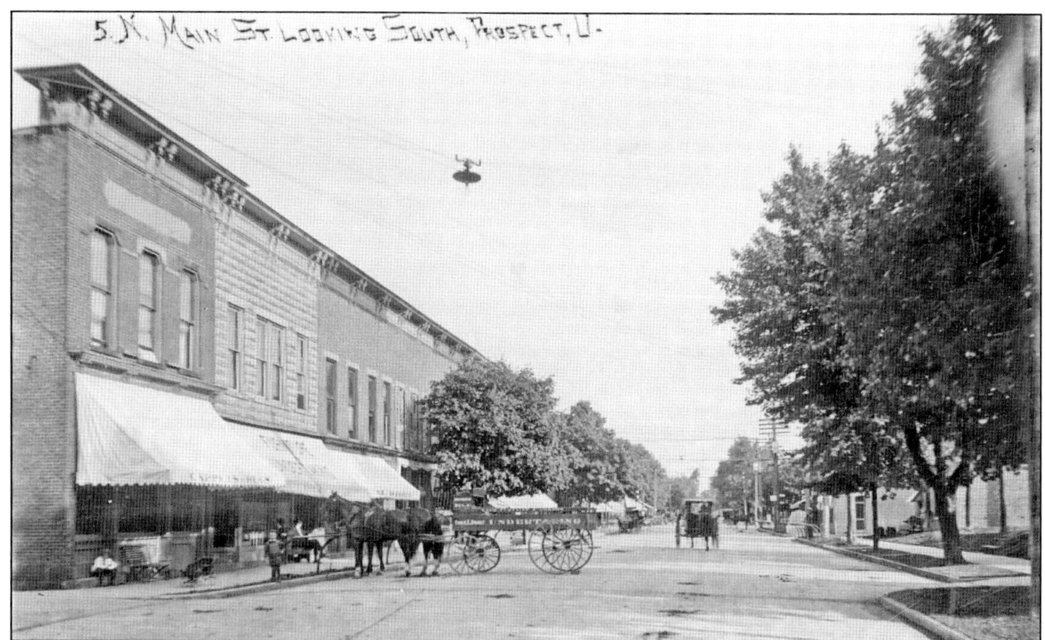

Business Was Booming. Prospect's Main Street was vibrant with a variety of businesses advertising their services on sidewalk canopies. These retractable overhangs protected shoppers from inclement weather and helped cool the interiors of the stores. Shoppers could purchase carpets or furniture while making final arrangements at Thomas E. Drake Undertaking, which had a delivery wagon waiting for whatever the cargo might be. (Courtesy of Richard Carey.)

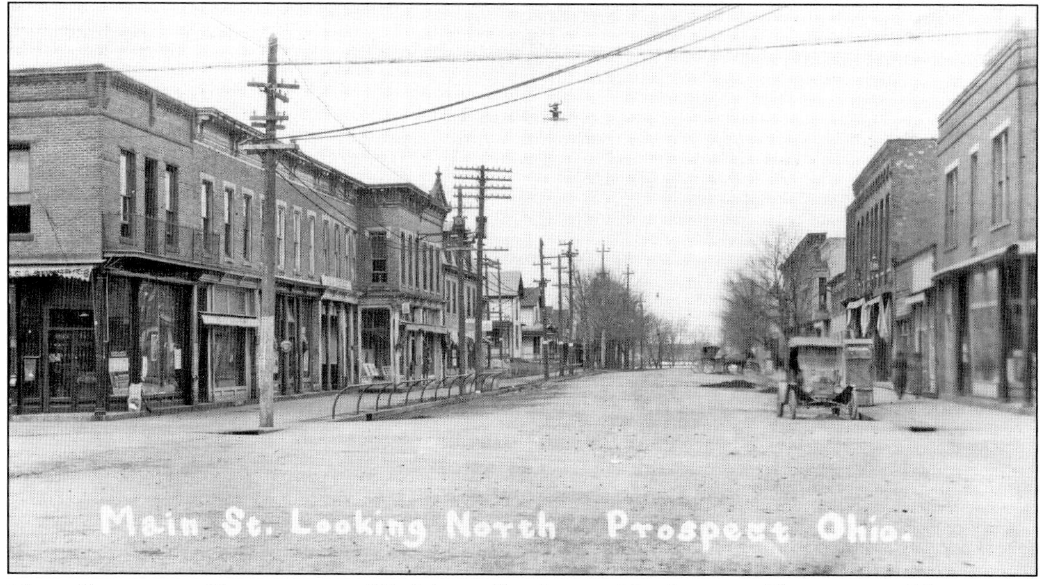

Main Street in Transition. Hitching rails, along with a horse and buggy, stood in contrast to the technological advances of electric streetlights, telephone wires, and automobiles. Prospect's telephone exchange was located on the top floor of the building with the iron railing (in the left foreground). During the 1913 flood, water rose to a depth that required the rescue of the telephone operators from the second-floor balcony by boat. (Courtesy of Ralph and Erdine Eaton collection.)

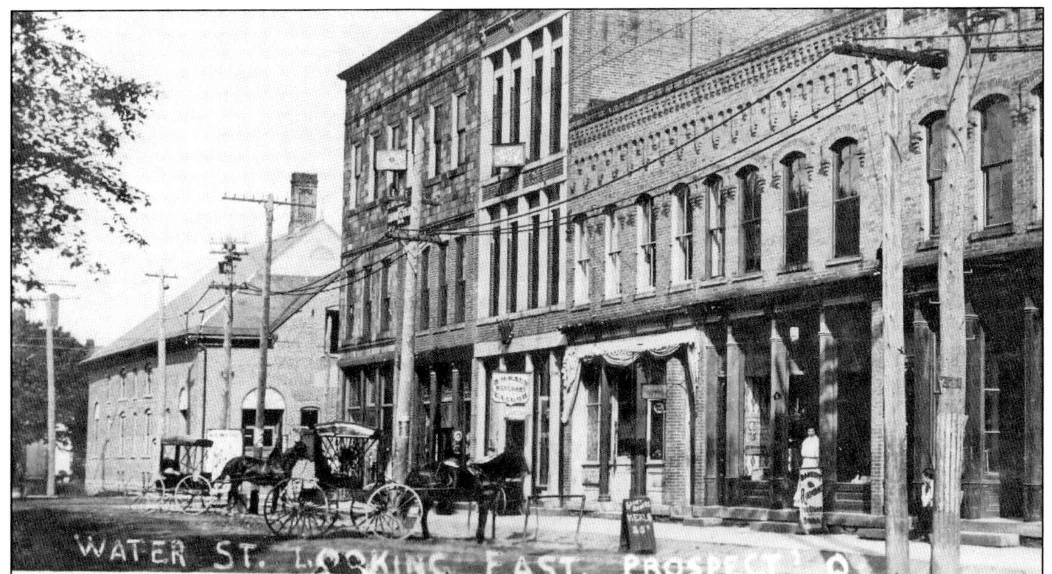

STOP AND SHOP. Patrons of this dining establishment on Water Street could purchase "Short Order Meals" for 25¢ followed by a scoop of ice cream. After a stop at the tailor's shop, people could perhaps pause in the Modern Woodmen of America lodge or visit with the Knights of Pythias. Lodges and fraternal organizations such as these, along with the Masons and Odd Fellows, played a major role in the social and business worlds at the beginning of the 20th century. (Courtesy of Ralph and Erdine Eaton collection.)

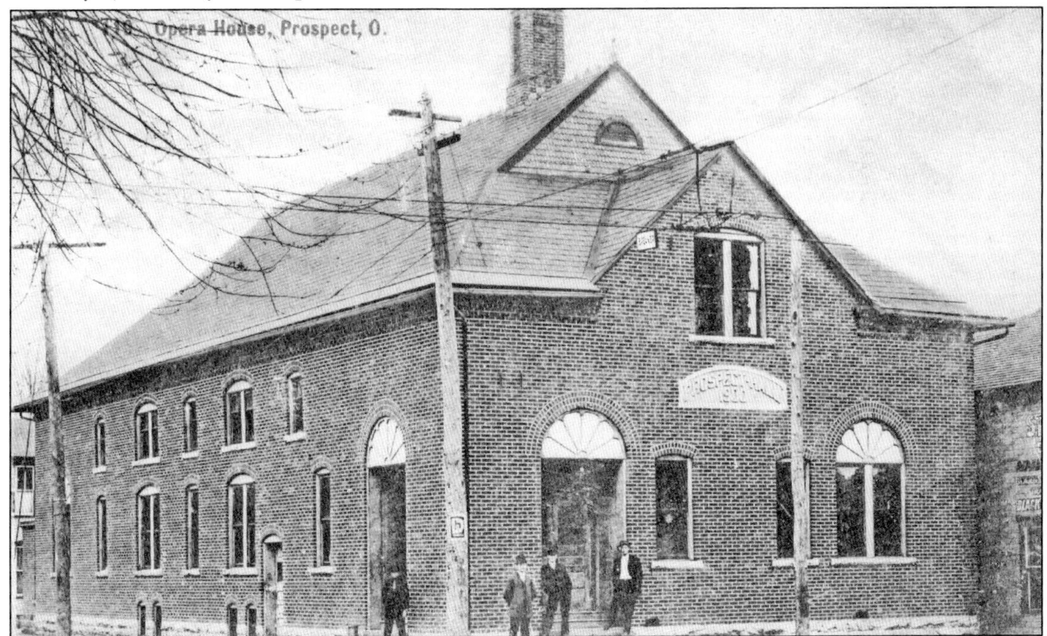

OPERA HOUSE. The Prospect Hall, opened in 1900, was the cultural center of the village. This opera house hosted lectures, concerts, school plays, and graduation ceremonies. Although it was advertised as having a seating capacity of nearly 1,000, it is doubtful that the true capacity was that large. Durwood Lodge No. 153 of the Knights of Pythias now occupies this building. (Author's collection.)

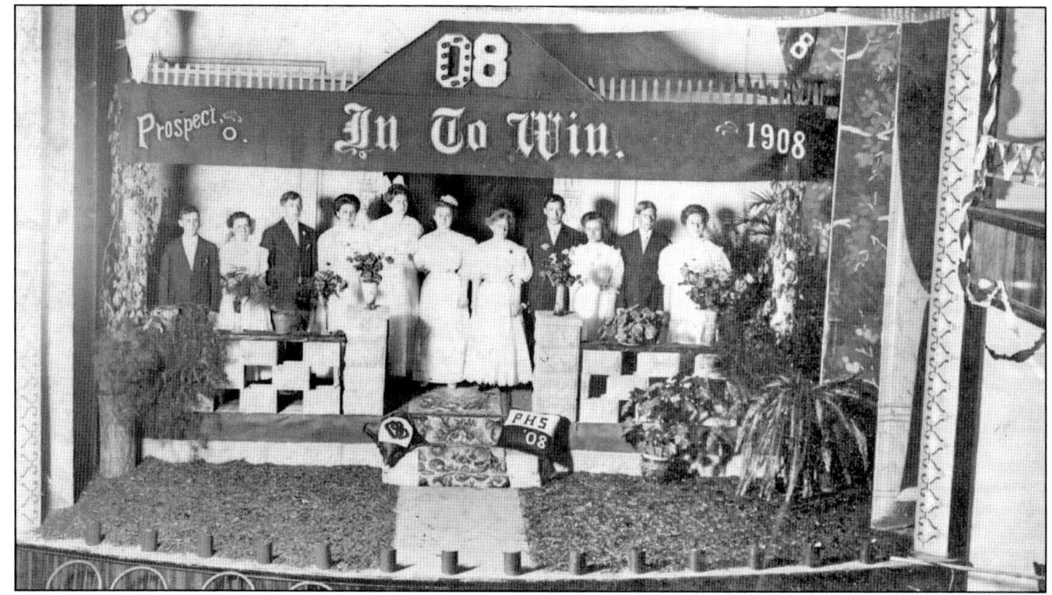

TAKING THE STAGE. Prospect High School's class of 1908, with its motto of "In to Win," is pictured on stage at Prospect Hall. Activities such as plays, musical performances, lectures, and debates were popular community entertainment options. Some schools offered students the chance to participate in a lyceum course featuring presentations by professional speakers who traveled the country entertaining and enlightening students. (Author's collection.)

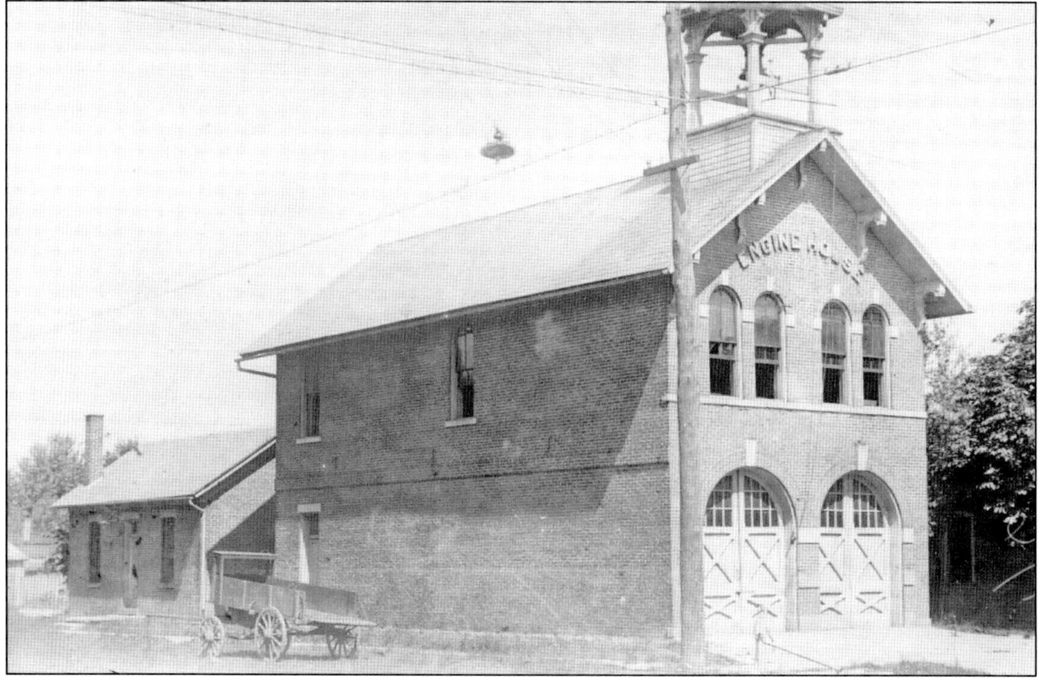

ENGINE HOUSE AND JAIL HOUSE. The residents of Prospect were rightfully proud of their engine house on Water Street. Designed for horse-drawn firefighting apparatuses, the structure also housed mechanized equipment for many years until a new fire station was built. The smaller building behind the engine house was the village jail. (Courtesy of Richard Carey.)

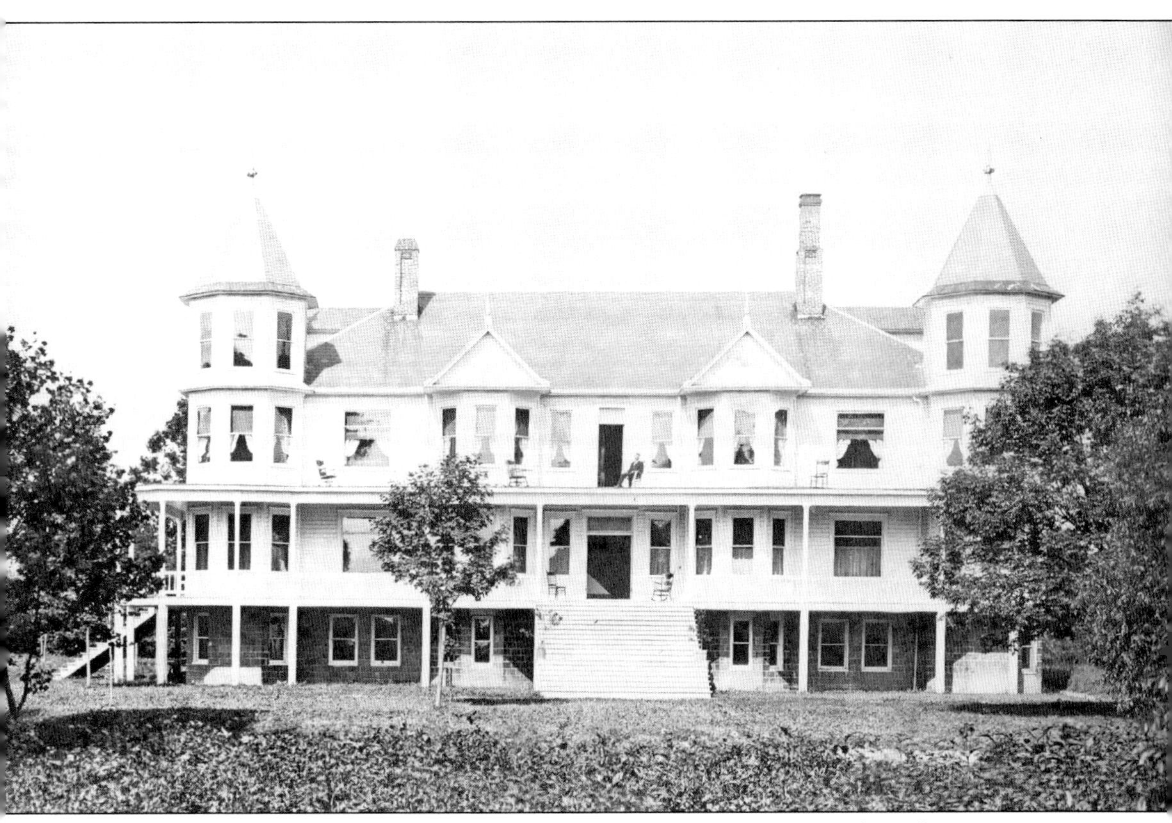

SULPHO-MAGNETIC SPRINGS SANATORIUM. Located on the west side of South Main Street behind Battle Run, this magnificent facility was a health spa and vacation destination. Its advertising clearly stated that it provided "the best care and treatment for all who apply, except those afflicted with contagious or infectious diseases." Patrons would find "a pleasant, healthy, and restful place to spend your vacation. Baths of all kinds. The spring water is remarkable for its purity and cleansing power. Use its crystal draughts and you will quickly realize that you are dealing with a powerful remedial agent, a great curative factor which is intangible to finite minds." Rates depended upon the size and location of the room, with the cost for room, board, and treatment ranging from $10 to $20 per week. Travelers could take advantage of the services for $2 per day. The building was destroyed by fire in 1905 and was not rebuilt. Nearby communities also touted the medicinal properties of their springs. Magnetic Springs, located a few miles to the south, developed rapidly when mineral waters, which were believed to have healing qualities, were discovered there in the 1880s. Hotel resorts sprang up, and the village grew rapidly. The discovery of modern medicinal cures eventually led to a general fading interest in natural healing. The resorts soon closed, and the hotels were eventually razed. (Author's collection.)

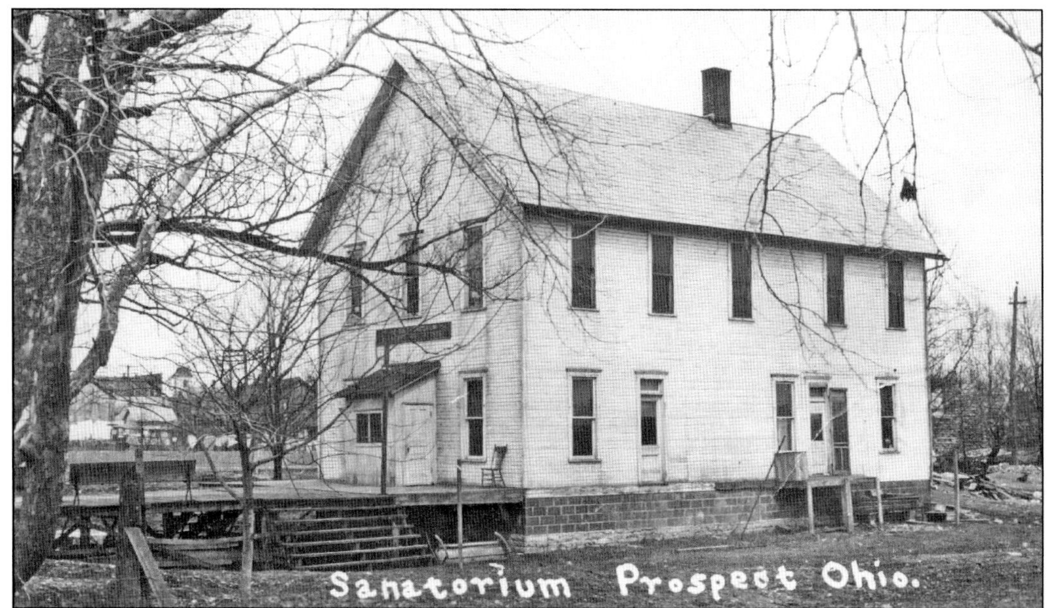

SANATORIUM, SANITORIUM, SANITARIUM? Confusion over what types of services were offered at facilities such as the Gast Sanatorium certainly could have existed considering the numerous and various spellings of the word. While the names were often used interchangeably, in general, sanitoriums and sanitariums were known for the treatment of diseases and illnesses, while sanatoriums resembled today's health spas. (Courtesy of Bob Turner.)

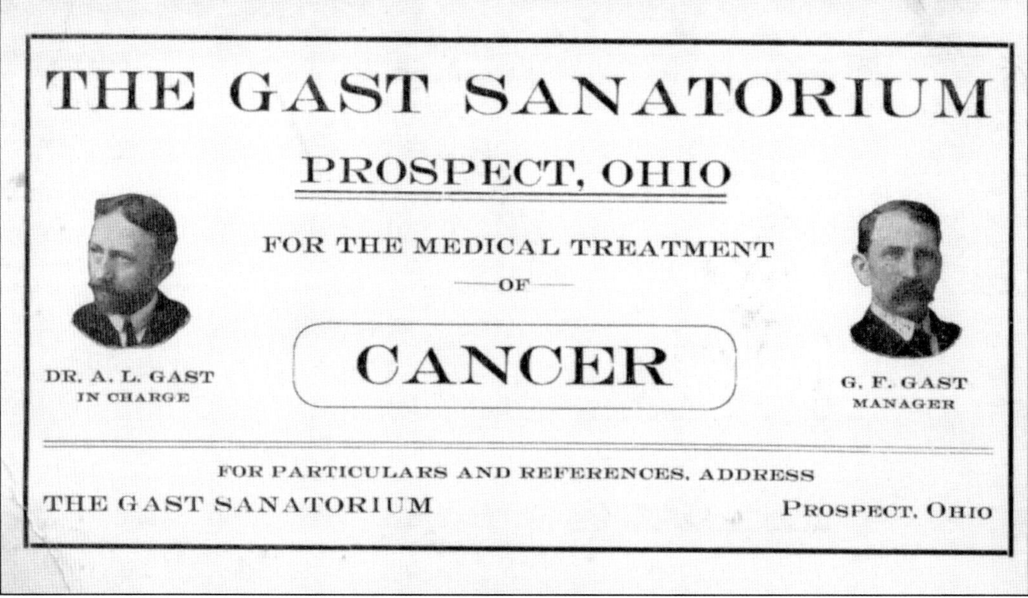

GAST SANATORIUM. Dr. Samuel Gast, of Scott County, Iowa, discovered what he believed to be a cure for cancer. In 1869, his nephew, David Gast of Prospect Township, began treating patients with the remedy. No records of the exact treatment protocol are known, but references to elderberry root poultices have been found. After David Gast's death, his son, George F., went into partnership with Dr. Arthur L. Gast to open and operate the Gast Sanatorium. (Courtesy of Bob Turner.)

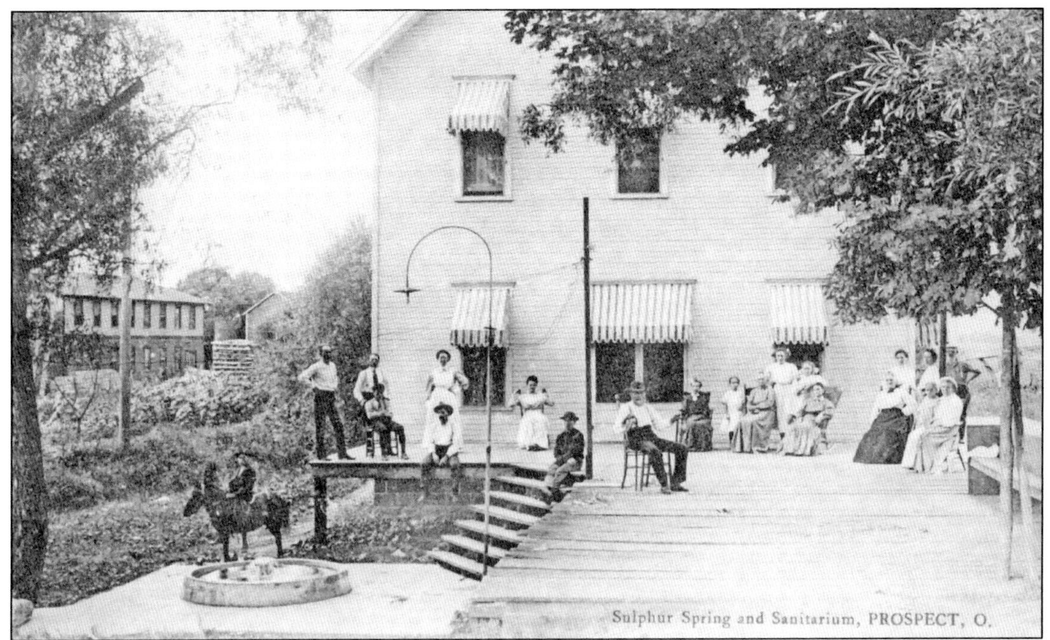

ENJOYING THE OUTDOORS. While it can only be surmised that many of these people were patients (usually called guests), it is apparent that time outdoors was encouraged, judging by this large seating area and lighting for evening use. Steps lead down to one of the many naturally-flowing springs in the village. The large building at far left is the Prospect Creamery. (Courtesy of Richard Carey.)

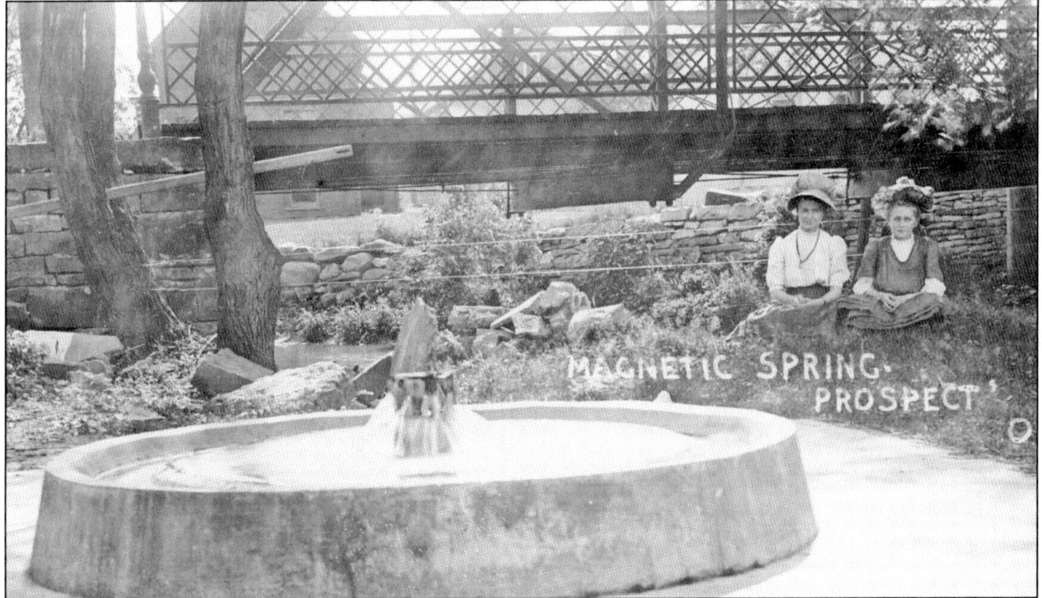

WATER CURES. Prospect was well known for its springs, which were advertised as "magnetic" or "sulphur." Visitors came from great distances to partake of the spring waters, which were very popular as a curative agent. One spring in the downtown area was developed into a "Roman bath." The bubbling spring shown here was adjacent to the Gast Sanatorium, while at least three others were scattered throughout the village. (Courtesy of Richard Carey.)

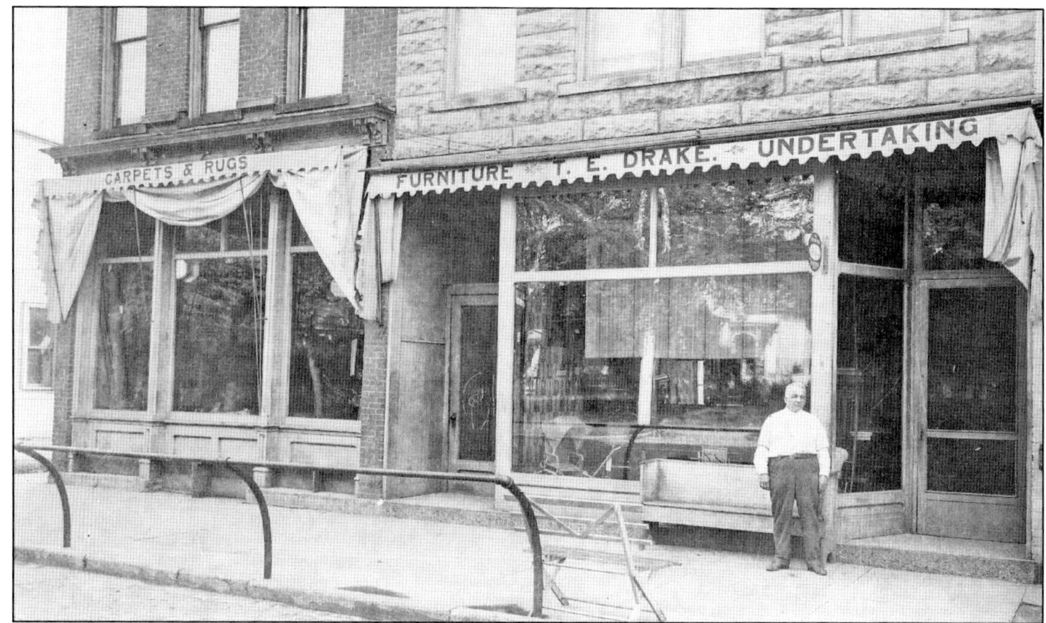

Table or Coffin? Thomas E. Drake's company on Main Street was similar to many furniture stores that utilized the skills of their furniture makers to also provide coffins. The combination was a natural one, as the creators of furniture often had beautiful showrooms full of furniture that could be also used for wakes. As holding viewings in the home began to fall out of practice in the early 1900s, stores often added specially designed parlors for use in displaying a body prior to interment. (Courtesy of Mike and Linda Perry.)

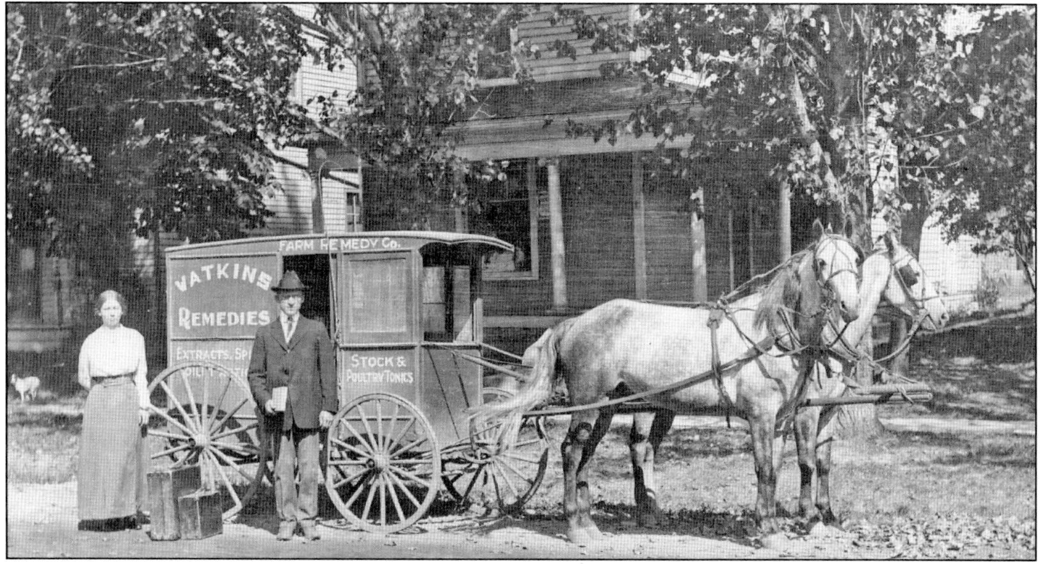

Medicine Man. Starting in 1868, Watkins products became some of the earliest to be sold door-to-door by traveling salesmen (like the one pictured) representing the Watkins Farm Remedy Company and its specialty, Watkins Vegetable Anodyne Liniment. Richard Watkins of Prospect became known for his success selling Mulsified Coconut Oil for Shampooing and, later, Dr. Lyon's Tooth Powder. These products were not associated with Watkins products such as the vanilla people use today. (Courtesy of Ralph and Erdine Eaton collection.)

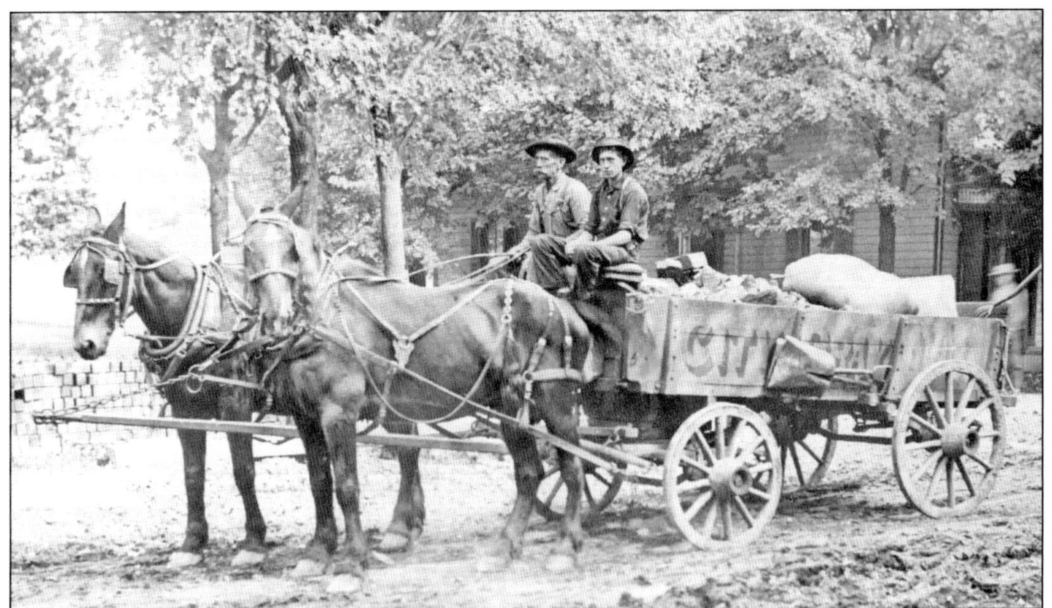

Delivery Service. The City Dray Company provided delivery services throughout the Marion County area. The business may have faced some financial difficulties with the advent of mechanized equipment. In 1916, it advertised in local newspapers the sale of "8 horses and mares aged 4 to 12; 3 dray wagons; 5 sets good heavy harness, at a bargain." (Courtesy of Jane Burkett.)

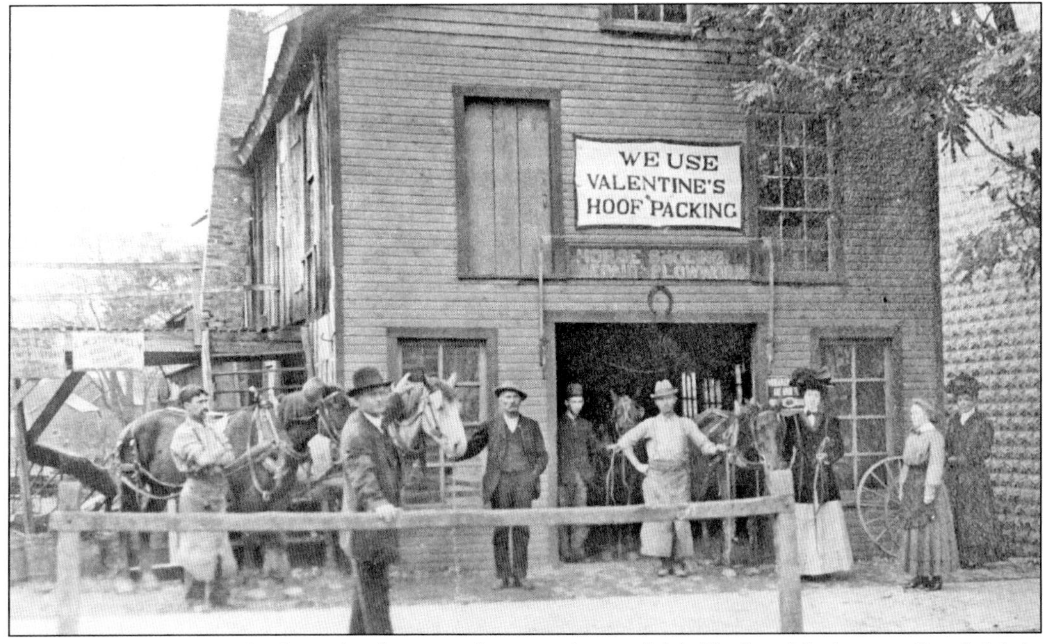

Service Station. Charlie Selanders was the proprietor of this blacksmith shop on South Main Street. The necessity of keeping horses well shod provided a steady business for blacksmiths, who also provided repair services for a wide variety of products such as plowshares and other iron items. Valentine's was the hoof packing of choice and was "guaranteed to soften any dry, hard sole and render it tough and flexible. After its use the foot can easily be trimmed." (Courtesy of Jane Burkett.)

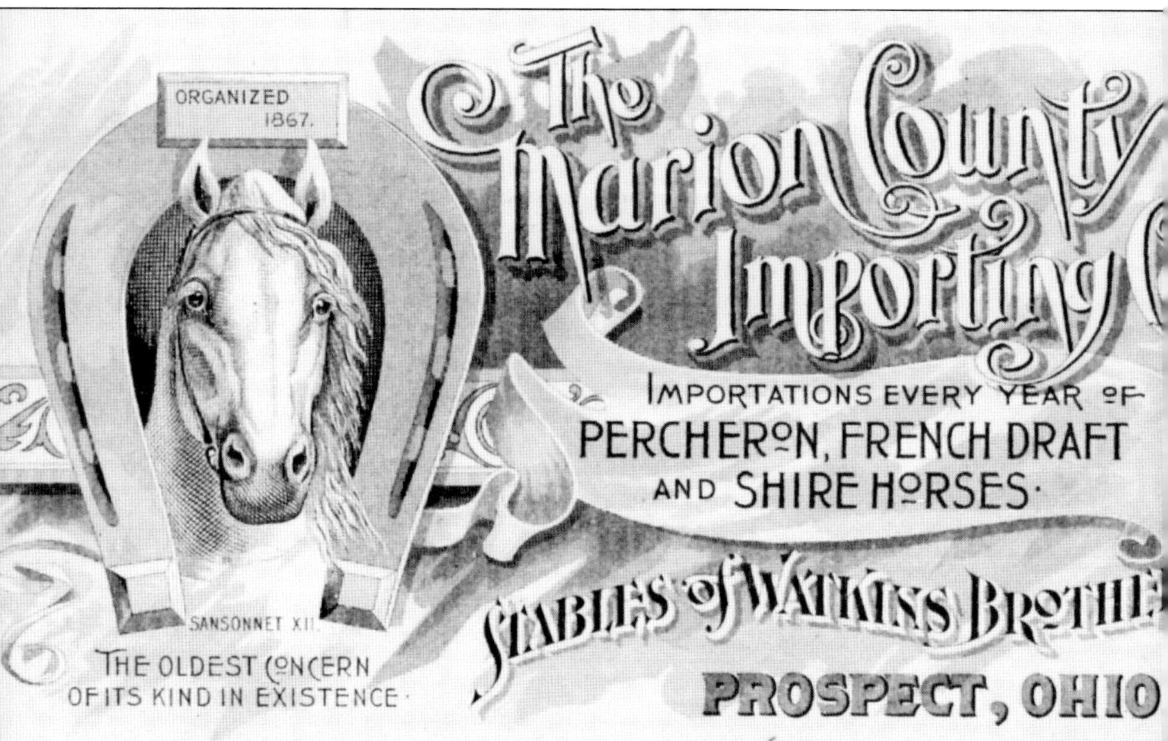

Marion County Importing Company. Jacob Howser and William Gilmore organized the Marion Importing Company in 1867 to bring Norman breeding stallions to the United States from France and Britain. More than 67 of the stallions were imported over the next 15 years, with sales generating more than $150,000 ($3.5 million in 2016 dollars). Watkin Watkins of Prospect operated a stable in conjunction with the importing company. Howser's most well-known import was a Percheron stallion named Prince Imperial, who came from the stables of Napoleon III. Howser purchased the horse for $3,000 in 1868 while on one of his regular trips to Europe to buy breeding stock for his company. Upon his arrival in the United States, Prince Imperial was exhibited at fairs and horse shows with the claim that his forelock and mane were the longest in the world. When the horse died in 1888, he was made into a taxidermy mount and exhibited by the Howser family at various events and venues. Prince Imperial now resides in his own stall at Heritage Hall in Marion. (Courtesy of Richard Carey.)

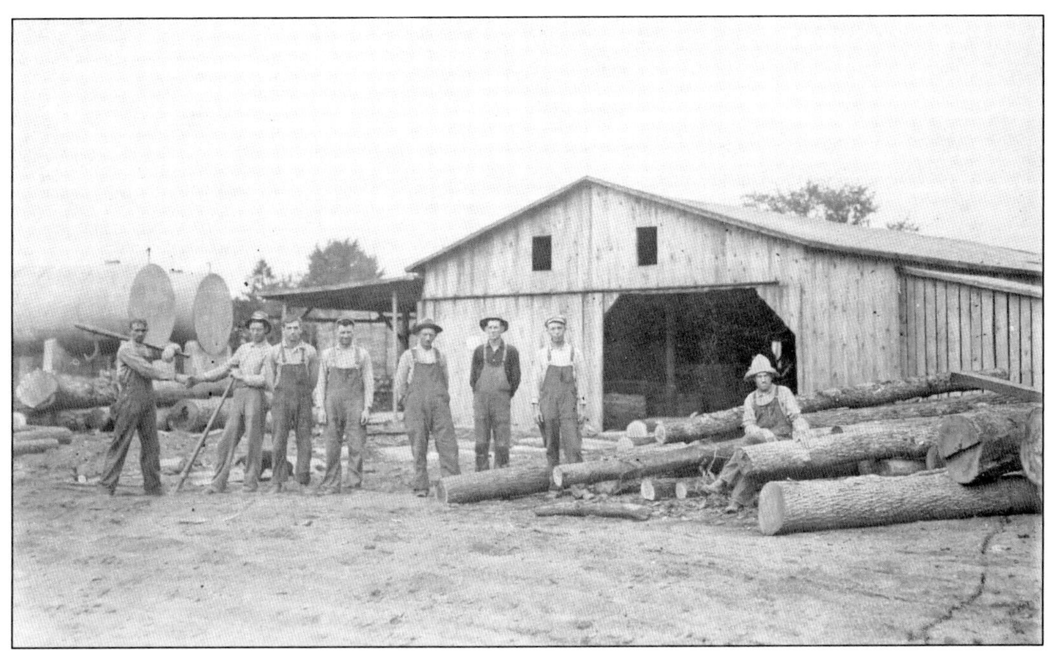

GAST'S SAWMILL. Located on State Route 203 just south of the village, Gast's Sawmill processed lumber from throughout the area. The open farm fields now in the area belie the large amount of wooded land that once stood in southern and western Marion County. Two of these men are holding cant hooks, which were invaluable tools for moving the heavy logs. The days of hand logging are largely gone, as mechanized equipment allows for the sawing, trimming, and loading of logs with just one machine and one operator. (Courtesy of Jane Burkett.)

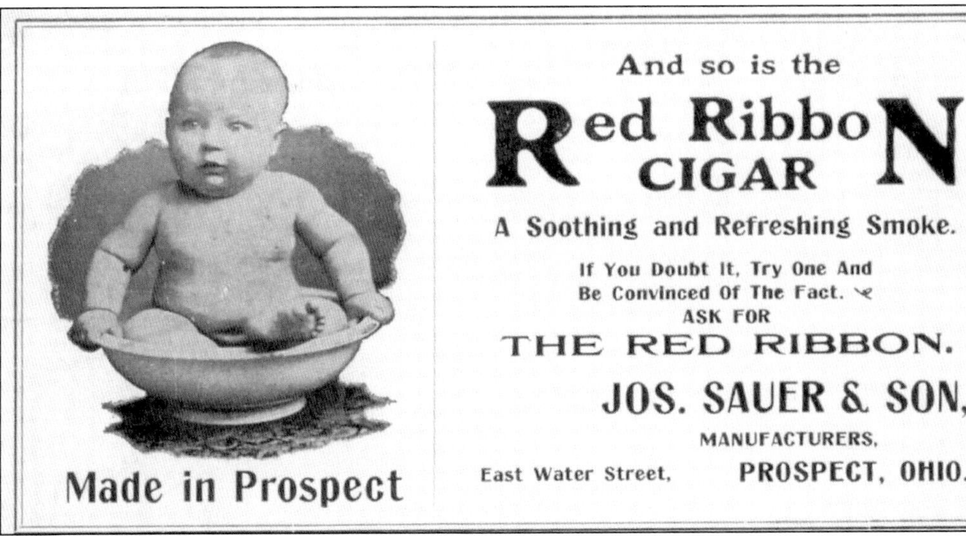

MADE IN PROSPECT. Using the universal appeal of a cute baby in their advertising, the Jos. Sauer and Son Company proudly announced that its tobacco product was also "Made in Prospect." Little is known about the company, but newspaper advertisements tout that its Red Ribbon cigar was "one of a few really good brands" that sold for 5¢ each at the Headley Drug Store in nearby Marion. (Courtesy of Ellis and Margaret Hudson.)

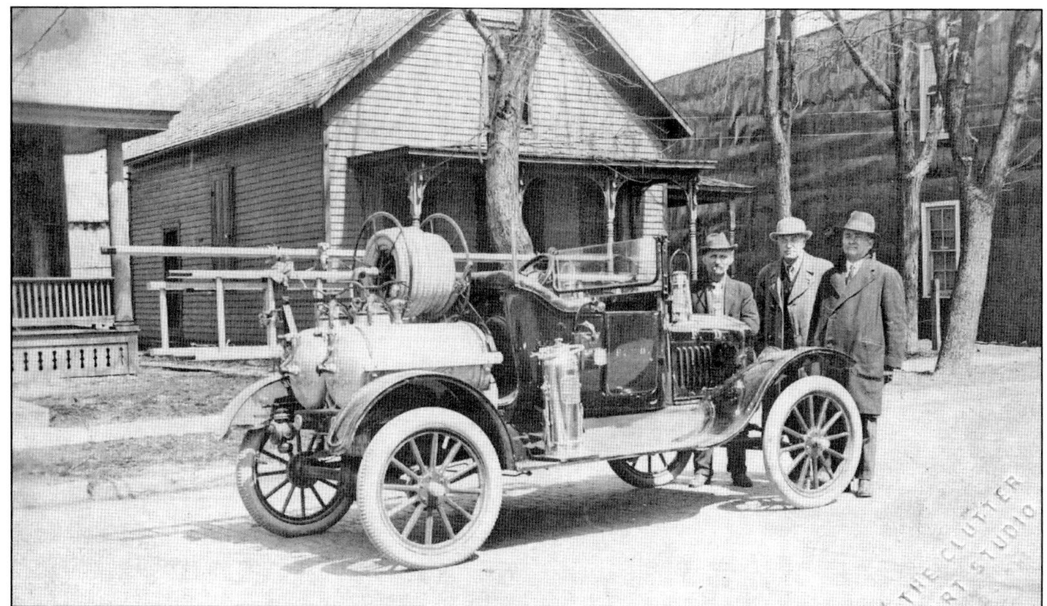

FIREFIGHTER. The Prospect Manufacturing Company was founded in 1911 to manufacture firefighting apparatus under the Deluge brand. Its do-it-yourself kits provided materials that customers could use to retrofit Model T chassis and included chemical tanks, hose reels, ladders, and other equipment. Later developments included water pumps, fire engines, and firefighting boats that used Hydrojet water jets for both propulsion and extinguishing fires. More than 100 of the boats were produced in Prospect for use around the world in World War II. (Courtesy of Wayne Apt.)

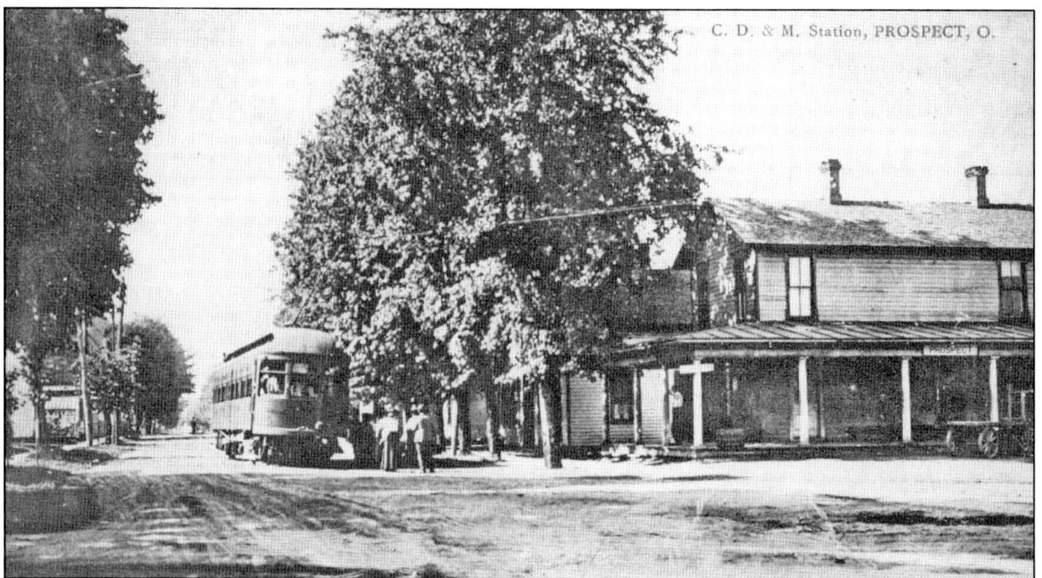

INTERURBAN SERVICE. The Columbus, Delaware & Marion Interurban provided rail service in Prospect from 1902 to 1933. The Prospect station stood at the corner of Park and Elm Streets. Powered by electricity from a coal-fueled generating plant at nearby Newmans Crossing, the cars could make the trip from Marion to downtown Columbus in just over an hour provided that stops along the way to pick up passengers were minimal. (Courtesy of Richard Carey.)

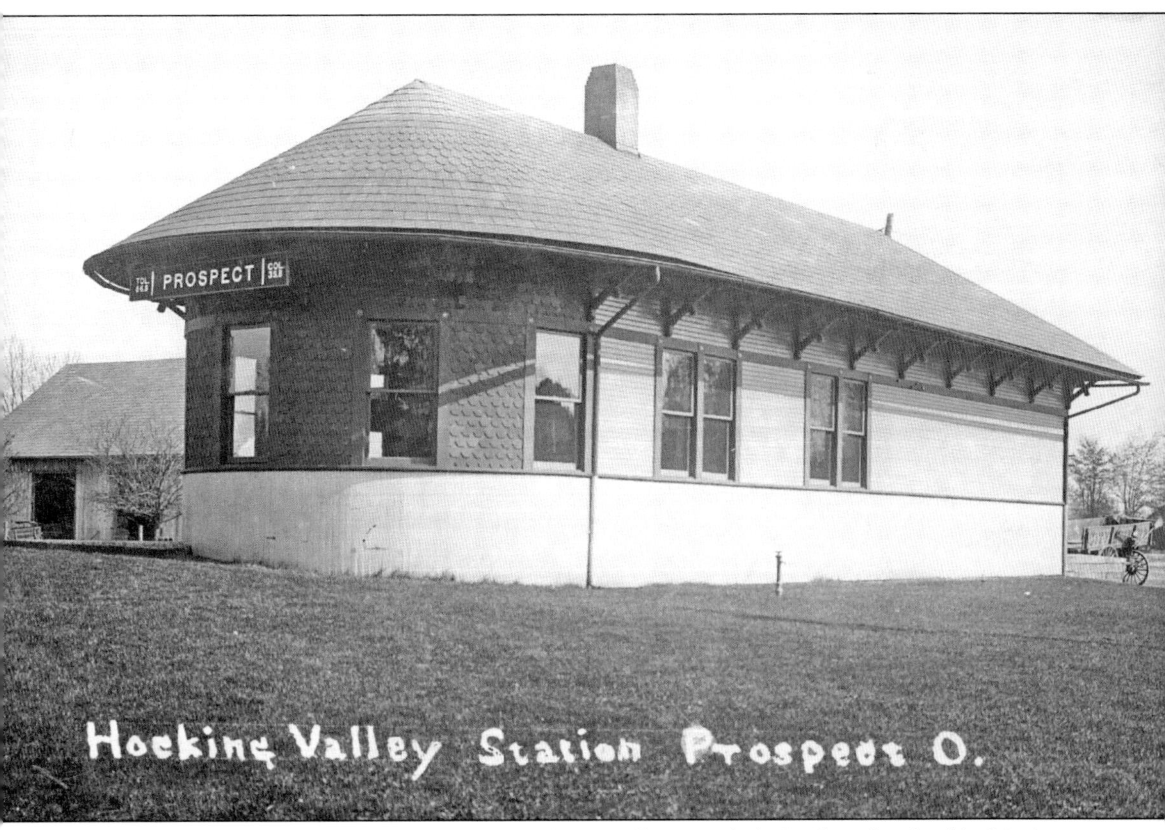

Hocking Valley Depot. The Columbus, Hocking Valley & Toledo Railroad arrived in Marion County in 1876, with service completed to Toledo in 1877. In addition to passenger service, the company hauled massive loads of coal and iron ore from the Hocking Valley in southern Ohio to docks in Toledo. Prospect was the site of this handsome depot built in 1901 on the west side of the tracks. It featured a waiting room with a rounded end and was nearly identical to a depot at Sugar Grove south of Lancaster. It provided a comfortable waiting area for passengers until the last passenger train came through town in 1971. The depot continued to be maintained by a rail agent for several years but eventually became vacant. Arnold Joseph, a former mayor of Prospect, purchased the station and had it moved to a different location in the village in 1978. The depot was converted to a restaurant featuring train-themed decorations and memorabilia. In 2011, it was sold again, completely dismantled, and moved to Gahanna, Ohio, where it was reassembled as a golf course clubhouse. (Courtesy of Richard Carey.)

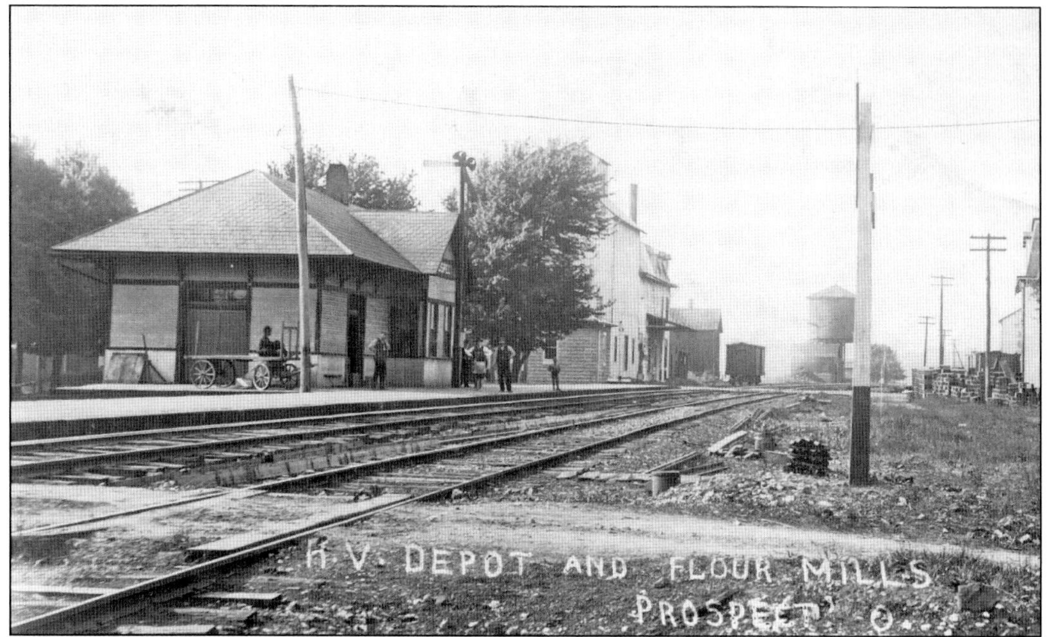

Depot and Flour Mills. In 1876, Christian Gast III, son of Middletown's founder, developed 60 lots along the railroad. He called his development Prospect, a name that was later adopted by the entire village. Two grain elevators, the Union Mills and the National Mill, were erected to take advantage of the rail service. (Courtesy of Richard Carey.)

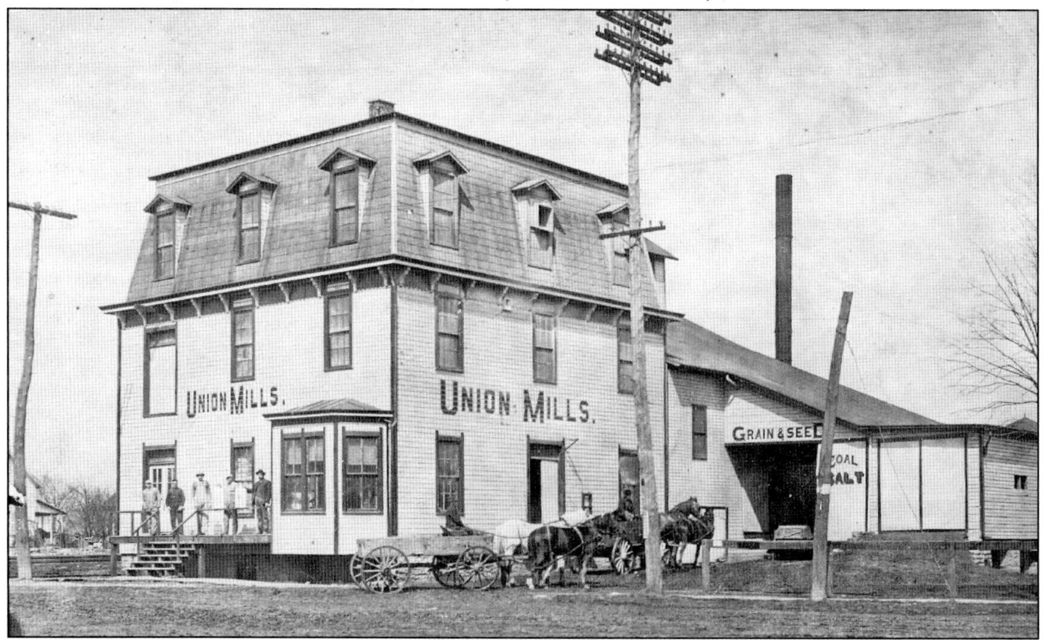

Union Mills. Customers waited in line at the Union Mills building adjacent to the railroad. Mill stores were much more than just places to have grain processed. They also sold animal feed, coal, and even household supplies. Union Mills was known for its Starlight Corn Meal and Starlight Patent Flour brands, which, according to advertisements of the time, were "sold by all grocers on a positive guarantee." (Courtesy of Jane Burkett.)

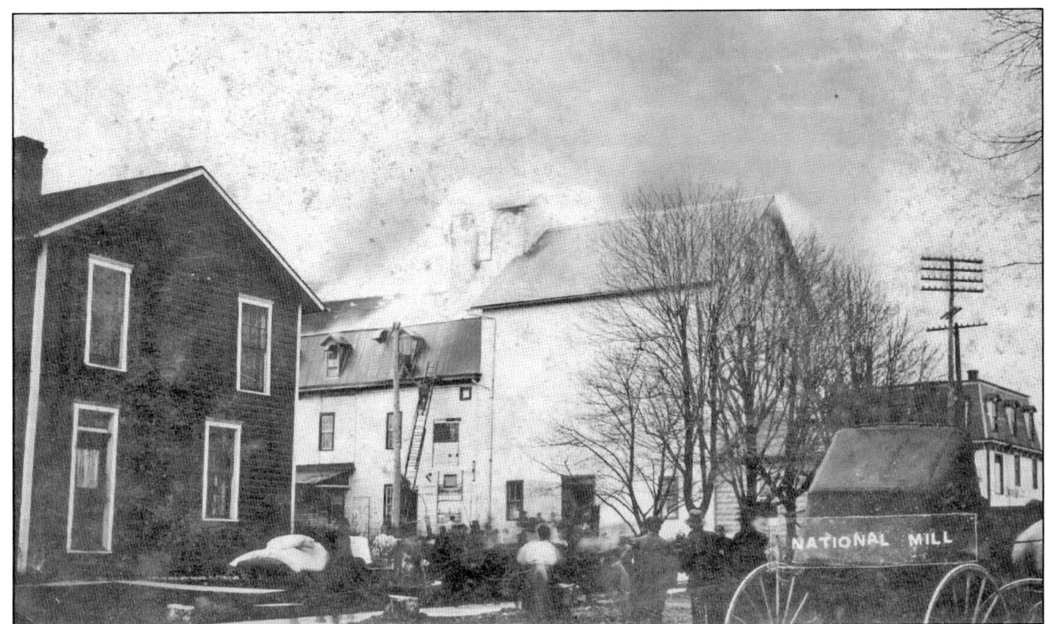

Mill on Fire. The National Mill caught fire on March 23, 1908, with a loss to the mill and adjoining property of about $40,000. The village had no firefighting equipment capable of handling such a blaze, although a bucket brigade (visible on ladders in the picture) made a valiant attempt to extinguish the fire. More than 12,000 bushels of wheat were destroyed by the inferno. (Courtesy of Jane Burkett.)

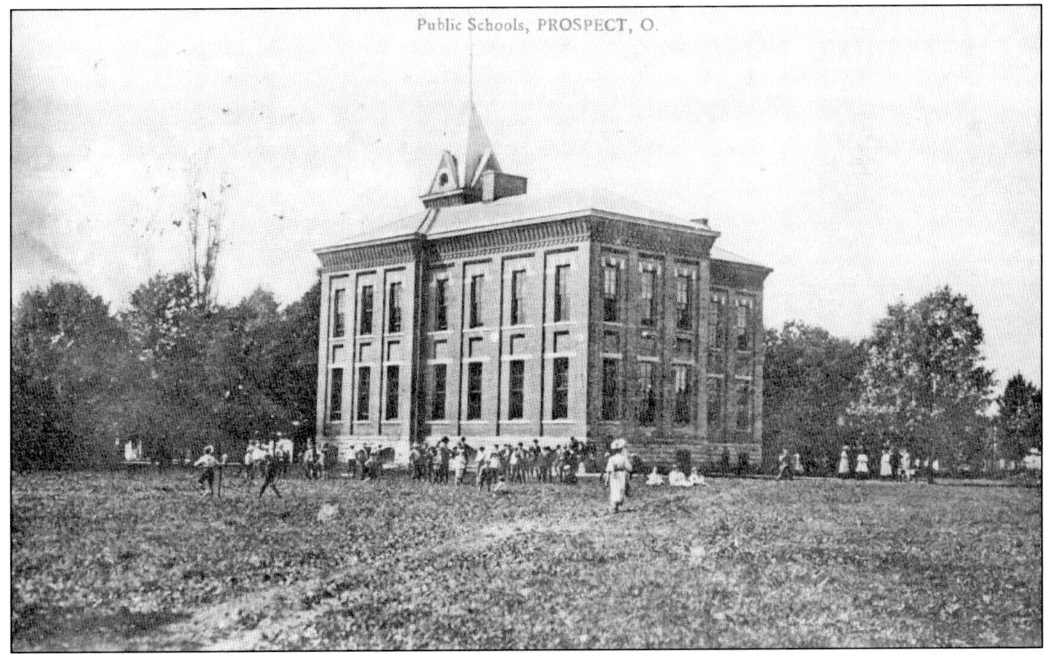

School Days. Prospect's impressive school building was constructed in 1884 at a cost of $10,000. Located on North East Street, it served a variety of grades until a high school was built on an adjacent lot in 1921. The old building then served as an elementary school until it was closed in 1966. (Courtesy of Richard Carey.)

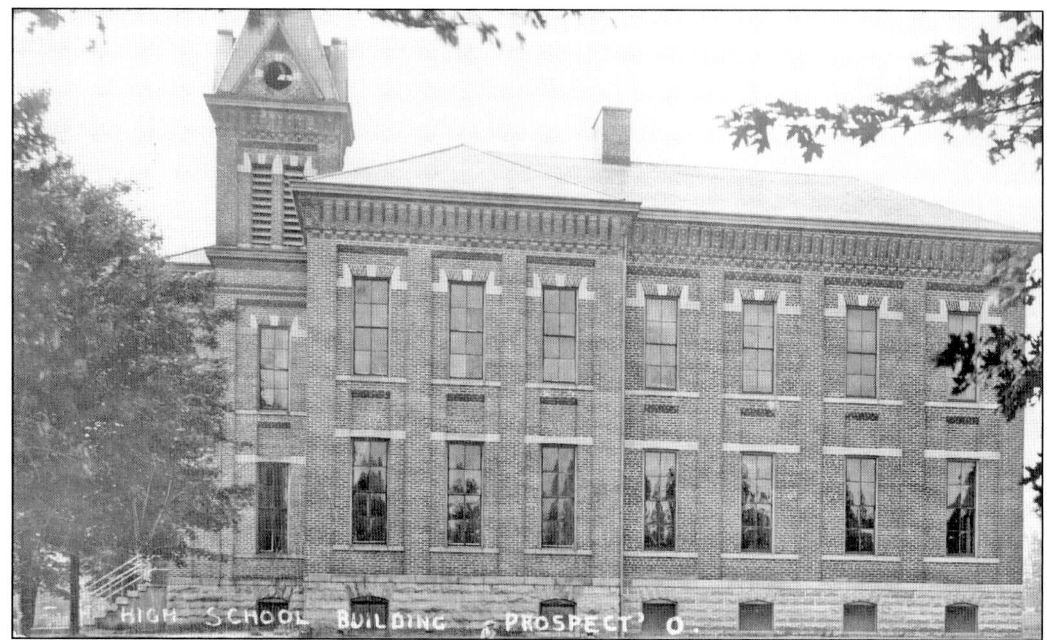

NORMAL SCHOOL. The Marion County Normal School, for teacher training, began in 1906 under the direction of T.E. Bolander. It was located in the Prospect School until 1917, when it moved to Marion. After completing an end-of-course examination, students were issued certificates to teach in Marion County for one to three years depending on their scores on the exam. (Courtesy of Richard Carey.)

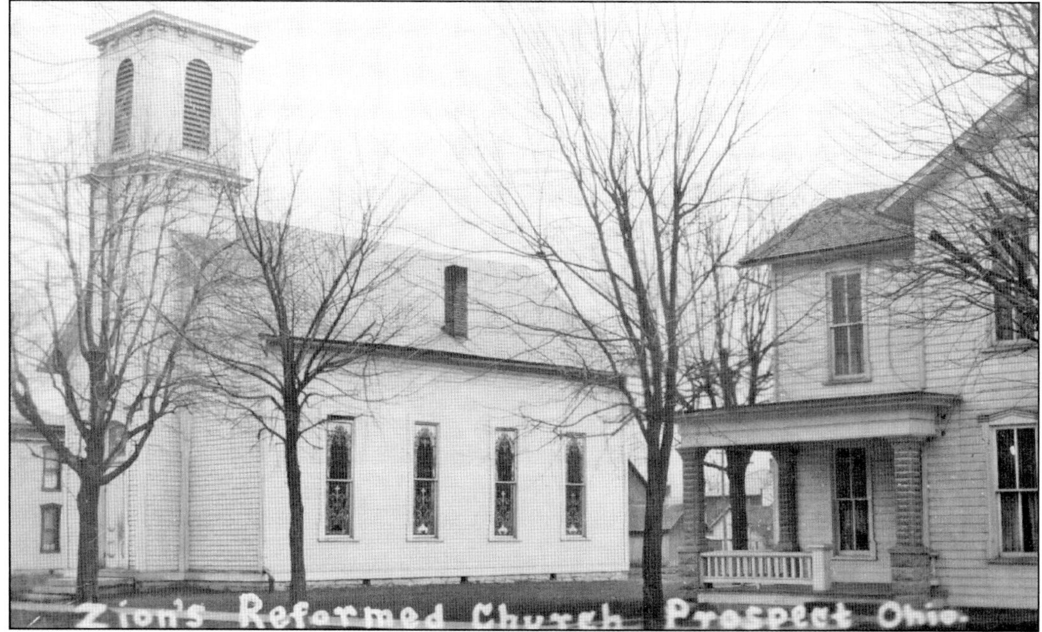

FIRST ZION REFORMED CHURCH. The German Reformed movement began meeting in Middletown in 1845. This church was built in 1874 at the corner of East and Water Streets. The foundation stones were dug from the Scioto River by David Mohr, a member of the congregation. (Courtesy of Richard Carey.)

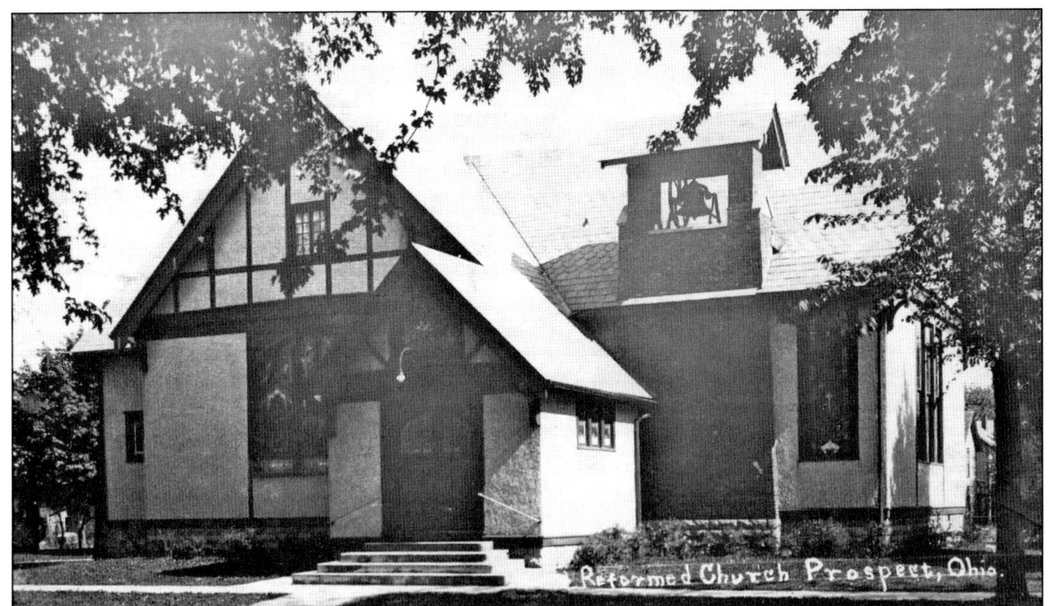

SECOND ZION REFORMED CHURCH. As the Zion Reformed congregation grew, so did its need for additional space. The members raised sufficient funds to tear down their original church and build this one in its place. It is still used as church by the Community Christian Fellowship congregation. (Courtesy of Bob Turner.)

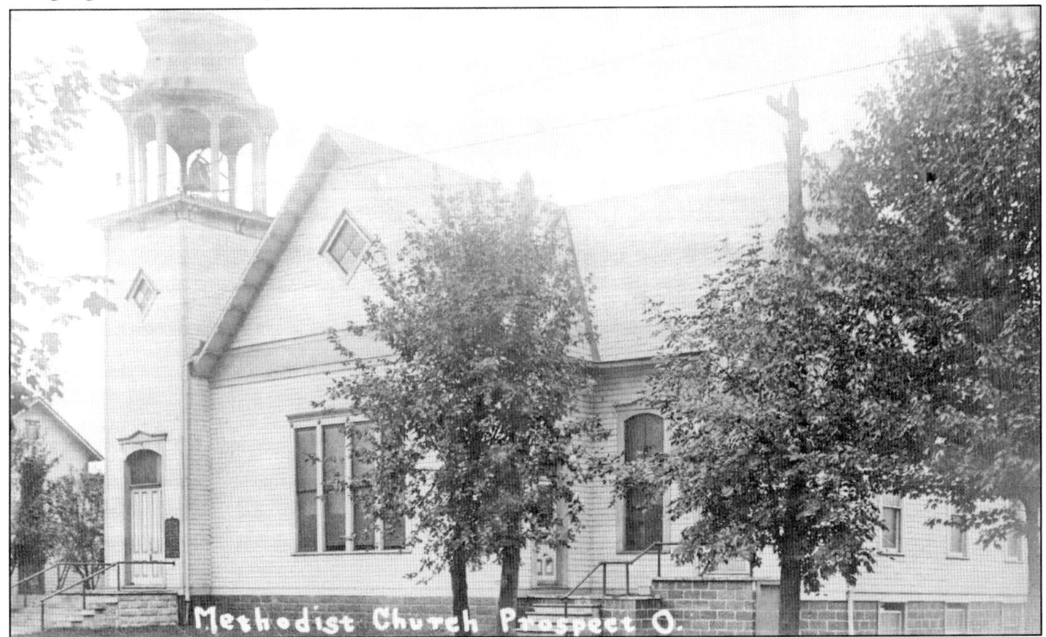

PROSPECT METHODIST CHURCH. Prospect's oldest congregation began meeting around 1816. In 1837, a church was erected on the current site, but it was moved around 1858 for use as a barn after it was replaced by a new building. The second church cost $1,650 to build and had a capacity of 450 worshippers. In 1900, a small basement was excavated, and in 1910, an organ loft and additional rooms were added. Other renovations over the years include stained-glass windows and additional basement space. (Courtesy of Richard Carey.)

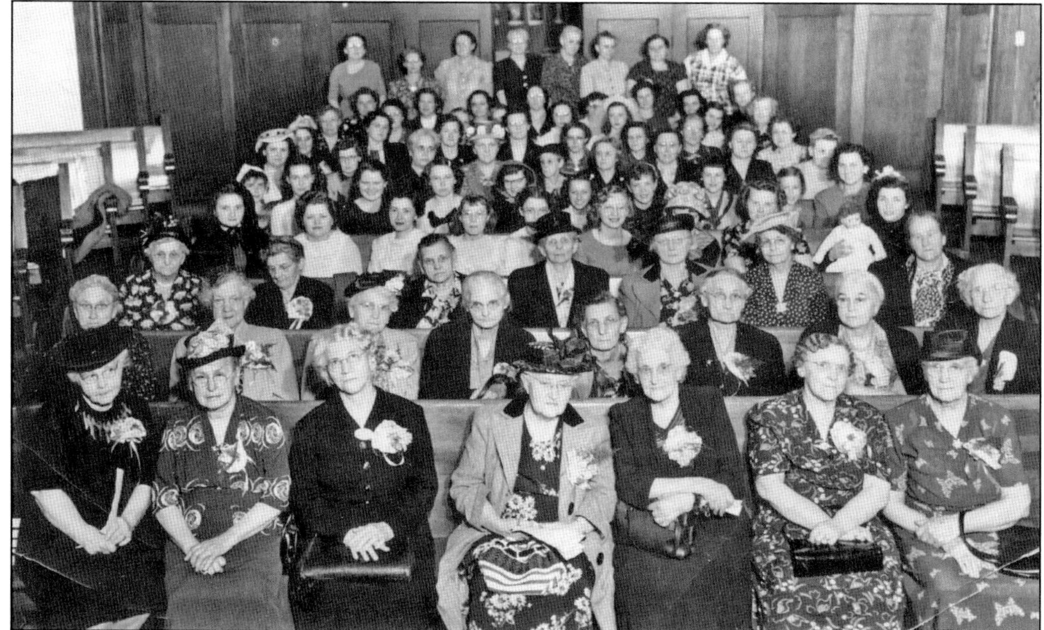

Women of the Church. The women of Prospect Methodist Church fill the pews in this 1950s-era photograph. While the exact occasion is unknown, based on the older attendees having corsages, it is likely a celebration honoring those who had obtained a certain status. (Courtesy of Jane Burkett.)

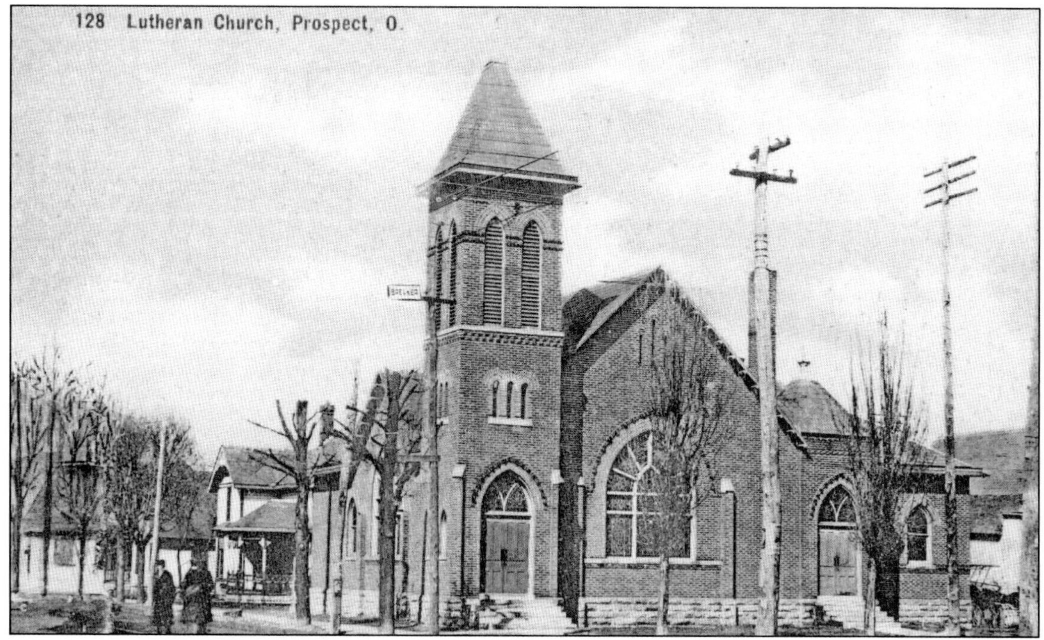

Lutheran Church. The Lutheran congregation first met in the home of village founder Christian Gast II around 1816. In 1849, a one-room brick church was built on the current site, but it was replaced after fire destroyed the structure. The current building was erected in 1892 at a cost of approximately $6,600. It featured a worship area measuring 54 feet by 36 feet and additional room for Sunday school classes. (Courtesy of Richard Carey.)

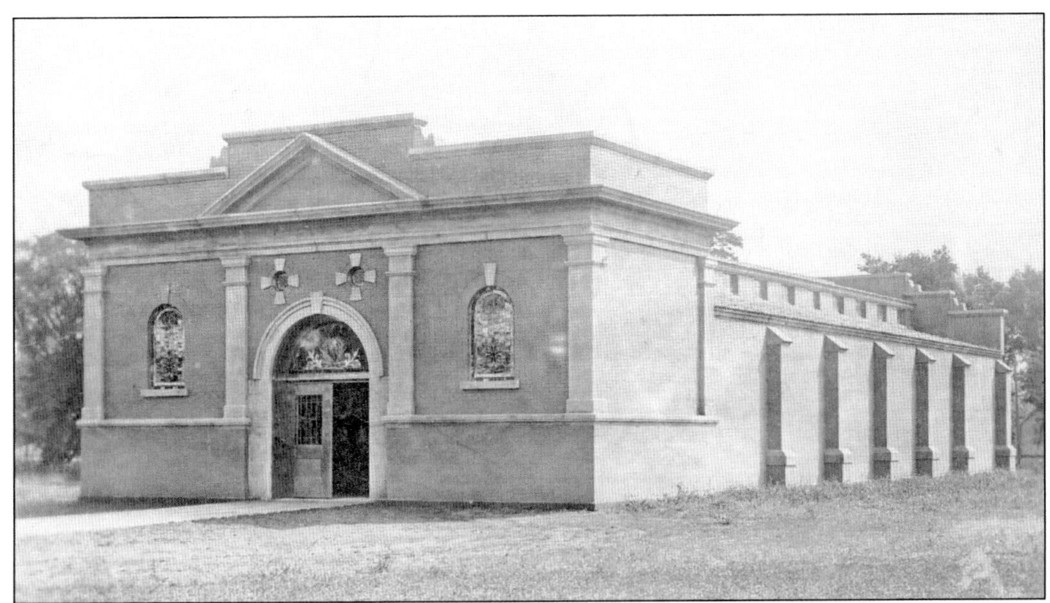

PROSPECT'S MAUSOLEUM. The first burials in Prospect Cemetery occurred in 1836. This mausoleum, located within the cemetery boundaries, was dedicated in August 1912. It featured stained-glass windows and marble floors. Due to structural weakness and less-than-stable ground, the mausoleum was razed in 1966, with the remains of those interred moved to a burial area in the back of the cemetery. Name stones from the mausoleum were reused as grave markers. (Courtesy of Rebecca Jacobs Rynders.)

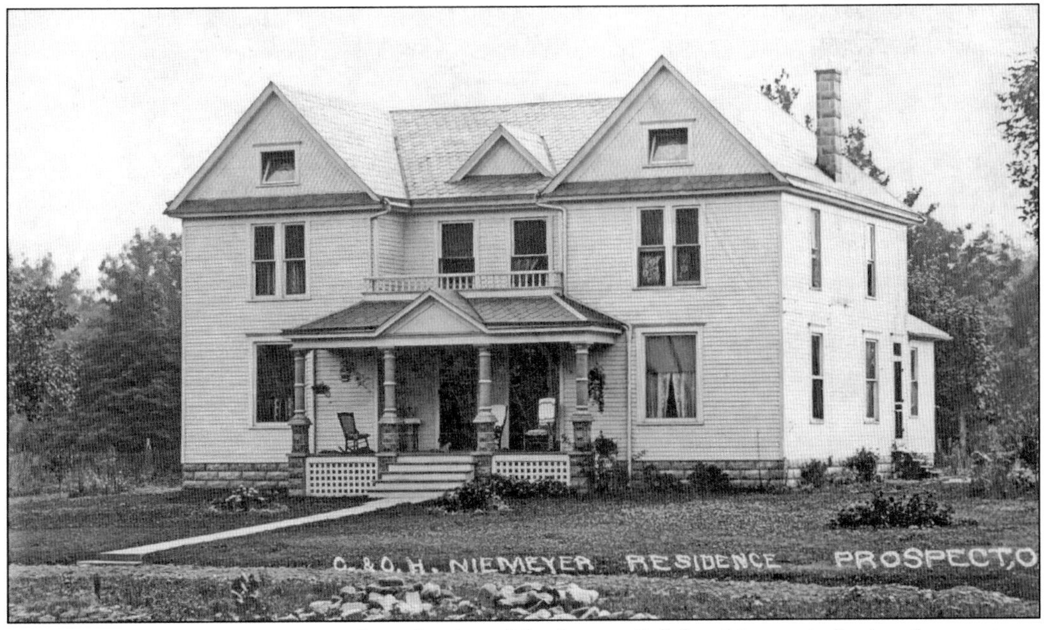

NEIMEYER RESIDENCE. Located on the site of the former Sulpho-Magnetic Spring Sanatorium, the home of Conrad and Sarah Neimeyer and their son, Oliver, is evidence of Conrad's success as a carpenter and hardware merchant. Oliver worked as a professional photographer and a state game warden. He also raced bicycles and trained hunting dogs while maintaining a small menagerie known as "Ollie's Zoo." (Courtesy of Bob Turner.)

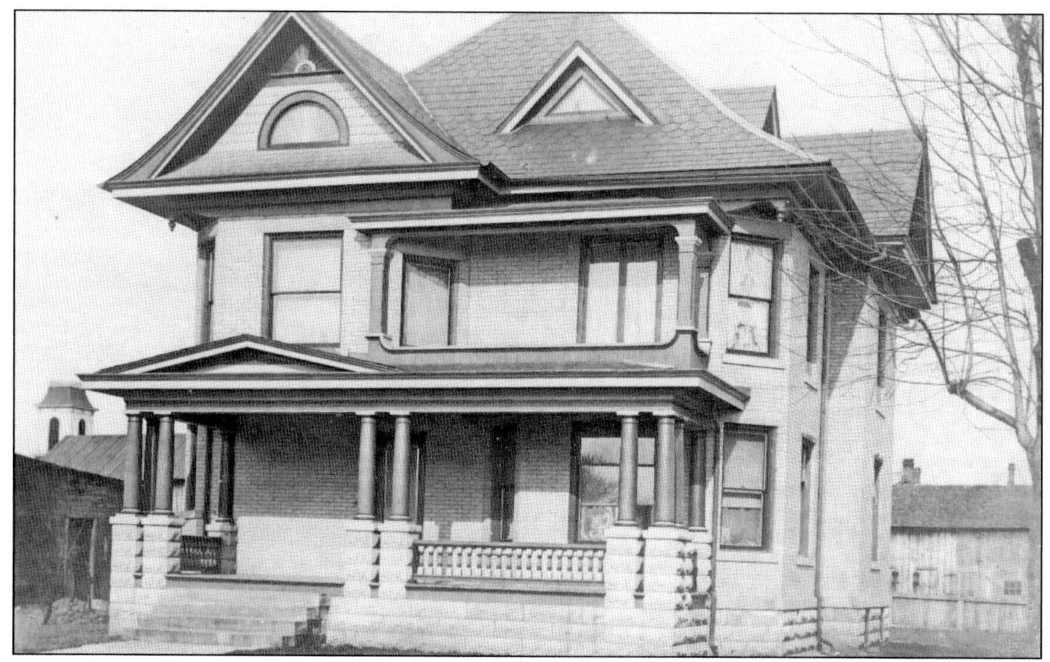

DOCTOR'S OFFICE. Dr. Robert T. Gray, who had his office in this building on South Main Street, provided medical care for generations of Prospect residents. Dr. Gray started his Prospect practice in 1938. In addition to his role as family physician, he served as Marion County coroner for many years. His involvement with the Boy Scouts of America earned him recognition on a national level. (Courtesy of Ellis and Margaret Hudson.)

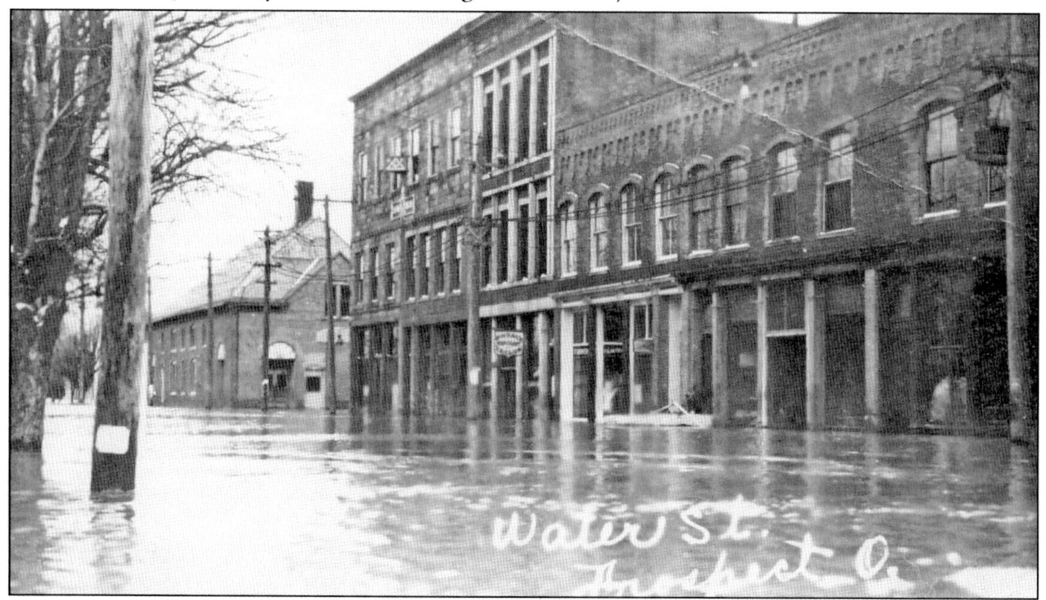

A FITTING STREET NAME. The village of Prospect experienced the worst flooding in its history after four days of steady rain in late March 1913. Streets in the downtown area (including Water Street, which is pictured here) were inundated, with more than 10 feet of floodwater from the Scioto River flowing through the village. Temperatures hovered around the freezing mark, making conditions even more miserable. (Author's collection.)

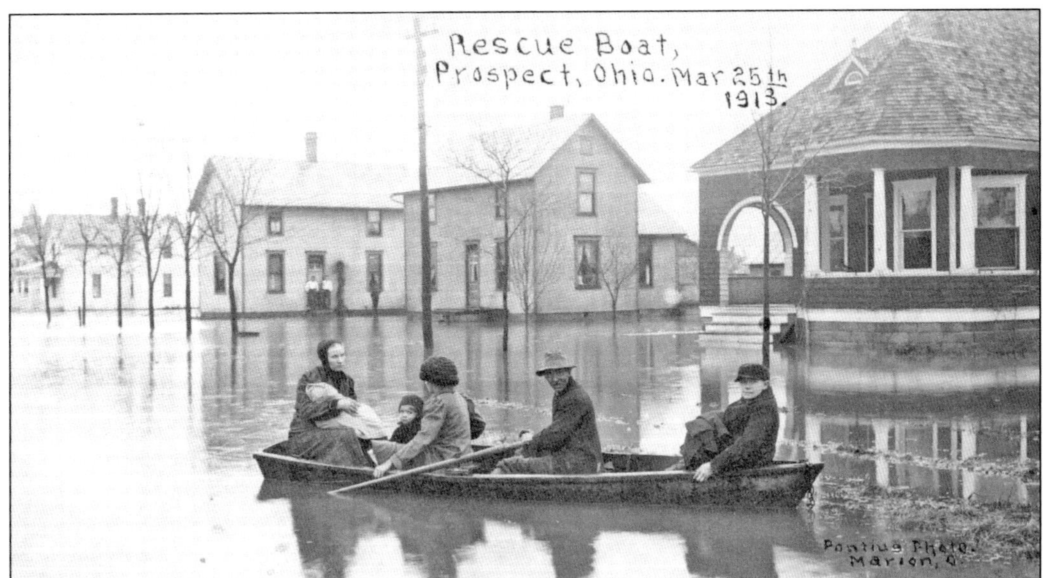

Rescue in Progress. In the course of the 1913 flood, residents moved furniture, themselves, and occasionally even their livestock to the upper floors of their homes to avoid the rising waters. Telephone operators at the second-floor location of the Prospect Telephone Company stayed at their stations until they were finally forced to leave the building through a second-floor window. This photograph was taken at North and Sixth Streets, where the water did not reach the depths found downtown. (Author's collection.)

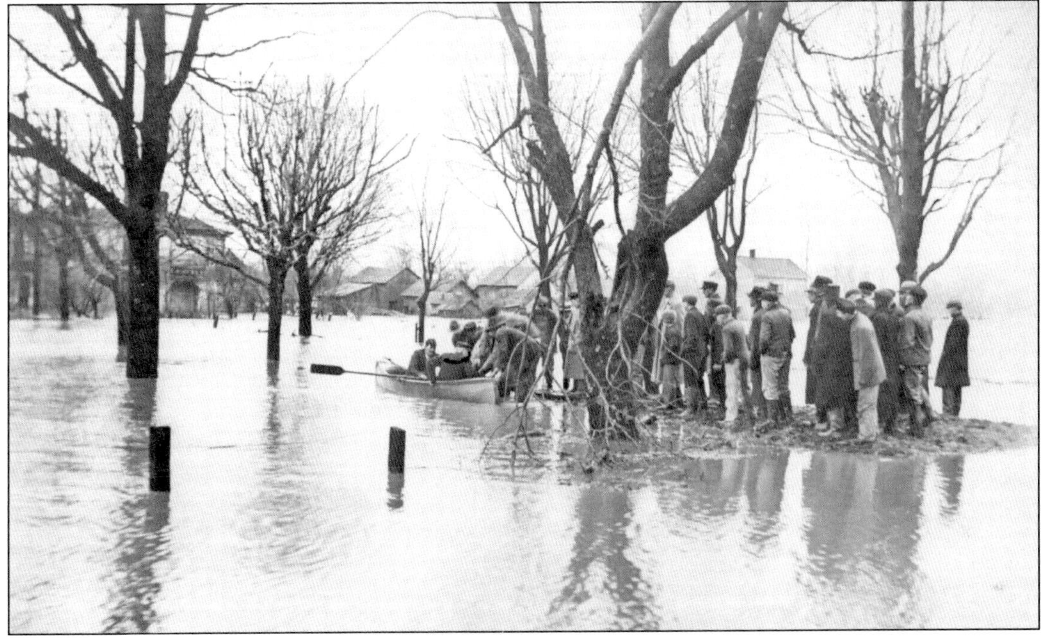

Stranded. Rescue efforts often relied on people with small boats. These were later supplemented by four lifesaving boats sent from Lake Erie by order of the governor. In more than one instance, boats were rowed into the ground floors of homes to rescue stranded residents. While no loss of life was reported in Prospect, efforts to save livestock were not as successful, with one farmer reporting the loss of 150 sheep and 80 hogs. (Author's collection.)

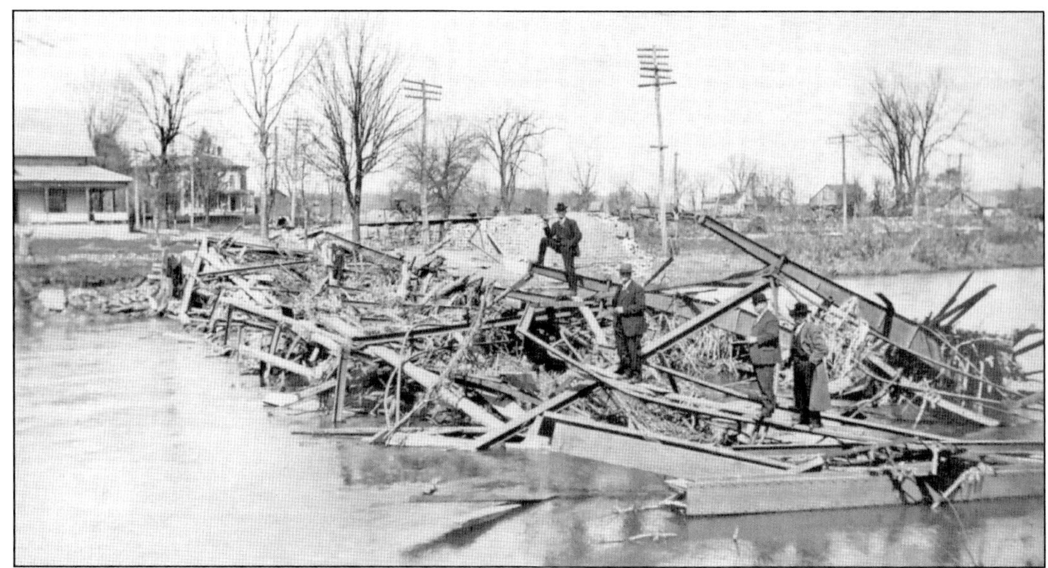

DEMOLISHED. Bridges along the length of the Scioto River were destroyed in the flooding, as demonstrated in this photograph of the remains of the Prospect bridge. From the Newmans bridge (north of Prospect) to the Fifth Avenue bridge in Columbus, only one bridge withstood the floodwaters. Residents of the Hoskins area captured their bridge as it floated off the foundation and secured it with ropes to prevent it from floating downstream and possibly destroying the Lavender bridge, which remained intact. (Author's collection.)

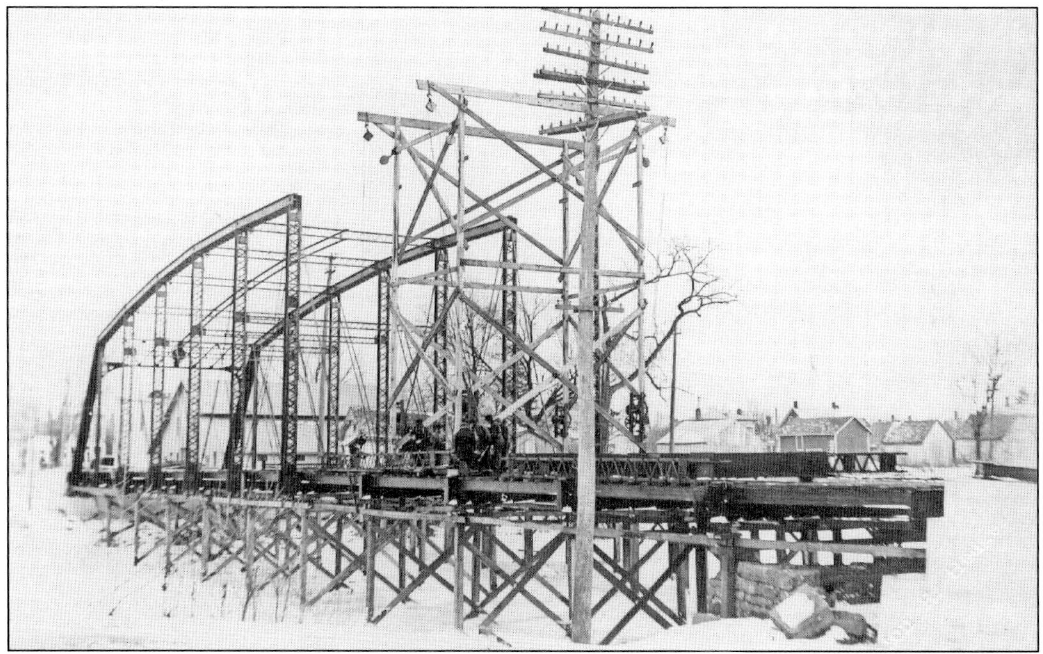

NEW BRIDGE. A new steel bridge spanning 217 feet across the river was soon started, with completion achieved late in 1913. The Parker through-truss design was used to help withstand the frequent flooding of the Scioto River. This bridge underwent a major rehabilitation in 1985. Continued deterioration, along with a heavy traffic load, led to it being replaced in 2007. (Author's collection.)

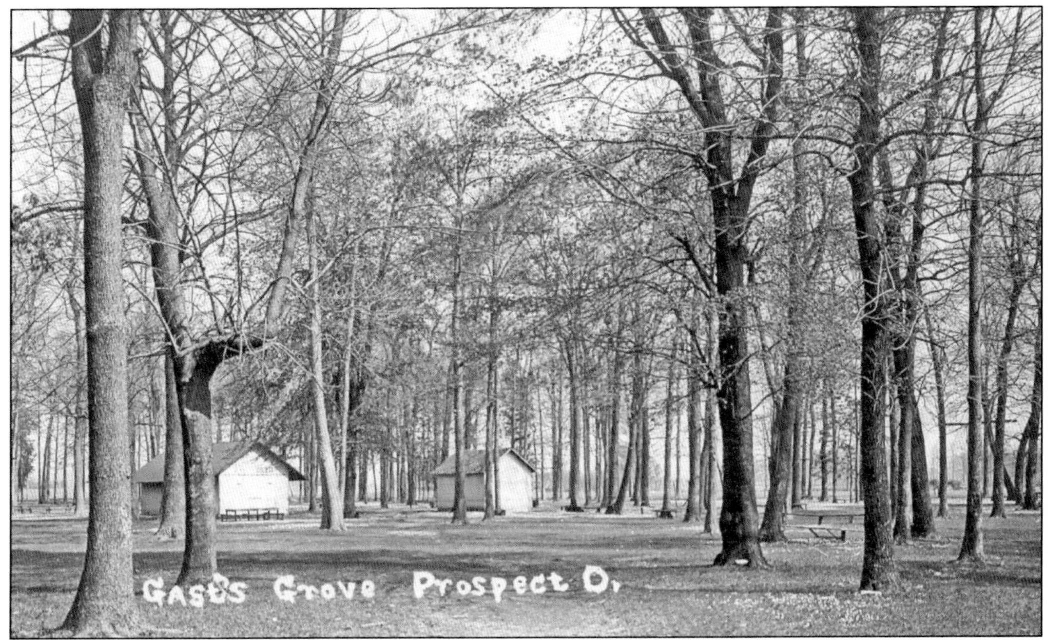

PROSPECT PARK. Situated on the south side of the village adjacent to Battle Run, Gast's Grove was an immensely popular area for gatherings such as the 1898 Marion County Farmer's Institute attended by more than 5,000 people. The village purchased approximately nine acres of the grove in 1926 for development as a park. In 1997, they paid $100,000 to purchase an additional 27 acres with funds raised from a park tax levy. (Author's collection.)

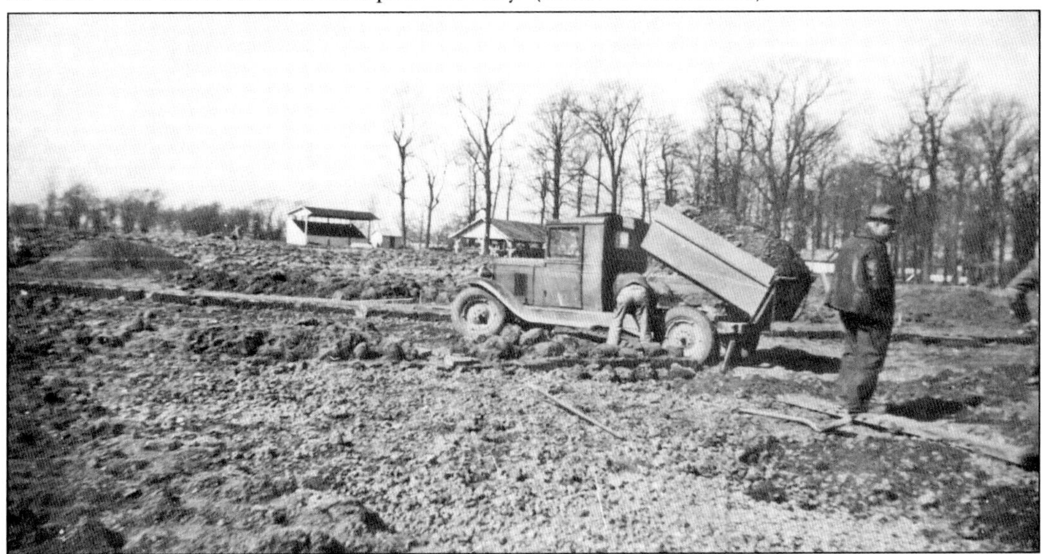

PARK IMPROVEMENTS. Improvements in the park (including a quarter-mile running track, stone fence, and grandstand) were completed in the 1930s as Works Progress Administration (WPA) projects. Additional enhancements over the years include three baseball fields, walking trails, an extensive playground area, and several shelter houses. There is also a large area of wooded green space and a veteran's memorial. Prospect Park is the site of several annual events throughout each year, including a Fourth of July celebration that attracts spectators from miles around. (Courtesy of Jane Burkett.)

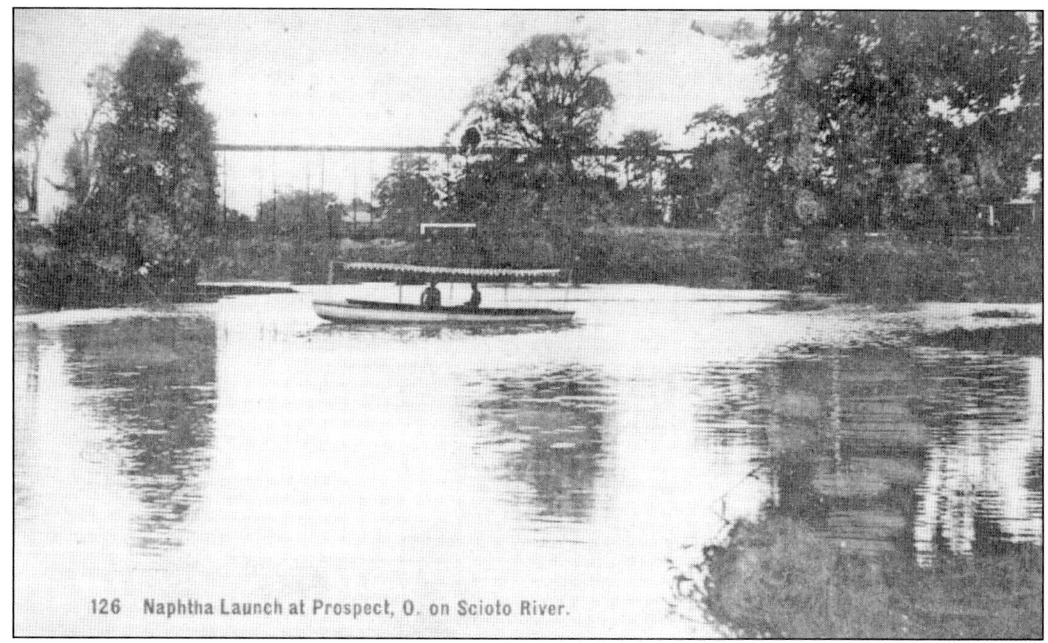

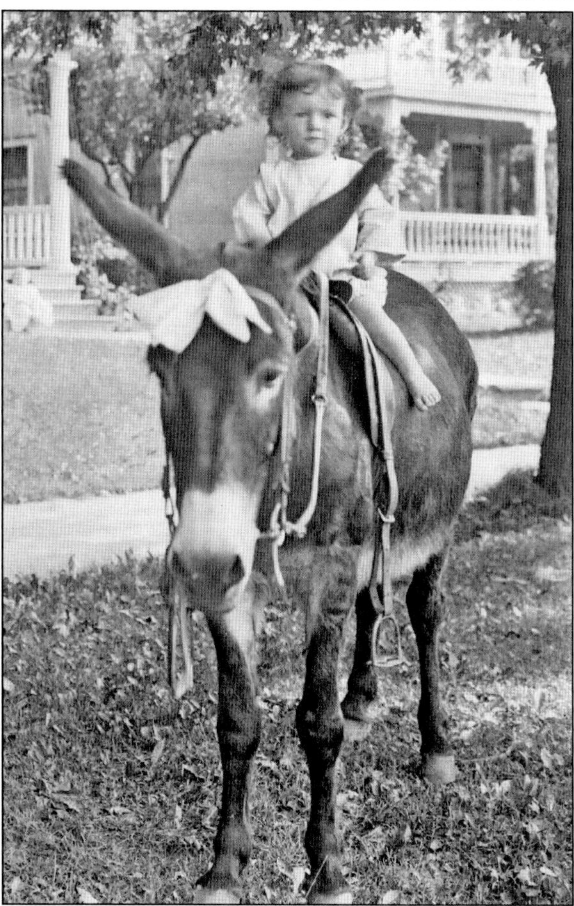

OUT FOR A RIDE. Taking a ride up the Scioto River from Prospect to Green Camp was an enjoyable activity around the end of the 19th century. In 1892, S.L. Wottring and W. McPherson of Prospect built a steam-powered boat and christened it the *Gazelle*. The boat was 30 feet long and had a 20-passenger capacity. In later years, another boat, the *Naphtha*, made the trip, which included a pass through the scenic Mirror Bend. (Courtesy of Ralph and Erdine Eaton collection.)

GIDDY-UP! With a look that perhaps says, "I think I like this," this youngster sits astride a mule that may have been having the same thought. Posed pictures taken by traveling photographers and featuring children sitting in wagons pulled by goats or perhaps eggshell carts "pulled" by chicks were treasured mementos for many families. Adults might be pictured "ascending" in hot-air balloons with scenic mountain views in the background despite a sign on the balloon basket that read "Flying High in Prospect." (Courtesy of Ralph and Erdine Eaton collection.)

Seven

WALDO AREA

In 1806, the Nathaniel Brundige and Nathaniel Wyatt families settled in Marlborough (later spelled "Marlboro") Township in what was then Delaware County. Brundige entered into an agreement with a land speculator for the purchase of land at an exorbitant price of $2.50 per acre, which was more than twice what the speculator had paid. The Brundiges soon established a homestead, and the development of what would become Waldo Township began. The Wyatts also established themselves with the construction of a two-story brick tavern near the banks of the Whetstone (now Olentangy) River north of present-day Norton. When the threat of hostilities arose during the War of 1812, the Wyatt residence was incorporated into a palisade fort known as Fort Morrow. The fort was to be used as a place of refuge as well as a stop for troops and other travelers passing through the area on a military road that ran from Delaware to Lower Sandusky (Fremont). After the war ended and the need for a fort was no longer imperative, Wyatt continued to operate the tavern as a gathering place and hotel for travelers on their way through the area.

In 1831, Milo D. Pettibone platted a village and started a new settlement about two miles northwest of the tavern. Pettibone, a Delaware attorney and a land speculator, once owned more than 900 acres in what would eventually become Waldo Township. Pettibone named his new settlement Waldo in honor of his son. Part of the land encompassed by the village had once been owned by Robert Hayes, father of Pres. Rutherford B. Hayes, but issues regarding nonpayment of taxes resulted in Hayes forfeiting the land. The village became incorporated in 1845. The village and much of the surrounding area below the Greenville Treaty Line became part of Marion County's newly established Waldo Township in 1848. The new township was formed with land taken primarily from Marlboro Township in Delaware County as "compensation" for territory that had been taken from the eastern part of Marion County to help create Morrow County. Additional land for Waldo Township came from Pleasant Township, which was located north of the Greenville Treaty Line, as the result of a petition to the Marion County Commissioners by Waldo Township residents.

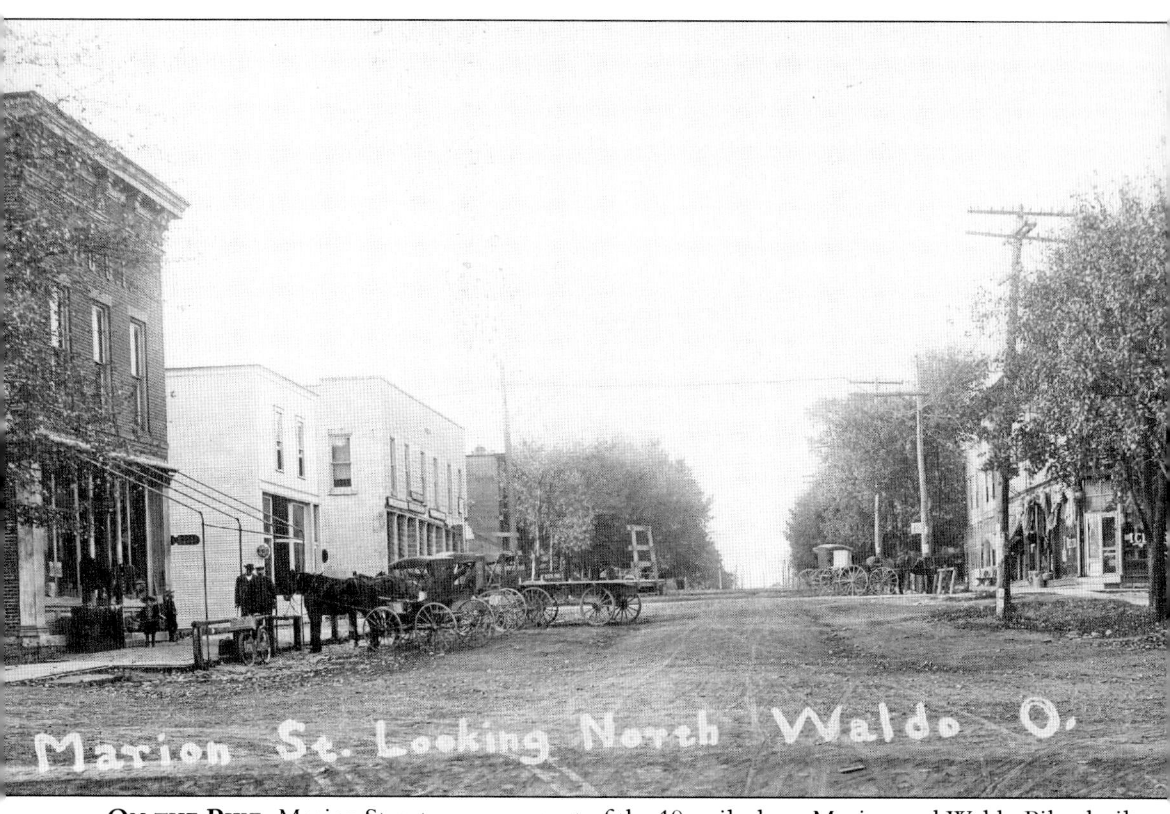

On the Pike. Marion Street was once part of the 10-mile-long Marion and Waldo Pike, built around 1868 at a cost of $21,000. Improvements to the roadway included ditching and graveling. Toll gates were erected to collect the revenue needed to repay investors in the Marion and Waldo Pike Company. Charges to travel on pikes varied: a four-wheel carriage with one horse was 15¢, a sleigh with two horses was 10¢, and each head of cattle driven in a drove was 1¢. Exempt from the charge were ministers or those on military duty, as well as those traveling to elections, funerals, or church. The pike eventually became Ohio State Route 23 and then State Route 423. (Courtesy of Ralph and Erdine Eaton collection.)

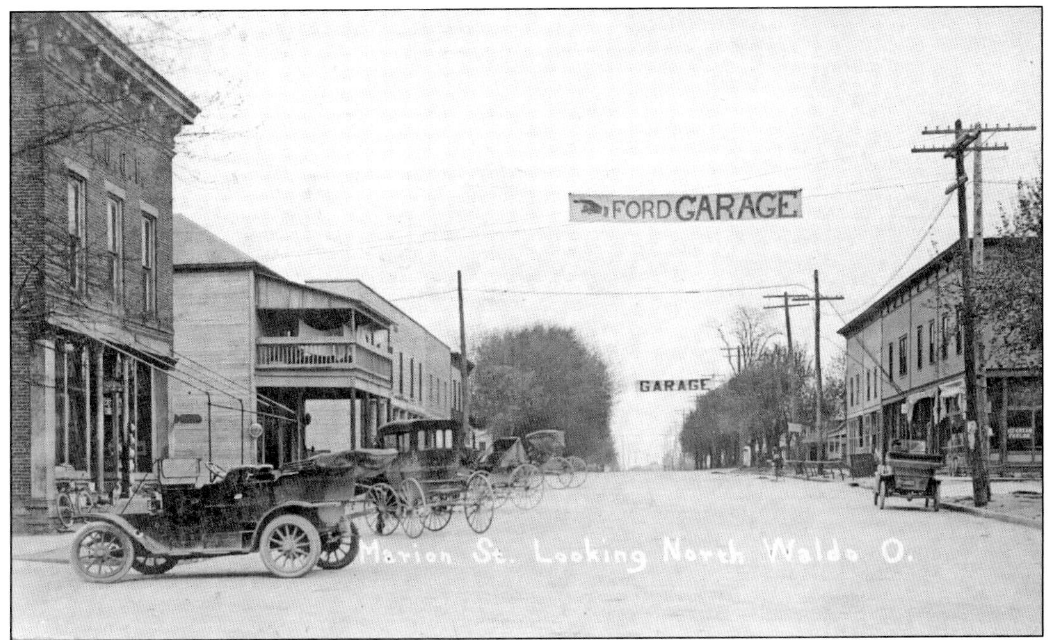

REPAIR SERVICES AVAILABLE. Automobiles, such as these Model Ts traveling through the village, could take advantage of well-advertised garages, while John Smith's blacksmith shop was available for buggy repairs. The building at left with the second-floor porch housed numerous grocery stores and restaurants over the years before eventually becoming the home of the famous G&R Tavern fried bologna sandwich. (Courtesy of Richard Carey.)

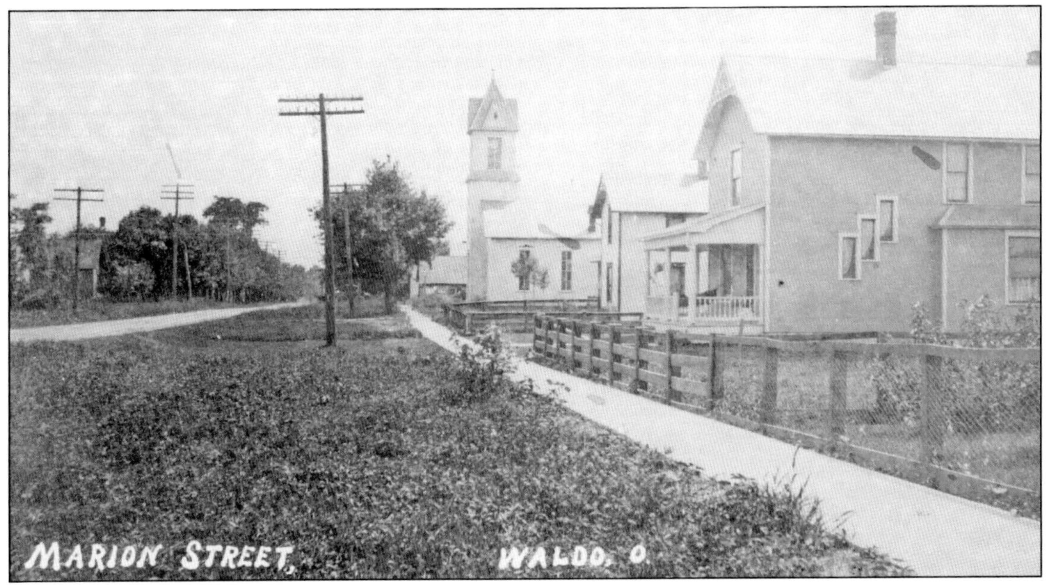

SOUTHERN VIEW. While the exact date of this photograph looking south on Marion Street from the current junction with State Route 98 is not known, it would have been some time after the 1894 installation of telephone service by the Central Union Telephone Company. A home featuring unusual staircase windows is shown at right, along with the Reformed church farther down the street. (Courtesy of Ellis and Margaret Hudson.)

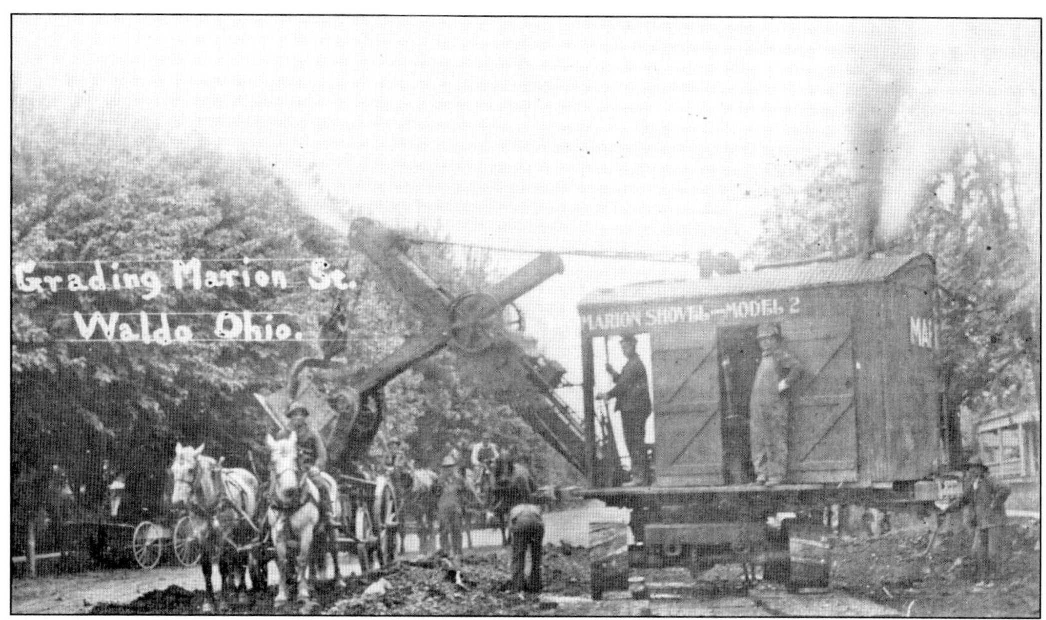

GRADING IN WALDO. Waldo is only a few miles from Marion, which was a mecca of steam shovel manufacturing. In fact, Marion earned the nickname "Shovel City" due to the number of steam shovels produced there. The largest producer of shovels was the Marion Steam Shovel Company; their Model 2 is pictured shooting smoke from the coal-fired boiler into the air while grading Marion Street. (Author's collection.)

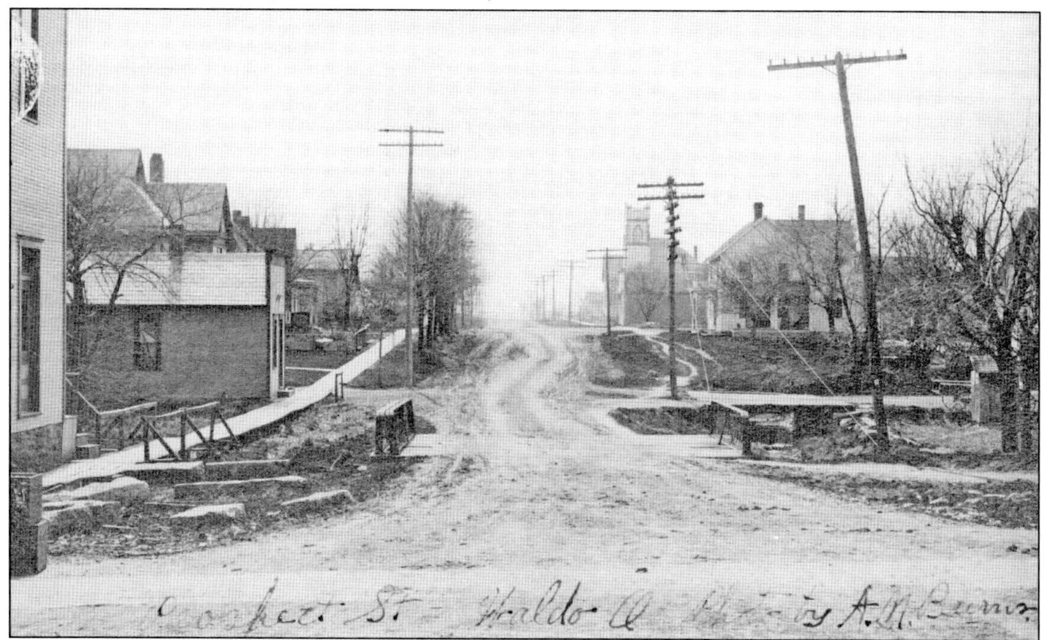

TOMAHAWK CREEK. Prospect Street (later renamed Main Street) crossed over the meandering Tomahawk Creek on the west side of Waldo. St. Paul's Lutheran Church is visible in the distance on its original site. The creek gained some local infamy as the site where several swine, which were then allowed to wander freely throughout the village streets, rolled into the water after becoming intoxicated on stale beer discarded from a local tavern. (Courtesy of Richard Carey.)

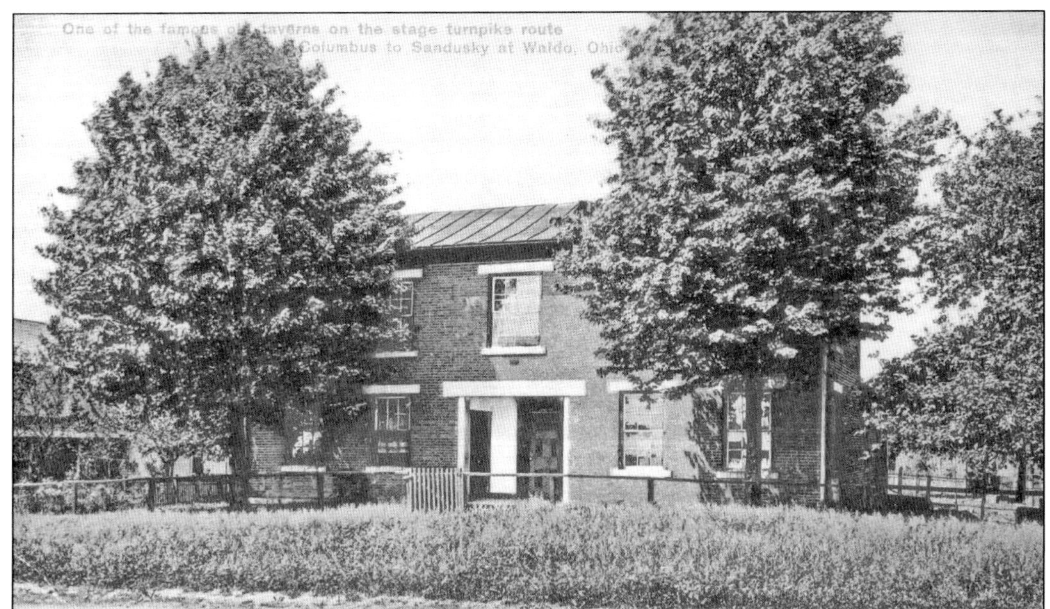

STAGECOACH INN. The Waldo Tavern, built around 1828, was a longtime landmark on Waldo's north end. The tavern served as a stop for stagecoaches traveling the Columbus-Sandusky Turnpike. The downstairs featured a "publick" room and a "common" room, with the upstairs providing lodging. Despite the efforts of local conservation groups, the building was razed in 1986, and the lot now stands vacant. (Courtesy of Richard Carey.)

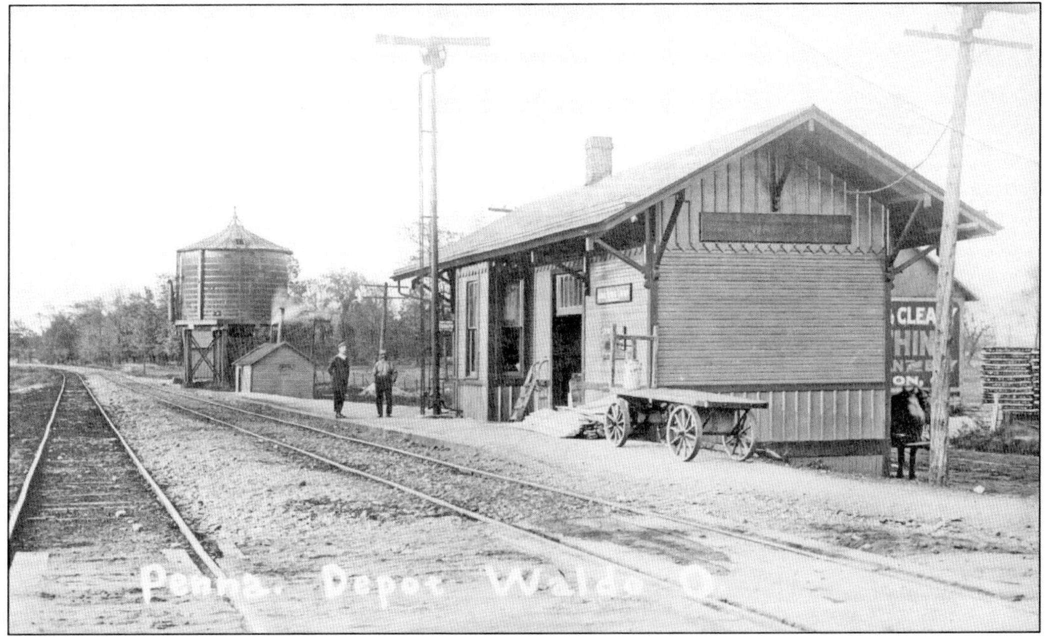

DEPOT. Waldo's train depot once stood on the Pennsylvania Railroad tracks on the west end of the village. A large water tank was available for replenishing steam engines, as were carts for handling items arriving via the American Express shipping service. After the depot was no longer needed for freight or passenger service, it served as a storage and work site for railroad maintenance crews for many years. (Courtesy of Richard Carey.)

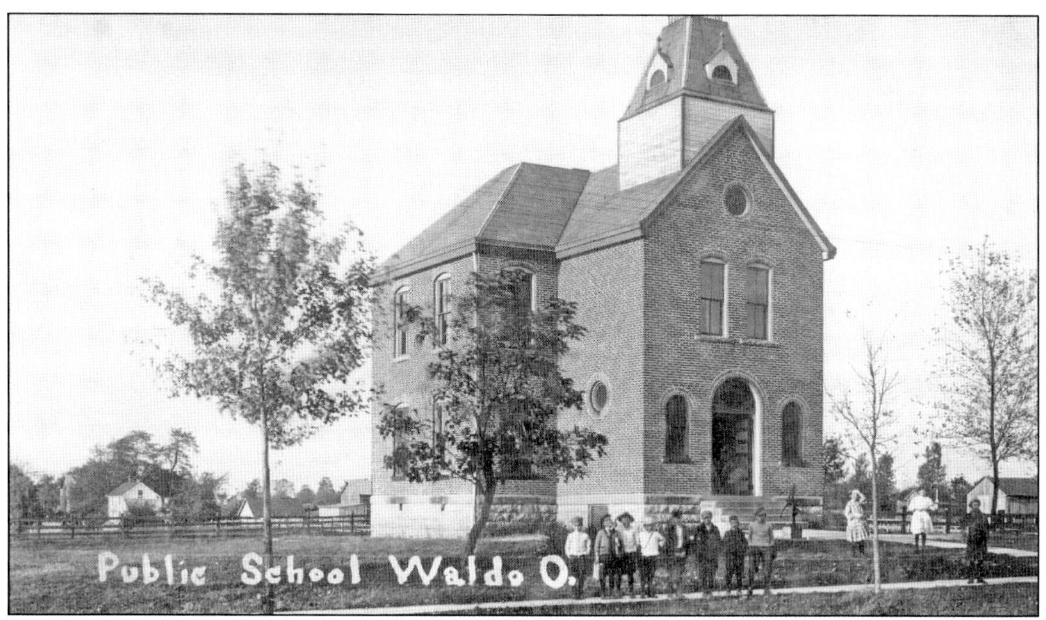

SCHOOL DAYS. Built adjacent to the Lutheran church on Prospect (Main) Street in 1898, the Waldo Union school featured two rooms on the first floor for students in the lower grades, while the second floor housed the upper grades. Classes for some high school students were also held in a small room under the bell tower. Eventually, overcrowding led to some classes being moved to the Waldo Township House. Today, the old school building is a private residence. (Courtesy of Richard Carey.)

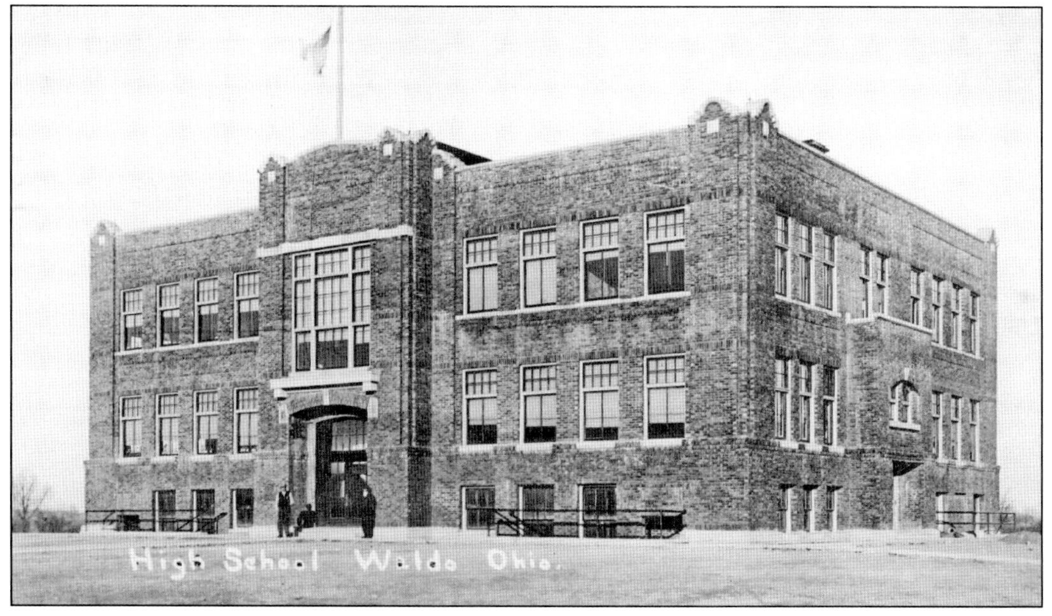

VILLAGE LANDMARK. Centralization of small schools as a result of state mandates led to the construction of larger school buildings such as this one built at the north end of the village in 1917. Expansions over the years included a gymnasium and cafeteria. It served students from the surrounding locale for more than 85 years, with the last high school class graduating in 1962. The building closed in 2005 and was eventually razed. (Courtesy of Richard Carey.)

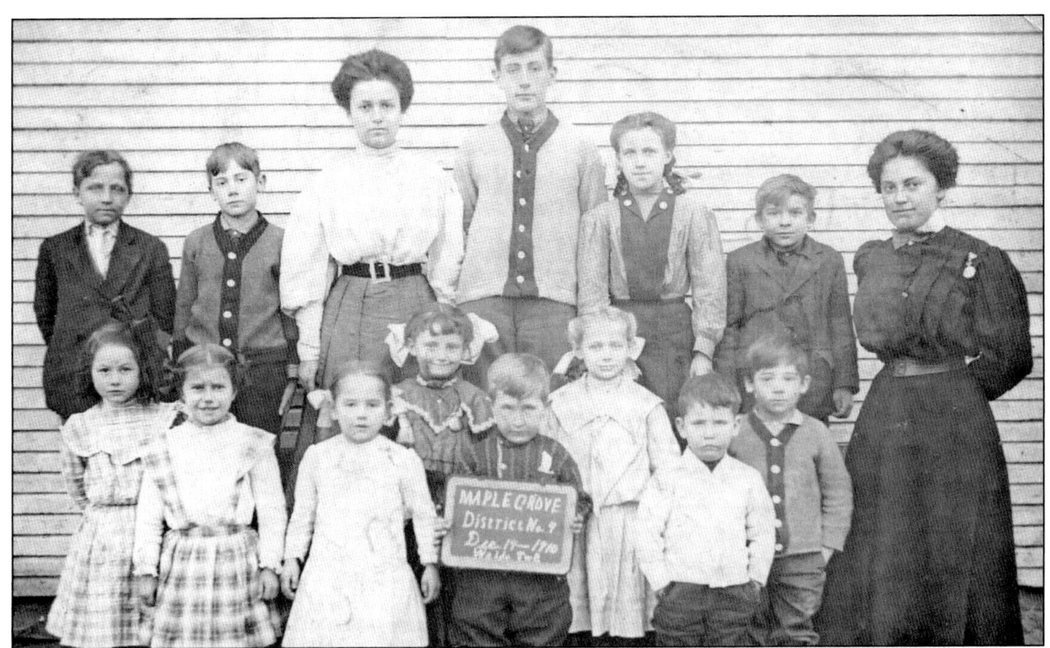

MYSTERY SCHOOL. Although the chalkboard clearly states the name and location of Maple Grove School in Waldo Township, no records of the school have surfaced despite extensive research. The designations of "sub-district" and "district" were often used interchangeably, resulting in confusion when trying to determine school locations. (Courtesy of Mike and Linda Perry.)

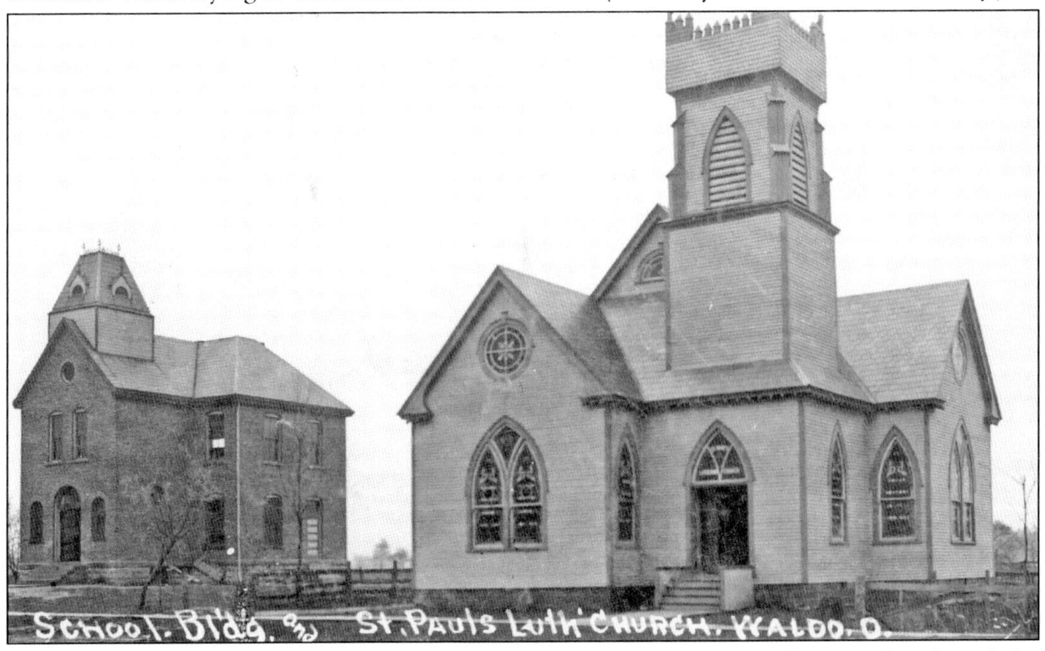

DUELING BELLS? While it is doubtful that the bells of St. Paul's Lutheran Church and the adjacent Union School were ever engaged in a dueling bells competition, their proximity would have made it quite possible. St. Paul's was completed in 1902, and renovations over the years included the raising of the building for a basement. It was used for services until 1972, when a new church building was completed. (Courtesy of Richard Carey.)

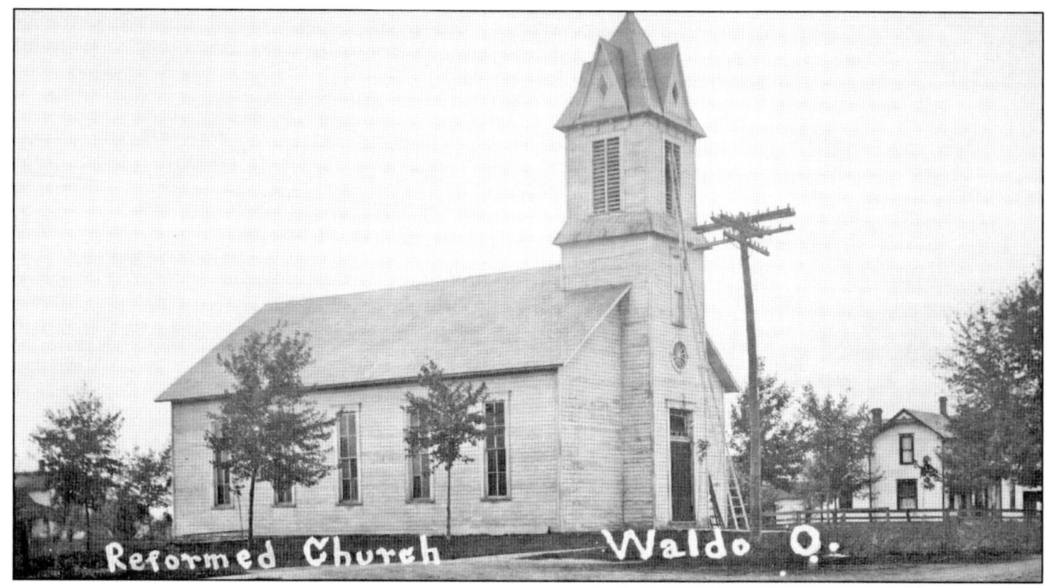

Reformed Church. The Reformed church in Waldo was known to village residents as the German Reformed Church. Located north of the village center, the building served the congregation well for many years before the church sold it after it merged with another congregation and moved to a new location. The steeple, which was apparently in need of maintenance in this picture (as evidenced by the ladders), was later removed, and the building was repurposed for retail sales. (Courtesy of Richard Carey.)

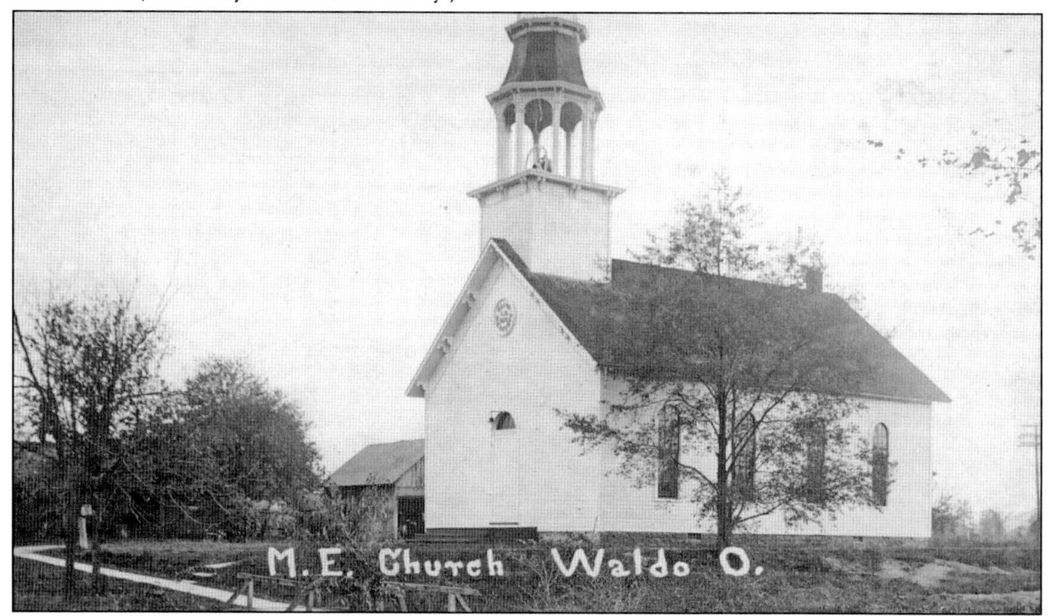

Methodist Episcopal. The Methodist congregation of the Waldo area began meeting in homes around 1834 and erected a church in 1838 at the south end of the village. The need for additional space led to them constructing a new building in 1877 at a cost of $2,000. It consisted of one large room with two stoves for heating. Over the years, more rooms were added, as well as a full basement. In 1953, the sanctuary was reversed so the congregation would face east while worshipping. (Courtesy of Richard Carey.)

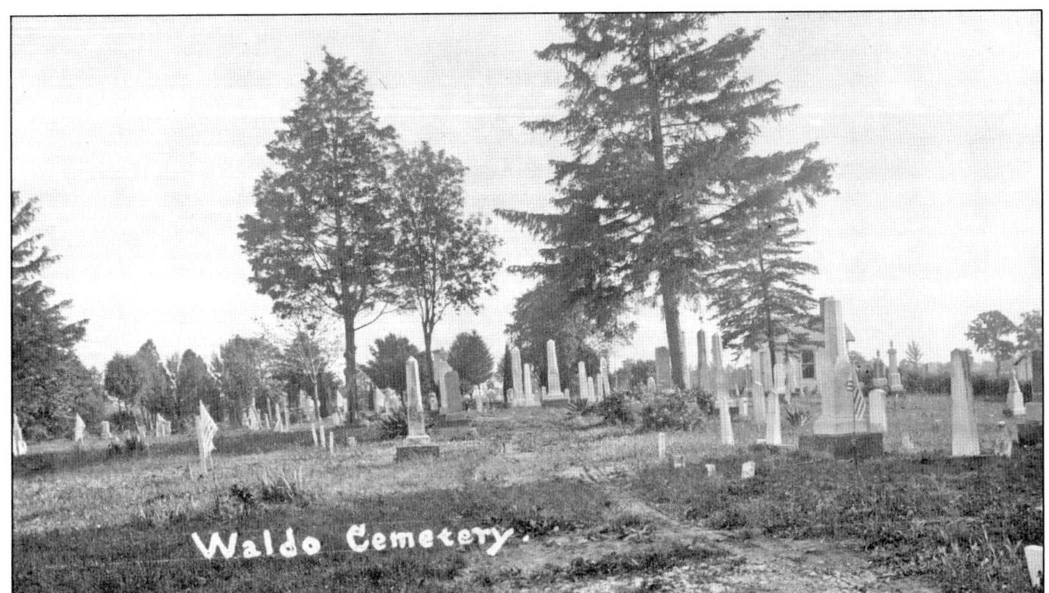

Final Rest. The Waldo Cemetery, located on Main Street across from the old Lutheran church, is a community cemetery not affiliated with any specific church. Nearby Wyatt Cemetery is the oldest cemetery in Marion County. Many veterans are buried there, including 13 unknown soldiers from the War of 1812. Ruth Wyatt, the first non–Native American child born in Marion County, is also interred there. Wyatt Cemetery is close to the site of Fort Morrow and a short distance from Mayfield Cemetery, another pioneer cemetery. (Courtesy of Richard Carey.)

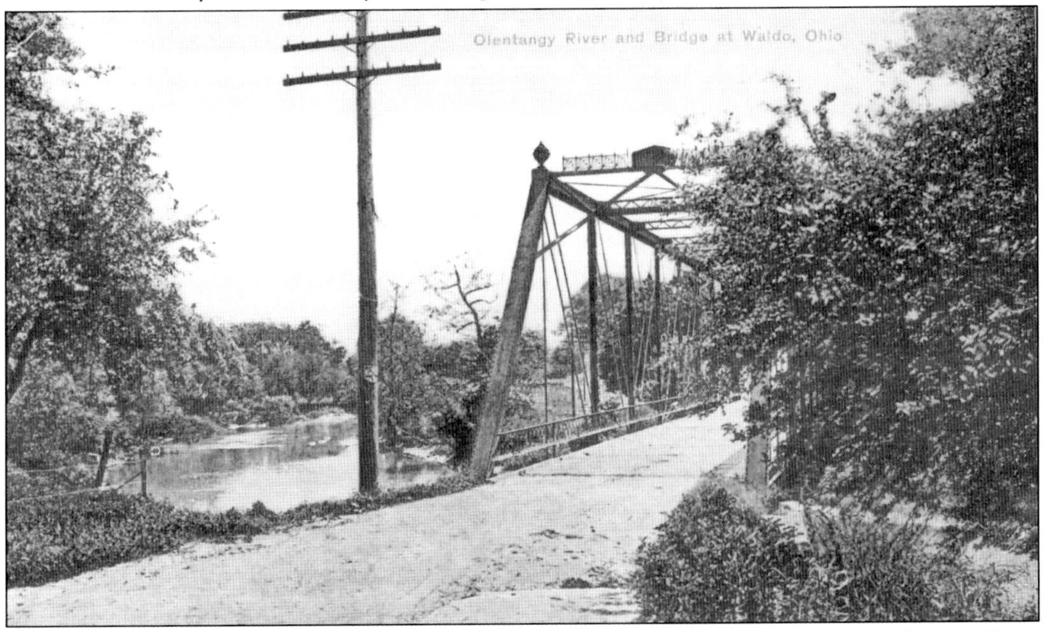

Crossing the Olentangy. Travelers heading east from Waldo through the village park on Main Street crossed this sturdy bridge over the Olentangy River for many years. The need for it was eliminated in 1951, when the US Army Corps of Engineers constructed a dam and levee as part of the Delaware Lake flood control project. The 3.5-mile-long project cost $4.3 million. (Courtesy of Stuart Koblentz Haley.)

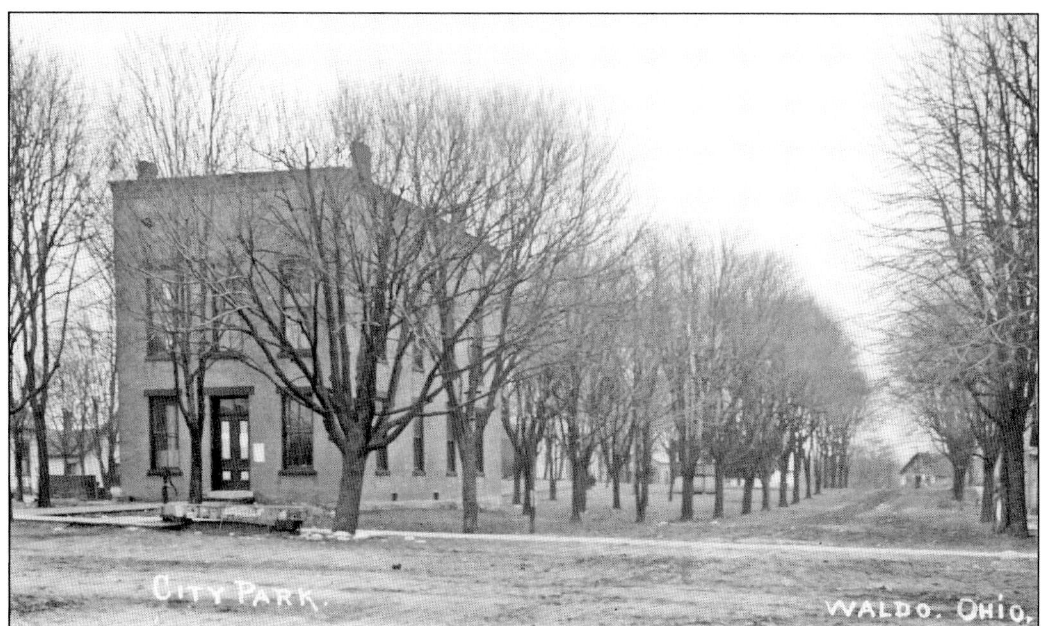

PEACEFUL PARK. Waldo was rightfully proud of its scenic park, which featured a bandstand and gazebos. The township hall, which was also used by the village, still stands at the north edge of the park location. The hall had meeting rooms and a small jail on the lower floor, with a theater on the second floor. The installation of a dam and flood control levee in 1951 virtually eliminated the park and several surrounding homes and businesses. (Courtesy of Richard Carey.)

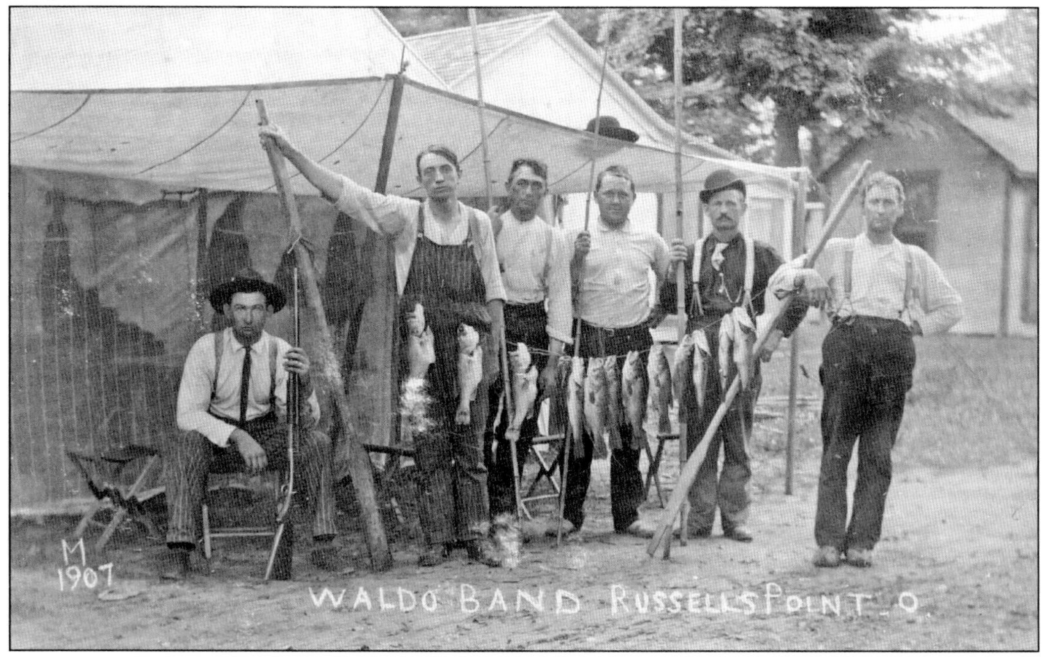

QUITE A CATCH. Members of the Waldo Band are shown displaying the results of a 1907 fishing excursion at Russell's Point on Indian Lake in Logan County. Apparently, their cane fishing poles were quite adequate to catch the evening's dinner. Many communities had small bands of which they were rightfully proud, and Waldo was no exception. (Courtesy of Richard Carey.)

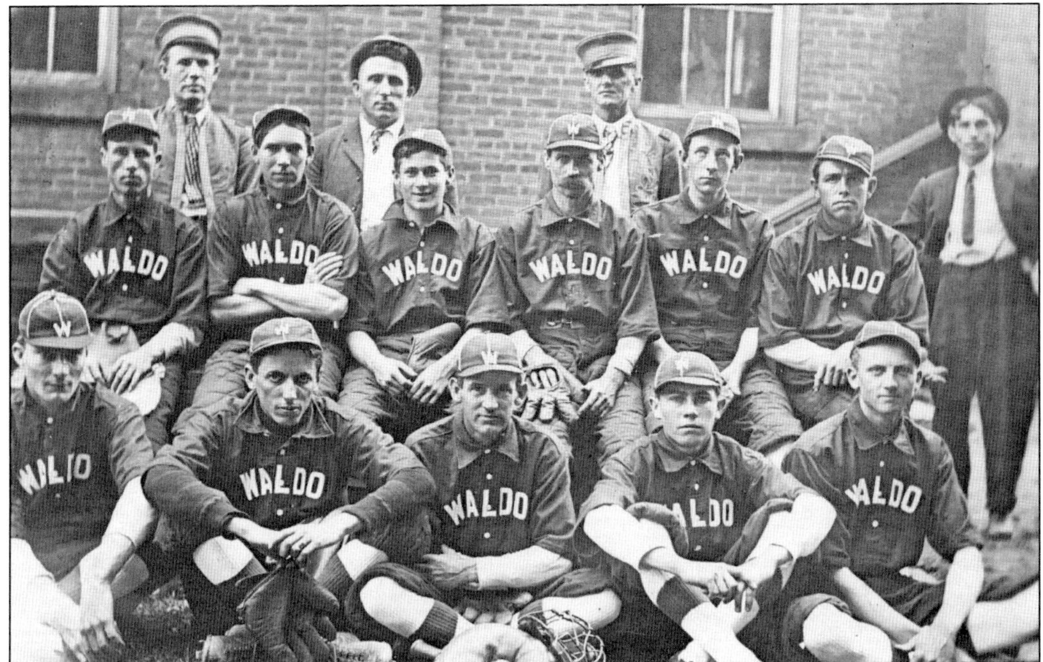

Batter Up. The Waldo baseball team posed for this team photograph around 1900. It is unknown why the two gentlemen in the back row have on what appear to be band or perhaps fire department uniforms, although the fire department was located nearby. (Courtesy of Richard Carey.)

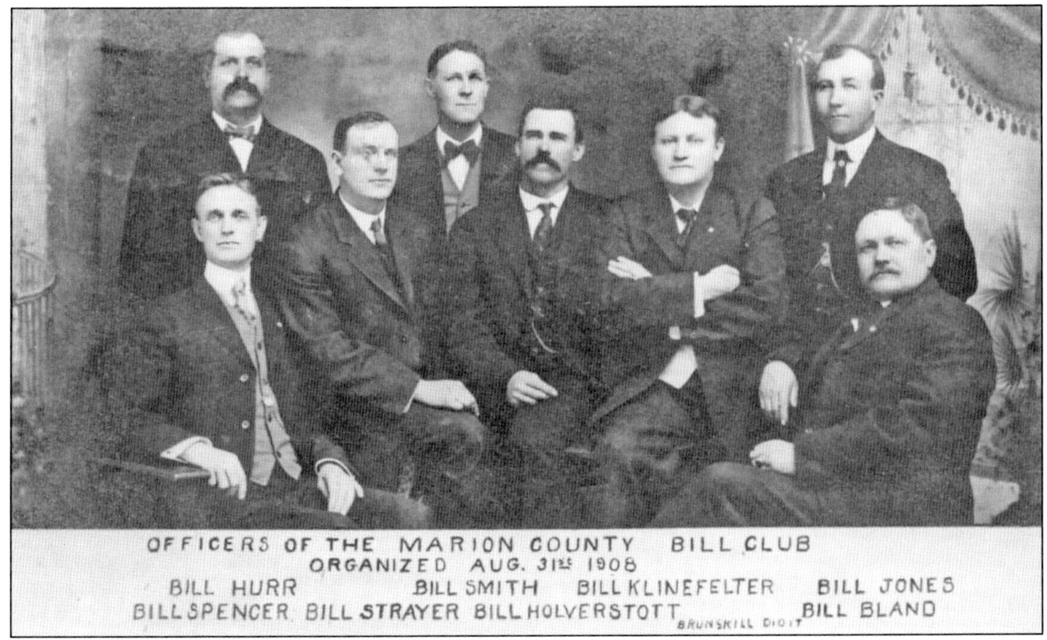

Know Anyone Named Bill? The Bill Club was certainly one of the most unusual social clubs in the area. Little is known of the organization other than that the primary requirement for membership was that one had to be named "Bill." The club began around 1908 and was in existence for at least five years. Both Marion and Waldo had clubs, with the Waldo club having at least 23 members. (Author's collection.)

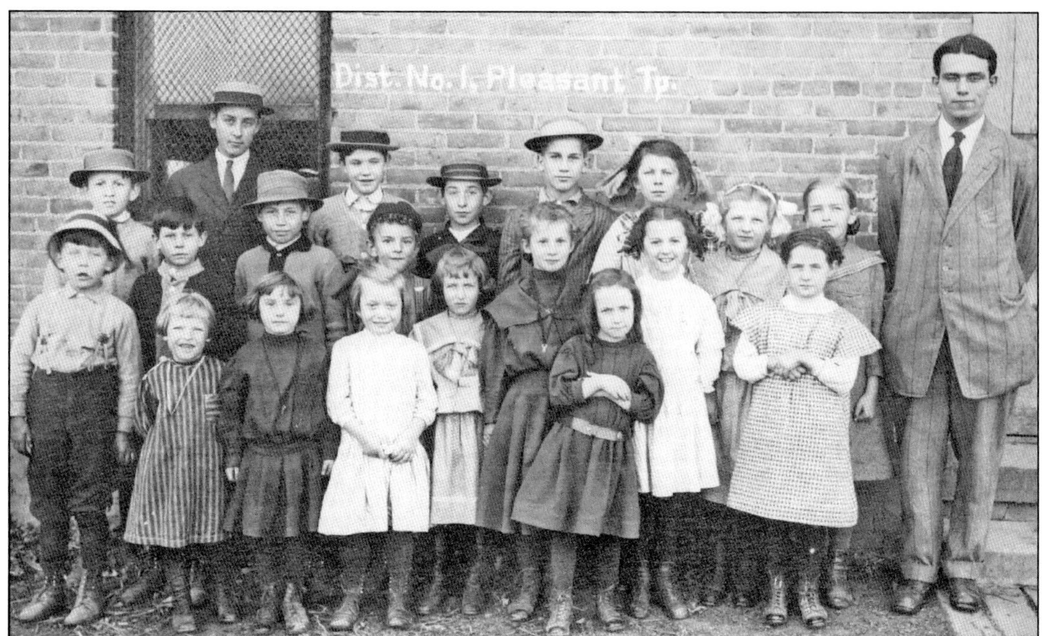

Pleasant Students. The students at District No. 1 School in Pleasant Township, also known as the Idleman School, were sporting their Sunday best while posing with their teacher. The school was located on Marion-Waldo Road south of Benzler-Lust Road. (Courtesy of Marion County Historical Society.)

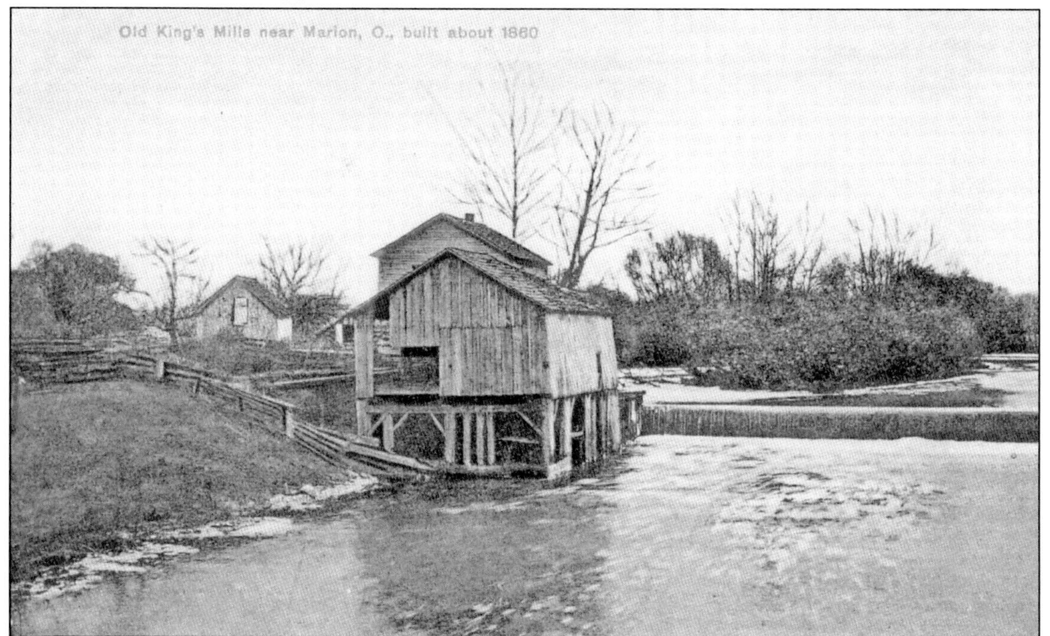

King's Mills. Titus King established a series of mills on the Olentangy River north of Waldo beginning in 1827. Among the services offered were carding, fulling, wood sawing, and grain grinding. Each of the mills had its own waterwheel fed from a communal flume. In 1907, the last of the mills was disassembled and moved to the Neidhardt farm in Pleasant Township. (Author's collection.)

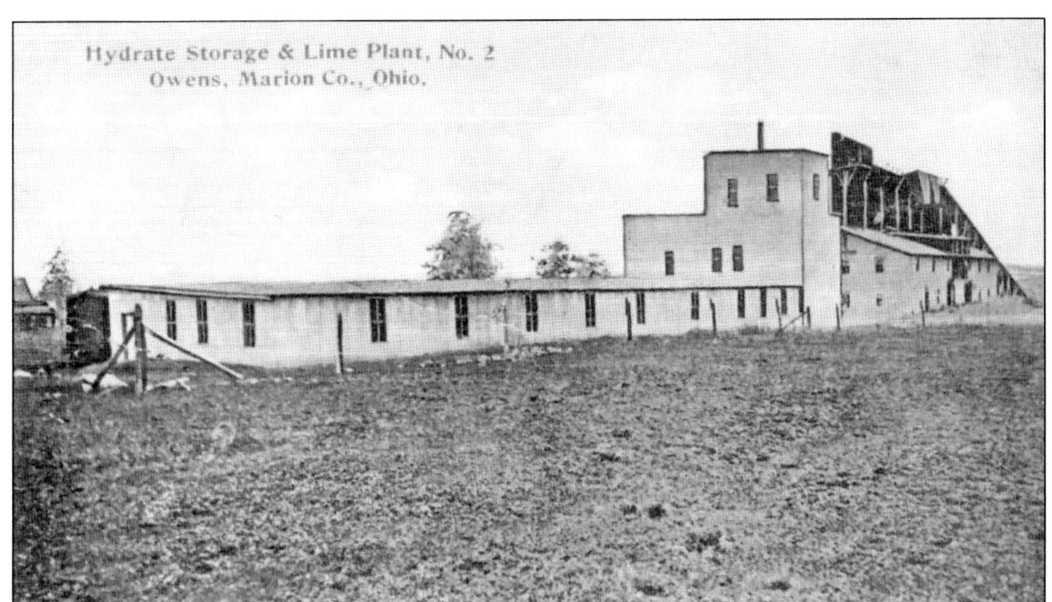

OWENS STATION. John D. Owens began quarry operations in Pleasant Township in the early 1860s. His business grew, and a company town soon developed around the quarry operation. In addition to more than 25 houses, a boardinghouse, an opera house, a general store, a train depot, a schoolhouse, and a livestock exchange were also part of Owens Station. The quarrying operation ceased soon after Owens' death in 1929, and the village eventually achieved "ghost" status. (Courtesy of Richard Carey.)

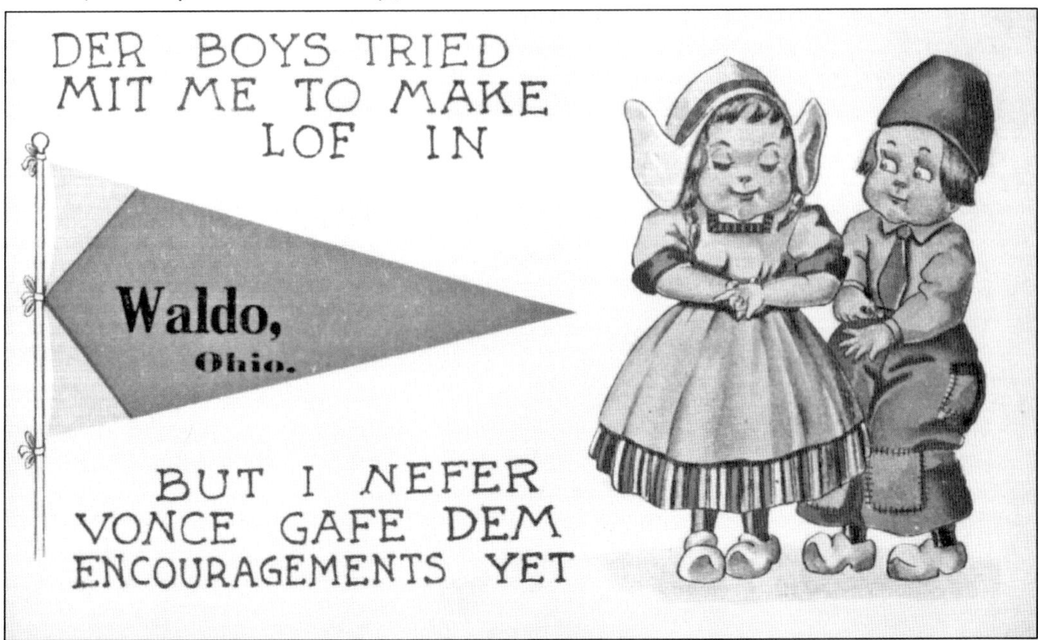

GOOD TIMES IN WALDO. Postcards featuring a little Dutch couple were very popular in the early 1900s. Cards such as this one, with its virtuous girl and hopeful suitor, would have been sold by local merchants who contracted to have cards printed with their town as the featured locale. No historical record exists of this couple's eventual status. (Courtesy of Bob Turner.)